White Supremacy

When did whiteness begin? Was its rise inevitable? In this powerful history, John Broich traces the emergence, evolution, and contradictions of white supremacy, from its roots in the British empire to the racial politics of the present. Focusing on the English-speaking world, he examines how ideas of whiteness connect to the history of slavery, Enlightenment thought, European colonialism, Social Darwinism and eugenics, fascism, and capitalism. Far from being the natural order of things, Broich demonstrates that white supremacy is a brittle concept. For centuries, it has been constantly shifting, rebranding, and justifying itself in the face of resistance. The oft-repeated excuse that its architects were simply "men of their time" collapses under scrutiny. With brutal honesty, Broich exposes the lies embedded in the grim biography of an invented race. *White Supremacy* calls for a deeper understanding of the past, that we might undo its grip on the present.

John Broich is Associate Professor of History at Case Western Reserve University. His previous books include *Squadron: Ending the African Slave Trade* and *Blood, Oil, and the Axis*, and he has written for the *Guardian*, *Washington Post*, and *BBC History Magazine*.

John Broich

WHITE SUPREMACY

A Short History

CAMBRIDGE
UNIVERSITY PRESS

CAMBRIDGE
UNIVERSITY PRESS

Shaftesbury Road, Cambridge CB2 8EA, United Kingdom

One Liberty Plaza, 20th Floor, New York, NY 10006, USA

477 Williamstown Road, Port Melbourne, VIC 3207, Australia

314–321, 3rd Floor, Plot 3, Splendor Forum, Jasola District Centre, New Delhi – 110025, India

103 Penang Road, #05–06/07, Visioncrest Commercial, Singapore 238467

Cambridge University Press is part of Cambridge University Press & Assessment, a department of the University of Cambridge.

We share the University's mission to contribute to society through the pursuit of education, learning and research at the highest international levels of excellence.

www.cambridge.org

Information on this title: www.cambridge.org/9781009627696

DOI: 10.1017/9781009627689

When citing this work, please include a reference to the DOI 10.1017/9781009627689

First published 2026

A catalogue record for this publication is available from the British Library

A Cataloging-in-Publication data record for this book is available from the Library of Congress

ISBN 978-1-009-62769-6 Hardback

Cambridge University Press & Assessment has no responsibility for the persistence or accuracy of URLs for external or third-party internet websites referred to in this publication and does not guarantee that any content on such websites is, or will remain, accurate or appropriate.

For EU product safety concerns, contact us at Calle de José Abascal, 56, 1°, 28003 Madrid, Spain, or email eugpsr@cambridge.org

For E.G. and D.B.

CONTENTS

INTRODUCTION

The discovery of a personal whiteness is a very modern thing . . .
W. E. B. Du Bois

When we use the term white supremacy, it doesn't just evoke
white people. It evokes a political world that we all can frame
ourselves in relationship to.
bell hooks

White supremacy is the unnamed political system that has made
the modern world what it is today.
Charles W. Mills

If a white man wants to lynch me, that's his problem. If he's got
the power to lynch me, that's my problem. Racism is not
a question of attitude; it's a question of power.
Kwame Ture

White supremacy is a total world, deep with history. It's
both a vast pattern of perpetuating white dominance and the belief
that that's justified. "Racism," as Robin Diangelo wrote, "can be
thought of as the systemic outcome of white supremacist ideology."[1]
Or, we might say, white supremacy is racism in action, racism built
into a society, in addition to racism as an ideology or belief.[2] And
while it certainly does, white supremacy doesn't have to look like or
manifest itself as racist *hate*. If it snarls, white supremacy can also
smile. It can soothe, or patronize, or promise. White supremacy
creates: it invents definitions for things like intelligence, civility, or

normalcy. And white supremacy is nothing without the *power* to invent and then enforce those.

Yet white supremacy can also embody *in*action; that is, historically white supremacy has also been about "waiting for the right time," about "not doing anything rash," about "looking for consensus," while nonwhite people suffer or die. Martin Luther King, Jr. put it this way: "I must confess that over the past few years I have been gravely disappointed with the white moderate. I have almost reached the regrettable conclusion that the Negro's great stumbling block in his stride toward freedom is not the White Citizen's Counciler or the Ku Klux Klanner, but the white moderate, who is more devoted to 'order' than to justice; who prefers a negative peace which is the absence of tension to a positive peace which is the presence of justice; who constantly says: 'I agree with you in the goal you seek, but I cannot agree with your methods of direct action'; who paternalistically believes he can set the timetable for another man's freedom; who lives by a mythical concept of time and who constantly advises the Negro to wait for a 'more convenient season.'"[3] White supremacy can even look like inclusion – admitting the Irish into whiteness, for example, to block the economic advancement of African Americans; or admitting some people of Latin American descent into a white identity movement to expand political power.

This book could have been titled simply "the origins of whiteness." That's because the superiority, the "supremacy" part, is baked into the "whiteness" part. Without one, you don't have the other. (Note that, since it's about whiteness, it's mainly not about how nonwhite people experience race-hate. I'm not qualified to do that. There are many good books about that, with a small but prime selection named in the suggestions for further reading.[4])

Any important history deserves to be told briefly. That means this book is far from comprehensive. And its extreme pace might make my professional colleagues shake their spinning heads: every page races through – sometimes even past – vast reading lists, vast fields of history. For example, I give the histories of minorities across the globe short shrift in favor of telling the story of whiteness. In other words, it focuses on the power of whiteness rather than resistance to whiteness. Scholars delve deep, deep into issues I raise in a mere sentence. But presenting the fine-grained details is not what's best for our shared particular goals in this book. My hope is that readers will find a helpful guide to more fine-grained history in my endnotes.

My aim is to offer a brief, readable synthesis of the best scholarship on the roots, growth, changes, and persistence of whiteness and white supremacy. I honor those many, many who've dedicated their professional scholarly lives, and often paid many costs, to doing this demanding work.

And why am I telling the history of the "English-speaking world" – to use an awkward phrase? Not only is it awkward, but also it can leave the utterly false impression that only English is spoken in the lands subject to English and British colonization or informal empire. Obviously, that's not true: Cherokee, Māori, Punjabi, and a wondrous variety of other languages are spoken there. This only highlights how whiteness is the primary focus of this book, which comes at a cost. (I could have used the phrase "English diaspora," but that's strange and awkward, too.)

Most importantly, the British Empire was the largest, longest-enduring force for creating, spreading, and sustaining white supremacy. The settler colonies and nations they spawned identified themselves as "white men's countries," and clung violently to the concept. And, as you'll read, they eventually imagined they were in an Anglo-Saxon union, defending the white race against racial challengers. You might already sense something like this in the world around you. Most readers of this book will have watched the near-simultaneous rise of Trumpism and Brexit (not to mention nativist movements and anti-immigrant violence in Australia and Canada). That's not a coincidence, but a clue about the global nature of whiteness. I hope, even as I write in a USA where this book will be banned in many states' classrooms, that my world-spanning approach might help readers think in new, comparative ways.

Would a history of individual global whitenesses be different? That is, would it change things if this were a story about the rise of white supremacy in the French Empire, or the Dutch or Spanish? They would share similarities: these empires inculcated a sense of superiority in the colonizers, they practiced ethnic cleansing, and they justified themselves with race science. Yet they'd be slightly different simply because of slightly varied histories. The Spanish Empire had its particularities: the role of the Catholic Church in race supremacy, for example. The French Empire had its own differences: say, the fiction common in the French Empire that colonized subjects were actually *citizens* of France. And the Dutch had a far smaller settler colony presence than these others. Meanwhile, there are things particular to the British case: they were the world's biggest-ever human traffickers; they also had far larger settler colonies than their European rivals. And the West Indies and their offshoot USA comprised the largest-ever slave society, where the very ideas of "white" and "black" were born. Perhaps my writing about a global whiteness particular to the British Empire and its antecedents will encourage scholars of other empires to think about different shades of whiteness.

As we proceed through the centuries in this book, we'll observe whiteness emerge, grow, mutate, and survive by burrowing into various niches. But this history doesn't mean evolution *had to* work out this way. It wasn't inevitable. Choices were made by people, not inalterable forces of nature. And, while people worked to reinforce the power of whiteness, people also resisted. So, as we observe white supremacy change, we'll see it attacked, suffer losses, regroup in new forms. It had to – *has* to – fight to survive.

White supremacy, then, has history: it's not a timeless force of nature. Nor is it some inborn (imagined) human nature like "hate" or "distrust of the 'other.'" As the first two chapters show, it had a beginning in relatively recent times; that means, unlike things outside time, it *can* have an end. That's heartening, at least. Yes, white supremacy is stubborn and old like a granite monument of the Jim Crow era; but it's *not* a mountain, incapable of being moved. There are people, institutions, trends, wealth – an ugly, tangled mass of chains – that every day cling onto it for dear life, anchoring it in place. And the second half of the book, in particular, shows the forging of these chains that barely hold, creaking and moaning.

White supremacists always had to invent and re-invent white supremacy because, everywhere and always, there were people of all flesh tones calling it out as wrong, stupid, or monstrous. Today, people with an interest in doing so argue that, if you look into the past, you'll only find racists; thus, their racism was excusable or even justified. White supremacy, then, is supposed to have been the sole option available to white people in the past. That's ridiculous at best, and clearly serves a present-day political agenda.

So, this book will highlight plenty of non-racist, anti-white-supremacists. It's far from true that they didn't exist or weren't vocal; it's rather that white supremacists consistently ignored, silenced, outspent, or brutally suppressed anti-white-supremacists. What's true about the past is true about our present.

In the end, there probably was no better observer of whiteness than James Baldwin. So there's no better voice with which to end these introductory remarks. Baldwin, fighting despair to do so, pled with his fellow citizens for decades to abandon whiteness and white supremacy for *their* own good in 1968. And he might as well have been speaking to the people of Australia or Britain or Canada. And he might as well have been speaking today.

> I'm not trying to accuse you, you know. That's not the point. But ... all that can save you now is your confrontation with your own history ... which is not your past, but your present. ... Your history has led you to this moment, and you can only begin to change yourself and save yourself by looking at what you are doing in the name of your history.[5]

Part I

The Long Evolution of a "Master Race" and "Slave Races"

1 BEFORE WHITENESS, 400S BCE-1600

We know that white supremacy isn't timeless or a force of nature because we can point to its beginnings and a time before it. In the words of some leaders in this field, whatever the race, "it came into existence at a discernible historical moment for rationally understandable historical reasons and is subject to change for similar reasons."[1] Scholars, in fact, can show us long millennia before the very categories of "white" and "black" existed as we know them. And you can't have white supremacy without an idea of "whiteness" itself.

Like I've said, the superiority, the "supremacy" part of white supremacy, is baked into the "whiteness" part. Without one, you don't have the other. You can have xenophobia, you can have religious predominance, you can have hatred between groups. But none of these are the same – or, I would argue, as pervasive and enduring – as whiteness and white supremacy.

Did the Ancients Hand Down an Idea of Race to the English-Speaking World?

Was there such a thing as "race" in the eyes of the ancient peoples of the Mediterranean and European realms? Let's stick to the Romans, since we're going to be talking about Roman Britain in a little while and we're limiting our investigation to (eventual) English-speaking lands. When you imagine Roman Britain, do you see paler-skinned people in your mind's eye? Do you think of it as "white"? Why? Have films suggested that? Or did the books you looked at in school tell you so? You wouldn't be alone. And there've been infamous cases of public outrage when scholars have explained that prehistoric and classical "English" were far from all pale-hued.[2] It's not hard to see that such racial outcries had far more to do with whiteness in the twenty-first century than with genuine findings about the ancient past.

In fact, there's plenty of evidence for varied flesh tones in England's deep history. Yet written sources from the Roman era aren't particularly interested in telling the reader who was dark-skinned and who was not. (That changed after the historical evolution of the categories of whiteness and blackness that you're going to read about in the next chapter. Stay tuned.) In any case, the evidence shows that darker-skinned people lived in the Roman-era British Isles. Setting aside that the ancestors of some of its second-century people were richly brown-skinned like Cheddar Man,[3] archaeologists and classicists show us that there were plenty of African immigrants or African-descended families. Rome's empire was vast, cosmopolitan, and interconnected by trade and political administration. People from one end inevitably ended up at the other.[4] No one should be surprised that northwest African traders might have tried their luck in Londinium or Eboracum (York); just as they shouldn't be surprised that an England-born centurion would die and be buried in Roman Syria.[5] Garrisoned in a chilly keep on Hadrian's Wall, there was an army unit of what were called "Moors," possibly like today's Amazigh people of northwest Africa.[6] But there were also poor and middling sorts of Africa-descended or mixed-heritage Roman Londoners.[7]

The Romans, of course, were notorious slavers; but there's no evidence that the darker-skinned or African-heritage people of Roman Britain were more or less likely to be enslaved than others.[8] Roman slavery wasn't race-based in terms of color. Put another way, as much as the Romans thought they were the greatest, they didn't associate Roman-ness or slavery with flesh tone.[9]

Did they think they were a superior race? They didn't have the idea as we do. There was an idea that was close: *genus*. But we'd be imposing our concepts if we translated that as "race" the way we think of it. Today's expert classicists tell us that *genus* meant something like "tribe." It was a group of people who shared certain lifestyle-patterns and claimed a certain deep identity. They told themselves they were members of a historical group, perhaps united by a mythological past. Language could be part of it, but did not have to be. Body features – skin tone and so on – were not important to signifying *genus*. "Blood," that is, did not determine one's *genus*. Even the Romans, who were so proud of their Roman citizenship and limited it, did *not* try to limit Roman citizenship by keeping it within limited bloodlines or limited skin tones.[10]

European elites' obsession with categorizing, ordering, and ranking the peoples of the world would have to wait for the centuries of colonialism, as Chapter 3 will show. But, yes, the Romans, and Greeks before them, tried to group the peoples, the "genuses," of humankind around the Mediterranean center of their world. And we need to understand that because for many, many centuries – until the rise of early modern whiteness – these ancient ideas shaped what people thought of as "race."

Ancient Greek and Roman observers definitely made observations about the surface features of bodies. In our day and age, these indicate "race," a deeply meaningful, supposedly biological "reality" that shapes a person's destiny. (Of course, these things *aren't* inherently true, but are imposed.) But, for a Greek observer, these surface features did not carry all our modern baggage. For example, when Herodotus (c. 484–c. 425 BCE), a Greek geographer born in today's southwest Turkey, visited Egypt, he offered plenty of descriptions of the dark-skinned, curly-haired people there whom we'd call "Black." He definitely had xenophobic things to say about them; he thought Greeks were better, quite simply.[11] Herodotus, like Aristotle a century before him, seemed to think the tan skin of the Greeks was better than the skin of paler people and darker people. Tan, in the words of Goldilocks, was "*just* right," not too light and not too dark.[12]

At roughly the same time, around 400 BCE, Greeks like Hippocrates offered a theory of why different human groups looked and acted differently. It was part of a whole system of explanation based on climate and geography that we call today "Hippocratic theory." It's a fascinating subject that ranges from medicine to epidemiology to urban planning to arguments for "human nature" and beyond. But, in the interest of time, let's limit ourselves to the Hippocratic theory of human groups, what we today would call "race." Hippocratic theory told people like Herodotus – and later Roman, medieval, and early modern writers who relied on him – that things like the sun and heat shaped human body types through the

generations. Wet, humid environments would shape them differently. Humans' insides would be changed, too, because the humors –
blood, yellow bile, black bile, and phlegm – reflected the outside
environment: heat, dryness, wetness, and coldness. The balance or
imbalance of the humors would reveal itself in behavior. Too much
phlegm made one too dull and impassive, for example. Of course, the
Greeks told themselves that *their* cities enjoyed the perfect native
environment – mixed and in balance – and thus had the greatest,
"just right," humoral balance, explaining their "civilized" nature,
unlike that of the people from wild or extreme environments. Put
another way, people who lived far from the Greek (and later Roman)
Mediterranean heartland were supposed to live in extreme climates
that imbalanced their outward appearance and inward humors.[13]

Aristotle (384–322 BCE) had much to say about slavery,
since he thought a lot about the proper ordering of city-state society
and governments – rulers, voters, subjects, masters, slaves. For
Aristotle, race as we know it had nothing to do with who was
inherently worthy of enslavement at the level of blood. What mattered to his thinking was the question of who was civilized; that is,
which peoples practiced lawful, republican politics where persuasion
was a matter of speeches in the city forum, not the spear. (This, of
course, was a rosy, idealized vision.) When Aristotle looked beyond
Greece's hinterland at strange, bearded foreigners who couldn't
understand Greek, he saw spear-throwing "barbarians" – men who
lacked the essence of civilization. These men (and their imagined
lessers: women), then, were suitable for enslavement – whatever their
flesh tone or gods.[14]

Ancient and early medieval people frequently enslaved their
prisoners of war (POWs). That was perhaps the biggest driver of
slave-making. Or take, for example, the later Vikings' notorious
slave raiding and slave markets.[15] It didn't matter what the color of
their victims' skin was.

From this, it's easy to see how Hippocratic theory and
Aristotle's ideas didn't lend themselves to ideas of race based on
something timeless in the blood or what we'd call genetics.[16] The
inward and outward nature of the body responded to the environment, and thus those features would change down the generations of
people as they moved around the Greek or Roman world. Or,
according to Herodotus and his followers, someone born in
a "bad" environment – that resulted, say, in laziness or excitability –

could be cured of those bad qualities by moving to a good environ-ment with ideal laws like a republican – Greek, of course – city.[17] Meanwhile, a "barbarian" captive's children could be raised as proper Greek republicans, with no taint of slavery in their blood. And, sure enough, the Roman emperor at the turn of the 200s was himself a dark-skinned North African as shown in contemporary portraits.[18]

The preeminent expert on the Greeks' ancient race thinking is probably Dr. Rebecca Futo Kennedy, and she's stated these things pretty efficiently. Greeks, she wrote, believed that "specific peoples were bound to specific lands, that the characteristics of particular lands and climates had determinative effects on human appearance, behavior, and moral character, and that some geographic and cli-matic locations were superior and others inferior." Greek observers didn't look around their world and catalogue peoples mainly for the purpose of making a hierarchy of races. Nor did they understand the world through race logic as white supremacists would much later. But they thought about groups of peoples for a variety of reasons, "including curiosity, wonder, and fear of difference or the unknown."[19]

Why do we care what the Greeks and Romans thought? First, to appreciate that race ideas changed dramatically over time. Second, as much as there was change, these ideas of environmental determinism were incredibly pervasive and powerful, lasting many centuries and resisting rival ideas.[20] When early modern and modern slaveholders needed to justify their activities, they often had to fit justifications into Hippocratic theory or Aristotle's ideas. When that just wouldn't work, and enslavers needed to justify holding humans captive down the generations, they had to create or embrace new theories, namely the race-science of the 1800s and 1900s.

Africa-Descended People in Medieval England

Perhaps, after the Roman Empire mutated into separate post-Roman kingdoms and princedoms, there was less opportunity for the circulation of darker-hued people to what we call the British Isles. Counting Africa-descended people there is very hard because there were no censuses or centralized, reliable birth records as we know them during the Middle Ages. Intermittent parish church records of baptism, marriages, and burials – just a priest or clerk

entering a line in a book – made no mention of "race." But archaeologists show us that there were still darker-toned people about, and
not just in the bigger port towns. Archaeologist Caitlin Green offers
evidence that, very roughly, as many as a quarter of medieval English
villages had at least one resident descended from someone born
somewhere in Africa.[21] Early signs point to a sub-Saharan origin
for a young woman who died in the 900s in west-central England;
while a lady of African origin was buried in the churchyard next to
her neighbors in Elmham, East Anglia, around the year 1000.[22]
There's no basis for or against thinking that these women were slaves
or particularly disadvantaged on account of their skin tone.
Meanwhile, early medieval sources tell us that the celebrated abbot
of Canterbury, Adrian (637–710), was a "man of the African
nation." He inspired a mini-Renaissance in Anglo-Saxon England,
traveling the land, gathering a flock of students, and teaching things
like Greek, math, and astronomy derived from Plato and Aristotle.[23]

Later, from the 1200s, sources tell of an expert crossbow-
maker, a free man living in London, who was a Muslim of Africa or
the eastern Mediterranean; but at the same time tell of a Muslim man
escaped from slavery, a so-called "Ethiopian" named Bartholomew.[24]
Then there's a case from the later 1200s of an African man who may
have been purchased as a slave in a market in Tunis by crusaders
returning to England, but ended his life a member of London's
Greyfriars monastery in some capacity.[25]

Medieval Religion and Hints for the Future of Race-Based Slavery

Medieval Christianity and a concept of a realm called
"Christendom," historians tell us, were a piece of the puzzle that
would eventually become white supremacy. But we shouldn't push it
too far, too fast. Encounters between Muslim lands and Christian
didn't create a slave race and master race and didn't create whiteness,
even if they nudged its evolution.

Firstly, there was war-making between people who believed
that their religion made them very different. For example, Christian
kings and nobles and their soldiers fought Muslim kings and nobles
and their soldiers in what's today Spain from around 700 to 1500;
the same went for the eastern Mediterranean lands (let's call this area

"the Levant" as a shorthand) from around 1100 to 1300. The reasons for these campaigns were many and mixed, and fill library shelves. On the Spanish, or Iberian, Peninsula, it was a war of expansion by Christian nobles who believed they were "reconquering" Christian lands lost to Arab and Berber/Amazigh invaders from 711. (The majority of people had remained Christian and Jewish under new Muslim rulers.[26]) In the lands around Jerusalem, Christian armies fought to take over holy sites to please their God, perform a kind of armed pilgrimage, win personal glory, and seize land and loot. Traders like the Venetians and Genoese followed the crusaders into new ports in the eastern and southern Mediterranean – they even expanded north into the Black Sea – and trafficked in Muslim POWs and others to stock slave markets.[27] Whether in Spain or the Levant or elsewhere, most scholars don't find fighting and slaving based on the "white race" targeting a "nonwhite" race.[28]

What the Crusades did was to bring people from Europe into greater physical and, if you will, mental contact with a big, powerful rival.[29] The imagined rival bloc proved quite strong, confident, often wealthy, and quite happy to keep their own religion – thank you – and reject Christianity. Writers of the day tended to lump these antagonists together under the word "Saracens," a term they borrowed from the Byzantines, which they used for desert peoples of the Arabian Peninsula.[30] Fighting or thinking about the so-called "Saracens" created a new *Them*; naturally, that encouraged thinking about a new *Us*. In turn, there was a Saracen, Infidel, Muslim quarter of the world over *there*; just as there was a Christian, right-believing quarter of the world *here*.[31] (Actually, the Muslim target lands of the Crusades were tremendously varied and often in opposition. They weren't really *one* rival.)

Today, you might imagine that the unifying idea of a place called Europe was always an important idea or identifier for the people who lived there. Not so. True, there'd been an ancient vague notion of a vast hinterland realm called Europe – like the vast realms "Africa" and "Asia." But people didn't go around calling themselves "European" as they do today. Yet the Crusades and the early days of more distant sea travel promoted the idea of a coherent Europe or Christendom. Mind you, the Crusades did *not* result in political or cultural unity among the countless little realms of the European peninsula.[32] Far from it.

In Spain and elsewhere in Europe, crusaders sometimes attacked ancient Jewish communities, because they were supposedly the enemies of their Christian God close at hand, because they might yield "legitimate" loot, or both. Jews had lived throughout the European peninsula for millennia by then. In fact, rulers often valued their presence since, unlike Christians, Jews were permitted to lend money at interest (meanwhile, many other trades were denied to Jews). Then as now, borrowing was how ruling regimes got things done, after all; and Jewish communities were also handy for taxing. In London and other towns, Jews enjoyed long stretches of going unnoticed by the far larger Christian population around them, generally protected by the nobles who used them. These quiet stretches were interrupted – yes, often around the times of Crusades – by terrible moments when opportunists or rabid mobs scapegoated Jews, as happened around the time of the Third Crusade (1189–1192), when 150 were murdered and some, besieged, burned themselves alive at York.[33]

Still, the new culture of crusading, and Us-versus-Them framework, didn't suddenly transform Jews into an unchanging, immutable "nonwhite" race as defined by blood in the English-speaking world. King Edward I banned money-lending at interest by England's Jews when he returned from crusading in 1273. Suddenly, they were of no more use to their aristocratic protectors (spongers). Their only option for making a living was to convert, and even then, they had to "buy" their conversion by surrendering their property to the king. Finally, King Edward demanded Jews either convert or leave the kingdom in 1290. They returned – or perhaps more accurately, returned to open practice – under Oliver Cromwell in 1655. He was very happy to have Jewish merchants come from Amsterdam to London bringing wealth, trade contacts, and taxable imports.[34]

Scholars show that it was useful for medieval leaders to maintain Jewish separateness.[35] Were medieval Jews, then, the prototypical "lesser race," whose inferiority carried down through the generations in the blood? Not quite. Their status was situational: it could end at the moment of baptism as a Christian. Contemporary Christian chroniclers who decried medieval pogroms as impious and "inhuman" wrote that Jews were targeted on religious, not racial, grounds.[36] We'll see when and where Jewishness became located in the blood in later chapters. (Still, you can refer to smart, well-founded arguments that medieval Europeans started imbuing blood, not environmental factors, with a sort of "mythical racial significance" earlier than 1700.[37])

***

Although this book mainly limits itself to today's English-speaking world, we need to take a detour down to the Iberian Peninsula and the proto-Spain and proto-Portugal of the later 1400s. Two things were going on there that foreboded grim things for future whiteness. As Christian forces completed their "reconquest" of the Iberian Peninsula ending around 1500, they began to demand the conversion or expulsion of native Jews and Muslims at the point of the sword.[38] From that point on, some in the new Spain and Portugal suspected that converted Jews and Muslims hadn't *really* converted. This was for a variety of reasons, whether genuine concern for the safety of their eternal souls and the souls around them, to steal from them and bar them from office, or because of periodic revolts by minorities. (Conquest and suppression also resulted in POWs, some of whom the conquerors enslaved in accord with longstanding tradition.)

But how could one identify those who might be secret Jews or Muslims and thus a threat to the new Christian kingdoms? To identify potential false converts, the Church set up offices to do things like investigate the bloodlines of the accused, to establish – in the words of the time, yet words with an evil future – their "purity of blood."[39] From this, it's easy to see how, over time, religion could connect to something more like our notion of race – something that circulates in the blood down generations.[40] But this story of hunting down race in the blood is far more important to Spanish whiteness in this period than whiteness in the English-speaking world. That would come later.

Early Seafaring and Distant Encounters

In the early mid 1400s, the Portuguese struck out by sea in search of resources and trade goods for profit, encouraged by their kings, who collected taxes on their imports. They stumbled onto Madeira in 1419, and landed on the Azores. In the mid 1400s they sought to set up ports in Morocco, sailed further down the West African coast, and started trading with the southern shores of West

Africa shortly thereafter. It made perfect sense to these Portuguese to think about slave trading, too, since the ageless trafficking in humans had never halted in the Middle Ages; it just shifted in form and location. Portuguese chroniclers described how their first slave raid was almost an afterthought. A Captain Gonçalvez was sealing with his crew on a cape off of today's Mauritania, in 1441. The expedition was already a success, but Gonçalvez saw a last opportunity. "We have already got our cargo," said the captain to his crew, "but how fair a thing would it be if we, who have come to this land for a cargo of such petty merchandise, were to ... bring the first captives before the presence of our Prince?"[41] They kidnapped around ten people and took them to Portugal. (Per the *Oxford English Dictionary*, the English word "kidnap" became common around the 1680s, defined as abducting a child from, say, an English city and sending them to an American colony to be an unfree laborer.) The Portuguese immediately saw a new, perhaps the most profitable, opportunity, and the rest is a vile history.[42]

Again, medieval European slavery persisted from the days of the Romans just like so many other things.[43] And throughout that period people in Europe debated who was fit to be enslaved – "*Saracens?*" *Heretics? Criminals? Was it alright to enslave Christians?* – and what were the rights of the enslaved – *whom could they marry? When could they buy their freedom? What rights did they have to their bodily autonomy?* The answers to these questions varied over time and between places. There were those, for example, who argued that slaveholders had the right of life or death over their captives; while others argued that Roman law never granted that.[44] In 1388, the bishop of Barcelona argued that Western, Latin Christians mustn't enslave Eastern, Greek Christians; but the merchants of Barcelona went around him to the Pope and won a ruling permitting them to do so.[45] Meanwhile, some argued that the enslaved were born with souls that were equal to those of the free in the eyes of God; and there were those, especially in the later Middle Ages, who argued from new translations of Aristotle that the enslaved tended to be born "natural" slaves – from barbarian stock.[46] In the Middle Ages, sometimes the enslaved could hold personal property that remained their own; sometimes they could marry free people; sometimes both the slaver and the enslaved expected that the captive would be ransomed, with slave status being temporary.[47] These questions had to be argued and re-argued over the generations. (And in a later chapter we'll see that one of the things that distinguished slavery in the Americas is that these questions got settled along the harshest lines there.)

So, what to do about the rights and expectations of the new victims of Portuguese human trafficking as they sailed down the west coast of Africa and invaded places like Madeira? These people, unlike victims in Iberia or other edges of Europe, were far, far "outsiders."[48] They were well outside any sense of being "civilized" or familiar at all. From 1452, Pope Nicholas V and his successors granted the Portuguese king's permission, via papal bull, to conquer and potentially enslave "the Saracens and pagans and any other unbelievers" they found on their African journeys. This might sound like these Popes invented the African slave trade – and made it racial – out of thin air. But it wasn't like that. The 1452 bull simply combined two deep, ongoing traditions – enslaving non-Christian POWs and crusading.[49] To repeat: the Portuguese and Spanish slave trafficking on the African coast or nearby Atlantic islands was a *continuation* of ongoing trends in new places due to new opportunities.

On the other hand, these papal permissions no doubt contributed in some way to the prehistory of new kinds of slavery from around the later 1600s, of two connected things: first, the roots of *race*-based slavery, an idea that flourished later in the New World over the Atlantic Ocean; and second, the roots of the idea that Europeans traditionally were the enslavers/masters and Africans or other Indigenous non-Christians were traditionally the enslaved.[50]

The Status of Africa-Descended People in 1500s–1600s England

How do scholars know, however, that things like the 1452 Papal Bull and Portuguese human trafficking south of the Sahara didn't flip a switch creating whiteness and blackness as we know them? We can see this by turning back to our main setting: England, Scotland, and Wales. Historians have been painstakingly extracting the lives of Black Tudors from scant and far-flung archival data. We already know that dark-skinned folk had been in England and surrounding lands since time out of mind. And most African or Africa-descended people in England were not enslaved.[51] Scholars do indeed find some dark-skinned enslaved people living in 1500s England; however, the trade had been illegal there since around 1100, and the status of slavery, except as judicial punishment – for anyone of any hue – was not recognized.[52] (Given the break with Rome in the 1530s, the English naturally didn't justify slaveholding in England by appealing to the authority of a 1452 Pope.)

Some have suggested that medieval Christians were primed to take dark-fleshed people captive into slavery by the Biblical story of the Curse of Ham. In that Genesis tale, Noah cursed his son Ham's offspring to be a slave-race with dark skin. Subsequent religious commentators suggested that those offspring were the peoples of Africa, this argument goes. But this is a bit of a red herring, a mainly 1800s argument projected backwards by some. In fact, this argument isn't supported by coherent medieval commentary, nor the evidence of art and decoration.[53]

So, who were the relatively few enslaved in Tudor England? Documents show that Spanish and Portuguese merchants and visitors would sometimes bring their enslaved victims to London or Edinburgh. Sometimes, then, these people would stay with their slavers: whether because they had no other means to survive, because their slaver had fathered their children, or because they simply didn't know they could walk away. Other times, they did just that and even testified in court against their former captors.[54]

Far more often, Africa-descended Tudors were not enslaved and lived roughly the same variety of lives as non-Africans. There was a crafty manufacturer in London who made the best needles, while a successful silk weaver thrived just over in Southwark.[55] There were plenty of Black sailors in a number of port towns.[56] There was probably at least one Black or Berber/Amazigh Tudor knight, even.[57] There's an argument to be made that Tudor monarchs wanted Black servants, musicians, and other staff in their courts because it mimicked the most powerful, cosmopolitan court in Europe: the Spanish.[58] But life for the hundreds of Black Tudors and Stuarts was probably about as glamorous and comfortable as it was for most of their lighter-skinned neighbors; that is, unglamorous and uncomfortable. Most were probably pretty humble or of the servant class, like most folks. As one historian wrote, "the majority of the African servants were not curiosities, neither were they oddities nor status symbols."[59]

So, if "black" did not equal "slave" in the England of the 1500s–1600s, how did things get to a point where the British were the world's biggest human traffickers by the end of the 1700s?[60] That answer will be tied up with the rise of whiteness and white supremacy over that time period. But we can point to one key component: the fact that the pre-modern English, Welsh, and Scottish learned the human trade from the Spanish and Portuguese. The English didn't have overseas colonies as early as the Iberians (we'll get to Ireland in a moment), but of course they were seafaring people. They signed onto Portuguese and Spanish ships, quite simply. They learned to navigate the vast empty stretches of the Atlantic, catching wind and current in the right season. They learned how to trade on the West African coast and in the new ports of the West Indies and Spanish mainland. They learned the route to India, where the Portuguese negotiated with sultans and princes (and sometimes battled them) to set up permanent trade posts. There were some English attempts, under John Hawkins, to set up their own slave trade in the 1560s, but they didn't come to much – at least in those years. That would come.

Then something else happened that helped change England from just another gloomy land drifting on the fringes of Europe into an important, potent entity. It became, roughly during the reigns of Elizabeth and James I (about 1560–1625), a target of the bigger, more mighty Catholic kingdoms and empires of Europe. This is a vast history, so we won't take a deep dive into it. I'll summarize: King Henry VIII (reign: 1509–1547) envisioned himself having the same independent, powerful status as the Spanish and Holy Roman Emperors, even though he truly wasn't as powerful. Again, the story is long and complicated, but ultimately it meant that he declared himself the highest religious authority in the land – even above the Pope. From then on, there was a deep tension: would England (later Britain) reconcile with the Pope (and by extension the crowns in Europe that controlled the papal crown) or not? Might England even go over to the radical, even revolutionary Protestants? When Henry's daughter Elizabeth (reign: 1558–1603) refused to marry a Spanish prince, tension rose even higher. When James I (reign: 1603–1625) embraced Protestant ideas, the break seemed unfixable. The results? The English Crown was excommunicated in the late 1500s, and the Pope authorized a kind of crusade against the kingdom. In other words, England now had a target on its back, and the Catholic king who brought England back into the fold via invasion would be a hero to Catholic Christendom.

Why this tangent? Because had history played out just a little differently, England could easily have become just a cold province of mightier Spain or France. If Henry's daughter Mary (reign: 1553–1558), betrothed to a Spaniard, had given birth to a Spanish prince and good Catholic, for example. Or if Elizabeth hadn't been dauntless Elizabeth and had married a Catholic king and had a Catholic prince that reconciled England to the Pope. But instead, England became a sort of Public Enemy No. 1 and had to go it alone. England also, naturally, had to build up a powerful navy to keep invasions from Spain and France at bay. Those navy and privateering ships sailed all the way across the Atlantic to attack, raid, and harass Spanish ventures (in their raiding forays, Francis Drake [1540–1596] and other Englishmen were quite happy to ally with communities of Africans in Panama who'd escaped Spanish captivity[61]) – still more training en route to becoming the world's most powerful seafaring people.[62] Isolated England also needed to establish its own colonies in the Americas to rival the Catholic Spaniards – more training at colonization. You can see where this is going.

Precursors to Race-Hate Were not the White Supremacy We Know

The centuries before white supremacy were no Golden Age. Far from it. Sticking just to English-speaking lands, society was divided into a tiny fraction of "haves" – the aristocrats – and the "have nots" – the great majority of people with little security, little food, and few life expectations. In 1300, about half the people in England and Wales were serfs. That meant that they were bound to the land they farmed and, without having a choice in the matter, owed rent, produce, or service to a landlord. (Serfdom was never equivalent to slavery and generally faded out in England in the 1500s.[63]) Being Jewish or Muslim was at least a legal or civil handicap, at best; sometimes dangerous at worst. And it almost goes without saying that if Church authorities thought your malpractice of Christianity was a threat to the eternal souls of those around you, you could end up in hot water, or in a hot pyre. Christians were preoccupied with who could be saved from eternal torture and who could not.

And, as ever, there is evidence of xenophobia or fear of the outsider; xenophobia was different from today's white supremacy, though.[64] Medieval or early modern xenophobia was not based on a concept that the outsider was *permanently different at the level of blood*. A satirical and anti-Jewish text from around 1200 written by a Winchester monk offers a familiar critique of the big city around seventy miles to the northeast. London was filled with "actors, jesters, smooth-skinned lads, Moors, … effeminates … belly-dancers … beggars."[65] In other words, a person complaining about "all those foreigners in London" wasn't arguing about inherent biological difference; they were arguing about the foreigners' babel, their outrageous clothes, their outlandish habits. Sometimes nasty observations were based on the sense that too many outsiders were arriving at the same time or had no prospects for a job and would end up beggars.[66] Yes, darker skin, as a less common superficial feature, might stand out in London or Edinburgh. But that didn't necessarily mean that in times when immigrants or minorities suffered, the mob targeted Africa-descended people. For example, Dr. Miranda Kaufman offers the case of a backlash against foreigners during a plague epidemic that focused on the Dutch and French, leaving Africa-descended and Jewish folks alone.[67]

Did English people think dark, African skin was ugly? Might that be part of the roots of white supremacy? There must be a connection of some sort, but one of cause or effect? The sources suggest it wasn't quite so simple as pale skin being associated with lightness and goodness and browner skin being associated with badness or darkness. When the English had more exposure to Africans on distant shores by the later 1500s and the 1600s, their reactions were mixed. Yes, some people writing about Africans said they had ugly features and that dark skin suggested impurity.[68] And, yes, historians have long pointed out that the ideal of courtly beauty for a woman was supposed to be ultra-pale.[69] And yet Shakespeare's narrator in Sonnet 130 – "If snow be white, why then her breasts are dun;/If hairs be wires, black wires grow on her head" – *loves* his dark lady despite her not being pale. Frankly, there's not a lot of evidence of broad condemnation of dark skin in this early period. And even the way observers often critiqued darker skin was suggestive: as in Sonnet 130, writers tended to state things like "she was black, *but* beautiful" or "she was black, *but* was good and pure on the inside."[70] So, the negative connotations about darker skin, in this early period, read more like superficial xenophobia, in sum, and are not based on the assumption that dark-skinned peoples were of innately inferior blood.

Ireland as the Training-Ground for Colonization and Race-Suppression

It might sound strange, but English oppression in Ireland – to our eyes, filled with "white people" – was far more important to the historic building blocks of white supremacy. That's because scholars explain how Ireland was a sort of laboratory in which the English refined colonization over a "lesser" people before the centuries of their New World colonialism.[71] The English landed near Dublin around 1170 and from that moment on established a foothold. Over the centuries their control – whether through building colonial castles or alliances with native Irish powers – expanded and contracted. At first, the appeal of conquering parts of Ireland and coopting its lords was simple: there was an opportunity for English kings to grant new lands to nobles willing to go there.[72] Then, naturally, Irish people resisted, so that the English had to fight uprisings to keep their footholds. And expand them: after crushing resistance, the English often declared the lands of trouble-makers were now forfeit. This would become a classic colonial cycle the world over in centuries to come. Through this cycle, the English started to envision the Irish, who spoke a different language even if they were Christian, as a "*naturally* rebellious" people who resisted law and order down the generations.

Still, the English didn't succeed in taking over the whole surface of the island for centuries. It's a long and fascinating story, but what finally led to the English oppression of the whole map was a series of colonies installed by Henry VIII and his descendants.[73] These looked like contemporary Spanish New World colonies based on aristocratic feudal landlords sitting atop a pyramid of sub-landlords and tenants all the way down to Irish peasants. These projects, since they were agricultural colonies meant to plant new fields, were called "plantations," lending the name to a sinister history.[74] By 1607, the English claimed the whole island, there were no more Irish lords, and the English monarch called himself King of Ireland.

But the cycle of conquest and rebellion wasn't the only thing that invented the – lesser, supposedly barbaric – Irish race in the eyes of the English. The other major factor was that, after the Tudor and Stuart monarchs' break from the Pope, the Irish overwhelmingly refused to go along with it. For the Irish, refusing to put the English king above the Pope as "defender of the faith" was a way of resisting the colonizers. For the English, this was a sign of the mulish obstinacy ingrained in the Irish people.

It was also dangerous. Recall, the Spanish and French eventually threatened to conquer England as a kind of crusade to restore rightful religion from the end of the 1500s. As the generations went by and most Irish denied the Anglican Church, the English feared that Spain and France eyed Ireland as a potential springboard – even source of troops – for an invasion of Wales and then England.

Again, we mustn't get ahead of ourselves. Ideas that race resided permanently in the blood and bone had to wait for later generations, and intermittent transitions. In the eyes of their English overlords in the 1500s–1700s, the Irish people *could* transform. For example, scholar William Thomas, writing soon after Henry VIII's death (and quite presumptuously), said that King Henry's policies had transformed the Irish race. (His children would establish the big plantations or colonial settlements, but Henry focused on coopting the Irish nobility.) The king, Thomas wrote, "brought that nation [close in meaning to "race"] from rude, beastly, ignorant, cruel and unruly infidels to a state of civil, reasonable, patient . . . Christians."[75] The scholar proclaimed the successful transformation of the Irish people a bit early indeed, and over the next two centuries the English Crown instituted more and more measures to get the Irish to "civilize." First were efforts to drive out Papal influence, literally driving out priests loyal to Rome, followed by laws denying the Irish civil rights if they would not convert to the Anglican way and stop resisting.[76] Denying the "beastly" Catholic Irish the ability to hold property, get an education, even speak their own language: these were all ideas the British would later export to the far corners of the world. Today we'd call them "enforced assimilation."[77]

Final Thoughts

There's no single key to unlocking the deep history of white supremacy. There's no one sole explanation or turning point or common denominator. Some historical writers have enjoyed big successes by reducing vast histories down into tidy little explanations. That makes sense: clever stories are easier to sell and read.

But these stories tend to be bad history. We call such stories "reductive" because they *reduce* outcomes with many causes into explanations with few causes, or even just one cause. But the world, and history, has many forces pushing and pulling and leading to the results we see. And in seeking the deepest roots of white supremacy, it's not necessary to be reductive. We can pick out multiple, varied genetic strands that accumulated and combined and mutated into the monstrous, seemingly intractable idea of the white master race. Naturally, we can't pick out every single one in something as limited as a short book, but we can investigate multiple strands over great spans of time and place even here.

These strands developed over generations and grew in specific contexts – that is, because *particular* histories were happening. None of these was self-sufficient, none of these was supremely determinative – none of these was a Big Bang, in other words. There were more factors than just these, but we have to prioritize if we're going to complete our task in about 200 pages.

In roughly chronological order the building blocks were:

- **An ancient tradition of local communities, cities, or kingdoms around the Mediterranean claiming that they were "a people," with some kind of common, unifying set of traits.** They shared a particular way of life that set them apart; they were descended from a legendary hero; they spoke a certain language and shared certain ideas. This easily combined with Greek and later Roman concepts that the climate and landscape of a place – its air, water, temperature, and so on – affected the elements within the human body. Thus, ancient observers – and those who later read them – could make sense of "genuses" of humans through environmental logic. No one should be surprised to find that these observers said their peoples' bodies reflected the best environmental conditions. And, while the evidence shows that even places like isolated England were multi-colored in skin tone, xenophobia persisted across centuries.
- **A deep history of enslaving, but not because of some "natural" drive to do so.**[78] In the ancient Mediterranean and then medieval Europe, people with power often made slaves of their POWs. Other than criminals, that's where slaves came from. Since wars often occurred at the frontiers of empires or kingdoms, it followed that people from "beyond the known lands" could be enslaved.[79]

That in and of itself wasn't sufficient to make a "master race" and "slave race." There was yet to be a "white race" and "black race." And there still wasn't a slavery that lasted down the generations. We might say "slavery was situational": it was due to the victim's situation and the kidnappers' opportunity; slavery overwhelmingly didn't pass on to the victims' children.[80]

- **Crusading and the idea of Europe.** Crusading was something new from the end of the 1000s, representing an original, common effort by the many different European kingdoms that shared a religious network headed from Rome. (Anti-Jewish attacks unmistakably rose during periods of crusade, motivated by, or justified by, the idea that "the infidels" were also very close at hand.) The Crusades were not a great success, and their limited successes were short-lived, but over time they helped build a sense of "Christendom" and a sense of Europe as a loosely linked realm. The converse of Europe was supposed to be the land of the Saracens or the Orient or Africa. Crusading certainly produced POWs that could "justly" be enslaved, but ultimately more importantly, these lands beyond Christendom were supposed to be suitable for slave-buying or slave-raiding. As one expert put it, as Europe became a "no-slaving zone," Europeans ventured into a "slaving zone."[81] On the Iberian peninsula, the so-called *Reconquista* shared crusading motivations. Conquering Christians often forced native Muslims and Jews to convert. Subsequently, for a variety of reasons, people investigated Spaniards' bloodlines for the taint of non-Christian blood. **New categories of Us versus Them were thus global and local.**
- **In Ireland, the English got their first practice at creating laws that denied rights to a race who refused to "civilize."** England broke with the Rome-based church hierarchy at about the same time, and the Irish declined to go along with this. This helped turn English concepts of the Irish people from merely xenophobic to ideas that there was something deeply deficient in, and suspicious about, the whole Irish race. This went beyond their being unreformed in religion.
- **When Spain and Portugal employed new ocean-going ships to strike west and south across the globe, the English were drawn out, too.** In part, this was because of a kind of arms race with rival Catholic powers. In the next chapter, we'll see the significance of this for the eventual rise of whiteness.

2 THE EMERGENCE OF WHITENESS – GRADUALLY AND SUDDENLY, 1400–1730S

No one was white before he/she came to America.
James Baldwin[1]

So, there was a time before white supremacy, the globe-spanning complex of forces and ideas. As something made in history, it's not intractable: if there was a time before, there can be a time after. In this chapter, we'll see the emergence of a new thing called "whiteness," gradually, then suddenly.

If someone thinks they know something about the roots of white supremacy, they probably know that it's tied to the transatlantic slave trade and American slave society. At a bird's-eye level, that's correct. But, even within that broad sketch map, there's room to be wrong in some ways. And landing in a pitfall at the start obviously means you can't proceed down the right path.

The first error that will stop one in one's tracks is the idea that whiteness or white supremacy preceded and *caused* the transatlantic slave trade. It's a natural mistake, since who would be so cruel to their fellow human being, after all, if they actually thought of their victim *as* their fellow human being?

But, having read Chapter 1, and even before you read about the infamous transatlantic trade in this chapter, you should already have a sense that this isn't true: kidnapping and trafficking of non-British people didn't follow *from* white supremacy.[2] But such ideas most certainly contributed *to it* in the centuries to come. Kidnapping people beyond the frontiers of Christendom or Europe, enslaving POWs, and trading for other kingdoms' enslaved victims fit long-standing patterns. Besides, dark-skinned people were ever-present in pre-modern England, and those people weren't slaves necessarily, so existing slavery wasn't linked to skin tone. Remember, the most reviled race, and the focus of punitive colonization from the 1500s, was the Irish, after all. And they weren't enslaved.[3] The particular circumstances didn't lead that way.

Spanish Precedents

The mere fact that European invaders enslaved the people they encountered in what they called the "West Indies" didn't flip the switch on white supremacy. Indeed, Christopher Columbus's nefarious kidnapping of the first people he found there is a striking parallel with the 1441 kidnapping by Captain Gonçalvez of the people of what's today Mauritania on Africa's northwest coast. Like him, Columbus really wanted precious metals; but, at first, he also kidnapped a small group of people to take back to the royal court as an example. He assured his sponsors that the new islands could provide "as many slaves as . . . Their Majesties may stand in need of."[4] Note that he *didn't* write to Queen Isabella to say "I've found a slave race." He wrote that the people of Guanahani/San Salvador couldn't withstand the Spanish militarily; he could dominate them with fifty men. In other words, they presented a good *opportunity* for enslaving.[5]

Let's back up for just a moment. Columbus didn't sail from Spain, didn't sail from some Castilian port in 1492; he struck west from the island of Gomera, one of the Canary Islands. If Ireland was Britain's "laboratory of Empire," the Canary archipelago, just off today's Morocco, was Castile's (eventually Spain's). Various European explorers had known of the Canary chain from the 1300s at the latest, and from 1402 vassals of the Castilian king invaded those islands. In the tradition of the *Reconquista* or Crusades, their goal was simply to take land for themselves, guaranteed by grants from the king in exchange for being his feudal vassals.[6] (The Portuguese, meanwhile, were also invading nearby Atlantic islands; Figure 1.) The invaders might have seen this as a good opportunity because the people living there did not have equal military technology. But, in fact, Indigenous inhabitants put up a fierce, multi-generational resistance right up to Columbus's day, roughly 1496.[7] Still the attraction of the warm, lush islands, perfect stopovers for ships, kept drawing shipload after shipload of attackers. And it didn't take long for the Iberians to realize the

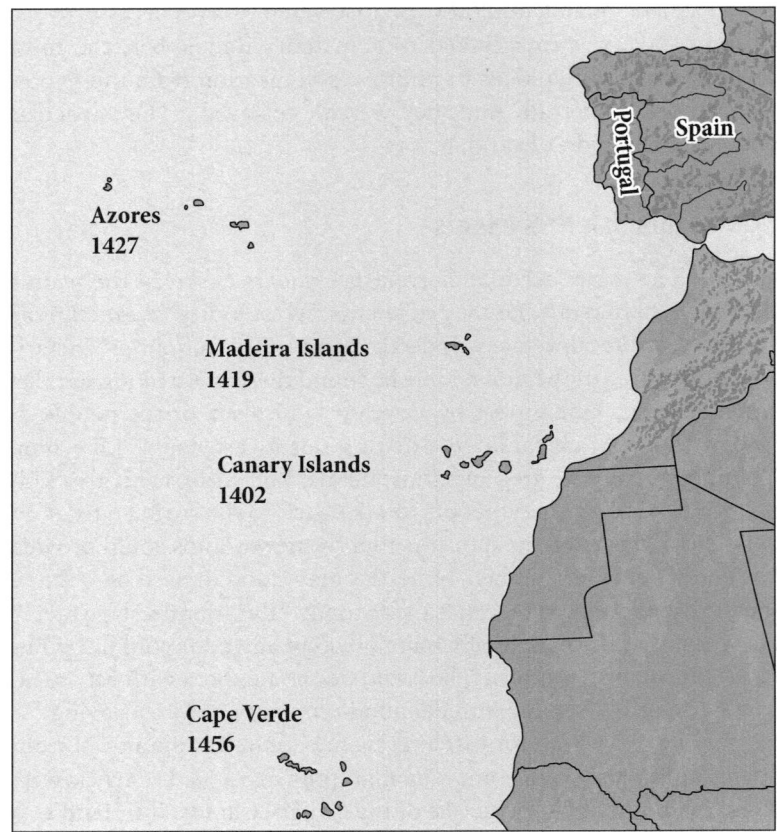

Figure 1 Map of the eastern Atlantic islands with rough dates of invasion by Portugal and Spain. (National borders are modern.)

extraordinary potential to grow one of the world's most valuable substances there.

And so, we finally come to sugar. Europeans had traded for it for countless centuries, but the Crusades brought Europeans into contact with Arab sugarcane operations more than ever. And when Crusaders briefly held lands in the Levant, they became sugar cultivators, in turn. Sugar operations proliferated to a number of Mediterranean islands and shores from there.[8] But the Canaries were sunnier still, and the Spanish created sugar farms and mills on those islands from the early 1490s, competing with Portuguese operations on the Madeira Islands just to their north. Within 30 years, sugar fields covered the main islands, and the colonizers sent over 4,000 tons of the substance to Spain per year.[9] Forget trading for Arabs' sugar: now they had their own.

As on the Iberian Peninsula, the Spaniards held people in slavery on the Canaries. But, with the new labor-intensive sugar industry, they desired *more* concentrated slaveholding. Below, we'll deal more with the bone-breaking industrial processing demanded by sugar. But, for now, suffice it to say that sugar refining took intense work on a scale with little precedent. The first people the Spaniards enslaved were their POWs, the Canarians who'd dared resist their invasion. But they weren't enough. And, as much as possible, free people avoided the horrible work of bringing in the sugar harvest and processing it.[10] So the Spanish trafficked people from Iberian slave markets, traded with Portuguese traffickers who raided or traded on the West Coast of Africa, or made their own raids and deals on the African coast despite the Portuguese monopoly.[11] It's impossible to fix numbers of the victims imported, but one of the main Canary Islands was populated by around 10 percent enslaved people in the 1500s.[12]

Already by Columbus's second voyage to the Caribbean, he took sugarcane shoots from the Canaries with him.[13] By 1515, sugar farms and mills took root around Santo Domingo, today's Dominican Republic. Why, when there were sugar operations much closer to Spain? Quite simply because the market could support it. Prices were high; consumers wanted it. Meanwhile, the Caribbean offered bright sun and often good rainfall.[14] It shouldn't be surprising, then, that the Spaniards repeated patterns established on the Canaries: try to enslave the local population, then reach further afield for more victims.[15] And just like on the Canary Islands, Spanish violence and disease combined in a population catastrophe for the Taíno people of Hispaniola.[16] From the first years of the 1500s, the Spaniards started raiding all around the Caribbean, then Central and South America, to kidnap people for the new sugar industry and other purposes.[17] So began the trafficking in the native inhabitants of the Americas that lasted for centuries.

But these weren't enough and, like in the Canaries, the Spaniards quickly began trafficking in West African captives to their Caribbean colonies. Scholars estimate the numbers of trafficked people from the start around 1513 to 1600 at 75,000–90,000, at least. That number's derived from official slaving licenses; given the activity of smugglers, experts think it's low. Meanwhile, places like Hispaniola and Puerto Rico didn't attract many Spanish settlers, so that very soon some sugar-growing areas counted ten enslaved Africans to one Spanish person.[18] We'll return to this extraordinary new dynamic in the pages to come.

The English Following in the Wake

It will sound like the English were left out of this history. And in a way that's right: in the first years of the 1500s, King Henry VII was consolidating his power and wasn't a real player in European power games. As mentioned before, his son Henry VIII tried to take his status to the next level, but couldn't determine his own fate without carefully considering his relationship to the mighty Spaniards and French. His break with the Pope was part of that effort to determine his own fate. That break made England the enemy of the bigger European powers and shaped things tremendously. For the purposes of this book's project, that means two main things: the English sailors would get drawn to the Americas as traders *with*, raiders *of*, and human traffickers *for* other empires; and the English would land on the coast of North America as competitors to Catholic rivals further south. English merchants took great advantage of new Spanish trade opportunities up until the reign of Elizabeth, when they realized England was taking the Protestant path. (Again, this story of England's parting with Catholic neighbors may seem like a diversion, but it helps explain the roots of its imperialism, to which we'll return in Chapter 4.)

Following the now-familiar pattern, the Spanish explored the southeastern seaboard of what is today the USA in 1521 and immediately kidnapped the local people, around seventy of them, at the first opportunity from somewhere around today's South Carolina or Georgia.[19] They sent some victims to Hispaniola and some to Spain, where most died.[20]

Encouraged by this first trip, the Spanish returned to the southeastern coast in 1526, quite conscious that they were replaying a role like the "reconquerors" of Spain, crusading knights come to expand Christendom.[21] Their plan was to create a base of operations, which they'd call "San Miguel de Gualdape," complete with seeds and farmers, doctors, and priests. It seems the Spaniards planned to leave local inhabitants in peace, provided they were "moral" and accepted Spanish dominion.[22] And, just as Spanish Caribbean colonies had started importing West African captives, so did these North American colonists from the very start. Thus, the first African enslaved people, around 100, arrived in what would be the USA, near what's today Georgia. But this 1526 colony failed, its people sick and hungry like so many other colonists. It's heartening, though, that the first Africans trafficked to North America were also the first rebels. Before the colony collapsed and the Spaniards sailed away, the captives set fire to a Spanish leader's house and slipped away into the forest. Some may have been integrated, then, into local Indian communities.[23]

We've been following the Spanish line because they preceded the English to the Americas and drew the English across the Atlantic first as traders with them, then as rivals against them.[24] Also, we've established that, by the time the English created their own New World footholds, the Spaniards had made trafficking of Indigenous people and West Africans routine. The English, then, didn't need to invent elaborate ideological justifications for such violence. There wasn't some hurdle for them to get over in order for them to "get over" the idea of brutally abusing their fellow humans. The pattern was well worn.

The English were very late to colonization in the Americas, agents of an investment company arriving only in 1607 (after a failed attempt in 1587), naming their outpost after their King James. Jamestown, planted in the middle of a land called Tsenacommacah by the people who lived there, wasn't a royal venture. The organization placed its fort deep up a river estuary in a defensible place precisely because they feared the rival Spanish might try to drive them out – claiming what we call Virginia for themselves, even though it was so far north from Spanish colonial centers. Like San Miguel de Gualdape's, it was a miserable experience for the first Englishmen who tried to set up there. Within a few years, nearly all of them had starved – in part because they acted stupidly with the people who lived there, the Powhatan Confederation. But, in part due to reinforcements arriving by incredible luck, Jamestown scraped by. It's worth mentioning here that the English intrusion could easily have been stopped by the Powhatan people, who numbered 15,000 to the colony's roughly 100. Not only did English "guns, germs, and steel" *not* help them – the Powhatans mercifully gave the starving men food.

One of the reasons we've spent so much time on the Spanish is because it helps us to understand the Englishmen's (and they were all men, at first – an important factor) plans and methods. Like the Spanish in the Caribbean and even more in what's today Mexico, the English were aiming for silver or gold, or at least a river route to the Pacific.[25] They weren't planning an Irish-style plantation, a sort of feudal farming colony. Such things would have to await the flourishing of religious idealists farther to the north. The Jamestown venture, like so many that followed it, was an investment. It was supposed to pay more in return than its 1,700 investors put in – the sooner, the better. This followed old historical patterns like companies that invested in trade to Moscow or the eastern Mediterranean in the later Middle Ages. And it followed newer developments like investing in sugar operations; for example, people in what's today Germany were investing in the Canarian sugar business already by the early 1500s.[26]

Native Americans and the First Large-Scale English Slaving

As with other patterns, English human trafficking and enslaving followed Spanish and older precedents. Even before getting a foothold in North America, individual English kidnappers took small groups of native inhabitants captive to send back to the royal court or for resale in a distant market, as scholar Margaret Ellen Newell describes.[27] Warfare created more captives. Naturally, native people of the Chesapeake region resisted as more and more English people arrived. The same happened in regions further north. From 1620, English people landed in what today is Massachusetts, aiming, unlike on the Chesapeake, to create growing plantations on the scale of Ireland's. Fighting between the people who lived there and the newcomers to the region tended to be small scale and local. But it resulted in Indigenous prisoners of war. Dr. Newell finds the Pequot War of 1636–1638, which was fought around what is today Connecticut and Rhode Island, a grim turning point. It was the biggest conflict to date between the English and one native society, and thus created the most POWs, around 300; but it also marked a moment when the colonists aimed to capture native people *for the purpose* of enslaving them.[28]

Was this because the Europeans defined slavery by physical appearance, now? No, not yet. Englishmen's perceptions of the physical characteristics of various Indian peoples were mixed. Some colonizers, for example, believed native peoples had darker skin chiefly because of exposure to the sun and elements. For them, indicators like Indians' dress or weapons, rather than flesh tone, were more revealing about their nature. Not surprisingly, Englishmen drew on comparisons to the Irish – or at least the Irish of their imaginations.[29] Yet, "the Indians," like the Irish, weren't a *slave race*, per se. Indeed, the colonists allied with regional Indian peoples against the Pequots and didn't propose to enslave all of them. They made distinctions. And the Pequots, in particular, provided what the Europeans viewed as a "just cause" and, again, an opportunity.

The Europeans wanted two main things from the Pequots. First, they wanted captive agricultural and domestic laborers, which they'd struggled to supply in New England.[30] By enslaving them, the English colonists could also sell their enemies out of the region and to the West Indies, including the tiny English colony at Providence Island (off today's Nicaragua).[31] Second, they also wanted to eliminate the Pequot as a people so they would never resist the colonists again. In an ominous sign of things to come, the English took some of the captives into their households on the theory that they could educate the Pequots – "civilize" or Christianize them – and then free the captives later in life once they were no longer a threat.[32] The term "assimilation" is ours, not theirs, but it fits, looking back on this tactic. It should also call to mind Ireland of the same period. English colonists in North America made explicit comparisons between the two and were motivated by the same outrage that native peoples rejected English customs and rule.[33] Meanwhile, in a treaty with their Indian allies against the Pequots, the English declared that no one should even speak the name "Pequot" again after their defeat.[34] They even renamed the "Pequot River" the Thames.[35] On a local scale, this was about elimination.[36]

Inevitably, this mention of eliminating the Pequots down to their very name brings to mind our concept of ethnic cleansing or genocide. Ethnic cleansing is defined as an attempt by one group to eliminate an ethnicity or religion from a certain region by force or fear, or by making their life impossible.[37] Yes, the Pequot War and its aftermath amounted to what we'd call determined ethnic cleansing.[38] Note that the English colonizers could and *did* distinguish between the Pequots – a people to be eliminated – and neighboring peoples like the Narragansetts – an acceptable group. They didn't view the various peoples around them as being of "one blood." And so, the colonizers didn't try to eradicate "Indian blood," the concept of a sole "Indian race" awaiting later generations. Indeed, in the pages to come we'll see the horrors of wholesale genocide in the US West in a later period based on that indiscriminate thinking.

(There's a quote, dated two or three decades before the Pequot war, attributed to King James I, that foreshadowed all of this. As he was planning to take Scottish Protestants and "plant them" in northern Ireland, to colonize, he is supposed to have ordered, "plant Ireland with Puritans and root out the Papists [Catholics] and then secure it."[39] The idea of rooting out – "extirpating," in the usage of the time – was very much a transplantable idea.)

After the Pequot war of elimination, the English adopted Pequot children and took Pequot women in order to transform them into something other than Pequot. The English told themselves they were saving Indian souls and demonstrating their benevolence.[40] Let's take a moment here to observe that, yes, adopting Indian children to transform them, "assimilate" them, naturally implies that English Christians thought their way was right or better. That's a hallmark of white supremacy, so we need to see that as an early building block, even if we haven't arrived, yet, in 1638.

So, yes, there was a specific sense of superiority at play, but adopting (which certainly harkened toward eventual "Indian Boarding Schools," too) was done out of fear or frustration at an enemy capable of resisting and even hurting the English. We're going to see that, ironically, fear that whites *aren't* supreme, or won't easily *stay* supreme, is completely woven throughout white supremacy. And that sense, explain scholars like Linda Colley, emerged from the earliest sustained contacts with foreign societies that had no intention of acknowledging English superiority.[41]

Perversely, in retrospect, Indigenous enemies of the Pequot took part in the spoils of war in the form of captives. That is, they took their share of enslaved Pequots, too. Historically, not all native communities held slaves, but some, like the Pequots' neighbors, did in small numbers, largely for symbolic reasons.[42] In this case, there were rules governing the treatment of the enslaved that kept them from the worst abuse. It's also highly unlikely that the Pequots' enemies understood that they were taking part in a practice that meant their enemies would be traded thousands of miles away, many to die from disease and abuse. They had no precedent for a globe-spanning traffic. (Thankfully, by the way, all of these efforts failed, and today the Pequots live on, despite it all.)

In a few decades, after making more war on native peoples, the New Englanders generated a large human traffic to what's today the American South.[43] During the same generation, colonists began paying allied Indian peoples to raid for captives among enemy Indian peoples. Again, for the colonizers, this was to get rid of enemies, produce unfree laborers, and generate trade to the West Indies, including to new English colonies there. These evils combined so that between 1670 and 1715, as historian Alan Gallay wrote, "more Indians were exported through Charles Town [Charleston] than Africans were imported during this period."[44] While arriving at the number is difficult, scholar Brett Rushforth calculated that from the early 1600s until the end of the traffic, Europeans in North America enslaved around 2–4 million Indigenous people.[45] Remember that when you hear arguments that Indigenous people were "eliminated by" disease as if colonists bore no more responsibility for horrors than bearing germs in their bodies.

Resisting These Trends

History shows that deep historical, and more recent Spanish, precedent provided justification for enslaving people in North America from the earliest days of English colonization. But the fact that we can pick out and, over time, follow these genetic building blocks that would lead to the evolution of white supremacy doesn't mean these *had to* result in white supremacy. People resisted these things. In fact, the deep history of whiteness and white supremacy can't be separated from a parallel deep history of resistance *to* white supremacy. Put simply, they came into being together and shaped each other.

The first and most important resistance came from kidnapped people themselves, of course. Already in 1521, African and Indian captives united in a sustained revolt at Santo Domingo in the Caribbean.[46] And you just read the story of the 100 or so African people who set a fire and bravely fled into the forest at the failed Spanish colony of San Miguel de Gualdape. These were only the first of countless escapes and revolts. For centuries, Indigenous people resisted through escape to neighboring tribes or into the vast North American hinterlands.[47]

Meanwhile, many non-enslaved people judged slavery as evil, too. For that, it's time for another diversion to Spain and one of the most famous cases of early anti-slavery in the mid 1500s. The story is important because it shows that the Europeans of that period didn't all assume that slavery was right or natural. "Men of their time," in fact, argued hard against it, and those arguments got a fair hearing, even "won," in the courts of emperors. Readers should help themselves to the dramatic tale of Bartolomé de las Casas, but I'll offer a quick sketch here. Las Casas showed up in Hispaniola in 1502 as a conqueror and colonist, even a slaver. But he quickly soured on the cruelty and joined the Dominican Order as a missionary to the native peoples. His travels showed him more Spanish slaving, cruelty, and murder and he started to campaign against it in the New World. The Spaniards benefiting from slave labor opposed him fiercely, trying to kill him on more than one occasion, and Las Casas struggled for decades against the slave system. (Unfortunately, for some years he advocated for West African slave labor to replace Indigenous before repenting of that, too.)

By 1550, after decades of campaigning and now a bishop, Las Casas participated in a days-long debate with a champion of New World slavery in the court of the mighty Spanish emperor. His opponent justified slavery by citing Aristotle who, while not the only ancient authority, and countered by other ancient authorities, argued that some peoples, barbarian peoples, were born natural slaves. Las Casas didn't say Aristotle was wrong, but denied that New World peoples were barbarians. Further, Las Casas said, Christian tradition said that Christians' first duty was to attract converts peacefully. Non-Christians outside Christendom could not be held liable for their lack of belief and most certainly could not be attacked and enslaved. In the end, Bishop Bartolomé de las Casas "won" the debate, and the Spanish emperor proclaimed that violent expansion must cease in favor of free labor and proselytizing.[48] At about the same time, Las Casas also published, with imperial approval, a book called *A Brief Relation of the Destruction of the Indians* (1552).

Yet the ultimate outcome is revealing, too: far over the ocean and well beyond the control of the imperial court, and motivated by the allure of silver and other impulses, conquistadores and other Spaniards continued their slaughter and slavery, emperor be damned.

As they did in all periods, whether as captives or not, Africans themselves fought against slavery. The central Angolan prince Lourenço da Silva Mendonça was exiled to Brazil with his family by the colonizing Portuguese in 1671. This may have been because of his royal family's refusal to pay a tax in enslaved people. When colonial Brazilian authorities feared the power of his family there, the Portuguese re-exiled Mendonça to Portugal itself, where he studied for years. He eventually joined a network of Catholic charitable societies, used that network and missionary connections to gather bloody evidence about the slave trade, traveled to Spain and Rome, and eventually, in 1684, won a case in the Papal court condemning Catholic countries of Europe for their participation. This included Native American slavery and Jews forcibly converted to Christianity. The Pope of the day thus called for emancipation. Yet, as with Las Casas, his words had relatively little effect in practice.[49]

Then there were non-Africa-descended Englishmen who opposed slavery. Experts find that this early outcry was based on the Golden Rule, which shouldn't be surprising in an era largely before a concept of race-based, or "racialized," slavery.[50] In other words, if the victims were *essentially* like yourself – human beings – they shouldn't be owned or brutally abused just because they had the misfortune of being POWs. Do unto others as you would have them do unto you. So preached Puritan leader Samuel Rishworth on Providence Island in 1633, who railed against enslaving trafficked Africans and may even have given them supplies to help some successfully escape.[51] His pro-slavery rivals, meanwhile, argued against him using the ancient argument about Africans' bodies: they were shaped by environmental-humoral factors to thrive in the heat, unlike English bodies.[52] On the other hand, the colony of Rhode Island rejected life slavery in 1652, stating that all trafficked people must be freed within ten years along the lines of indenture.[53] Aphra Behn's 1688 novel *Oroonoko* told the story of a noble African prince enslaved and brutally abused by Englishmen who were in all ways his lesser. Also from the 1680s, Pennsylvania's Quakers started proclaiming against slavery and for equal rights on a Christian basis.

By 1712, the colony forbade the trafficking of people within its borders, but the English Crown overruled Pennsylvania. Quakers' early anti-slavery, too, mixed Golden Rule sympathy for their fellow creations of God and self-concern that proximity to the degrading practice of slavery polluted them.[54]

(Meanwhile, broadly, the English told themselves that, whatever else, *their* colonialism wasn't the violent kind like the Spaniards'. Historian Michael Guasco wrote about this – while pointing out that the English made such proclamations shortly after the eliminationist Pequot War.[55])

People as Property: A New, Key Genetic Building Block towards the Evolution of White Supremacy

Did English-speakers, from their first days as New World slaveholders, believe that enslaved people were property for life? No. Or, at least, not exactly. Again, the record shows that slavery as a concept was familiar to English-speakers in the 1600s, even though there was essentially no slaveholding in England, Wales, and Scotland at the time. As historian Michael Guasco wrote, "slavery, for all intents and purposes, was alive and well in England, even if actual slaves were hard to find."[56] It was part of their past, a common part of the Bible retold by priests and depicted in stained glass, part of classical tales, and Portugal and Spain had been active slavers for a century by then. Yet English people who accepted some form of forced labor for criminals or POWs were not at all sure – at the beginning – that there should be chattel slavery – that is, that people, even their offspring, should be *possessions*.

The sources tell us different things, but there's good evidence that England, Scotland, and Wales's tradition of relatively unfree contract labor, indentured labor, largely framed people's thinking early on.[57] For example, some English human traffickers, like one William Jackson in 1645, sold kidnapped Africans as laborers with seven-year contracts to Bermuda.[58] Enslaved children were supposed to be subject to thirty-year terms of servitude. Yet, during nearly the same years, the late 1630s, there were traffickers who claimed they were selling people on ninety-nine-year terms. Ninety-nine-year, or "perpetual," contracts were utterly outside the norm.[59] This sinister side-stepping of tradition appears to have been opportunistic: it was the sort of thing that could happen when "indentures" had no recourse to justice, no one who could speak for them. On the other hand, some indentured POWs *did* have people who spoke up against abuses. In the 1650s, Scottish and Irish petitioners to Parliament complained about the abuse of indentured laborers in Bermuda, their countrymen, "transported" as POWs.[60] And scholar Margaret Newell discovered a case in which officials in Bermuda's colonial company located in England advocated for enslaved Indians on Bermuda itself. Those trafficked Indians were freeborn, they said, and should have been indentured servants, not enslaved. They should receive retroactive contracts (and be baptized), for "their enslavement was to the great dishonour of God and pulling down of His judgment against us."[61] But this effort seems to have come to naught.

And the evidence suggests that at least some of the first English promoters of slaveholding over indenture were quite aware that they were making a new case, a break from tradition. A writer like early Enlightenment courtier Balthazar Gerbier, who advocated for Caribbean colonization, knew slaving might challenge readers' "scruples."[62] So he wrote justifications to ease the consciences of his readers – and King Charles II, his main target. He argued that enslaved West Africans had already been enslaved in their own countries. Further, they were heathens, which called upon the ages-old justifications outlined in Chapter 1. Finally, citing a justification offered by slavers and apologists to this day, captivity by Europeans would improve or uplift West Africans by exposure to Christianity. (Mind you, for those without such delicate scruples, Gerbier also said they simply made good return-on-investment sense: you hardly had to clothe them and never had to pay them a penny.[63])

There were still other mixed views. An English Puritan writing in the 1670s, for example, believed that people enslaved for crimes should receive harsh treatment, while others should be viewed more like indentured servants.[64] Meanwhile, at first, in 1656, the Virginia colony was explicit about not enslaving Indians' children.[65] Then, in 1662, Virginia clarified in law that a child born to an enslaved mother *was* enslaved for life. A few years later, the Virginia colony's leaders were concerned enough about priests baptizing enslaved children, concerned that making captive children Christians might support arguments that they should be freed, that they issued an explicit declaration:

> Whereas some doubts have risen whether children that are slaves by birth ... should by virtue of their baptism be made free; It is enacted ... that the conferring of baptism doth not alter the condition of the person as to his bondage or freedom.[66]

This was a rather practical way in which the term "white" began to replace "Christian" as a distinction between free Europeans and captive Africans and Native Americans.[67] That is, quite simply, if the enslaved could also be a Christian, a new term was needed.

And records show that, by around the 1730s, British colonists regularly divided their world into "white," "black," and "Indian" or "red."[68]

Even as People Started to Be Classed as "Property," Resistance Continued

As much as proponents of Indigenous and African slavery won the day against their critics, there were still those who argued that English colonies, like England itself, were uniquely lands of freedom. The Virginia colony, for example, claiming in 1610 and Jamaica's new English rulers claiming in 1672 that they would never treat "Indians" the way the cruel Spaniards would.[69] As late as 1732, the new colony of Georgia tried to ban slave-holding as a vice that hurt a healthy society, along the lines of alcohol.[70] And there were those who argued that all humankind were common sons of Adam and should be treated with equal compassion.[71]

Scholars recently shared the story of one Indigenous man who sued for his freedom, showing that slavers couldn't always be confident of success. It was a victorious act of auto-emancipation *and* shows early English anti-slavery at the same time. An English slaver kidnapped a child of the Chesapeake Pamunkeys, Weyanokes, Mattaponis, or Chiskiacs, luring him away from home, and selling him as a lifetime servant to an Englishman around 1649. (The young victim was supposed to have signed an "X" on a lifetime contract of indenture which he couldn't read.) After decades of labor, the man, called "James" by his captors, entered a suit in Massachusetts Bay court.[72] While he seems to have had help in composing his filing, James's testimony was his own, and he succeeded in convincing the judge that he hadn't entered into the contract willingly, as an illiterate child. His captor appealed the case to a higher court, complaining that his "servant had been taken away."[73] James, he attested, had been a war captive and thus a legitimate lifetime slave, no matter what the contract suggested. Now more English colonists took James's side citing the Golden Rule, writing to the court that they were showing the same concern "as they would desire might be shown to them in the like case."[74] Unfortunately, we don't know the outcome of the appeal, or even whether the court ever heard it. James's captor's estate made no mention of him at the captor's death ten years later – perhaps James won his freedom, after all.

This early period offers cases of Africa-descended people winning their freedom in court, too. The evidence from England and Scotland of the 1500s–1600s frankly shows a consistent series of court losses by those who wanted to treat servants or indentured laborers like slaves outside of the colonies.[75] (The problem, of course, was getting the victim a day in court to begin with. They might need allies with the money and knowledge needed to access the court.) Judges said that there was simply no law of human property in English or Scottish legal tradition.[76]

As time passed and British wealth became more dependent on the existence of slavery, slavery-interests tried to get the law to guarantee their "property" in people. For example, slaving profiteers tried to get a guarantee from the British government that the enslaved remained enslaved in Britain and that baptism didn't change their status. And two high officials tried to placate them in 1729 with just such a declaration.[77] But, at least in England, Scotland, and Wales, it never really worked. The courts simply found no precedent for the new version of total chattel slavery – unassailable property in human beings. While poor servants *could* be mistreated like serfs, essentially, they could neither be owned nor trafficked as a parcel of property. Slavers could never be confident that their captives were truly "captive" on English or British soil and so they relatively rarely brought them there. That would have been a little too risky. Meanwhile, the evidence shows that slavers *did* use English legal tradition in the area of property rights to defend their cruelty *abroad* with more success.[78]

The idea that "England was too pure an Air for Slaves to breathe in," as a judge appeared to say in 1637, might have pushed the idea that England/Britain was a land of freedom-loving people –

pure – unlike other lands.[79] We'll spend more time on that in the next chapter.

Back to freedom suits in court, scholar Taunya Banks offers a revealing case of a woman and her son in 1655 Virginia. At least in that early period, an Africa-descended person might get their day in colonial court and claim that indenture, even for a person born to an African mother, was different from lifetime slavery. Elizabeth Key, of what we'd call mixed race, was sold into indenture by her father for a nine-year term. When the original employer-master died, the estate claimed that Key was in fact a slave. She successfully argued that she was an English subject like her father, a Christian, and indentured, not enslaved. She might have been motivated, too, by the birth of her son, fearing that he was doomed to a lifetime of slavery, as well. Instead, Key convinced the court, and she and her child escaped, thankfully.[80] But, unfortunately, between her success in around 1656 and around 1700, new laws roadblocked avenues like that taken by Elizabeth Key and James.[81]

A Large, Bleak Shift in a Sole Lifetime

In the first decades of slave labor on an island like Barbados or in Virginia, which preceded big sugar and tobacco industries, enslaved Africans lived a grim daily life similar to bonded servants, convicts, and so on.[82] That's not to minimize the horror of captivity, nor to say that servitude and slavery were the same – since people in one category had a solid expectation of release and those in the other could only hope. These changes help mark a distinction between that early period and a later period when there'd be powerful, all-encompassing concepts of a "slave race" and a sharp division between Africans and people deemed "white." White supremacy didn't lead to slavery, which was old; New World slavery helped lead to white supremacy, which was new.

Even if slavery, in the words of one historian, was "the product of many laws and policies," the change from uncertain status of, say, four- to ninety-nine-year indenture to slave-race-by-law was relatively swift.[83] Some scholars point to one man's lifetime as a good example of this quick pace.[84] Anthony Johnson was trafficked from southwest Africa around 1621 and sold probably as a medium-term indentured laborer, perhaps of fifteen years. Or, perhaps, his was a "perpetual" contract. In any case, he either completed his term or managed to buy it out. He married a trafficked African woman, had children, and received a significant parcel of land from the Virginia colony in exchange for sponsoring servants or tenant settlers. He grew tobacco for the market and corn/maize for subsistence. He even kept at least one captive laborer, probably a long-term indentured servant named "Casor." (Casor, in turn, kept his own cattle, from which he profited, owing a percentage to Johnson.[85]) He engaged in lawsuits, successfully appealed for a tax abatement, and swore legal oaths. By all appearances, in the mid 1650s, Johnson was a respected member of the community who could more or less depend on his rights as a productive colonist like his neighbors. Johnson lived to the ripe old age of around seventy, dying in 1670. And things would prove that 1670 Virginia was different from 1620 Virginia.

Now, his heirs could not inherit his property; instead, it reverted to the Crown because, in the words of Virginia officials, "he was a Negroe and by consequence an alien."[86] He was not a real subject, not a citizen; in sum, he was a social outcast. A generation or so later, his free, Christian descendants couldn't appear in court or swear oaths. By then, in many American colonies, not long after Johnson died, and even though his free descendants lived on, "being a slave" became almost synonymous with "being Black" or descended from Africans.

There's little to be gained by trying pin down an exact, limited date for the rise of chattel slavery. It's worthwhile to recognize that this moment was fuzzy and occurred at different times in different places. But a general shift around 1660–1700 has won favor by historians for a while.[87] We'll see at the end of the chapter the types of laws that, one by one, made this shift an evil reality.

There are two main reasons for this shift to human-as-property. First, Englishmen and other Europeans wanted a truly captive labor force. "Free Blacks," as they were called, were of no use to them. And while it's probably correct to say the Indigenous people of North America were the first mass group enslaved by Englishmen, Amerindians had some recourse to retreat, escape, and diplomacy. (The colonists sometimes had to maintain good relations with the native people around and within their encroachments.) Africans didn't have such potential recourse. As historian Lorena Walsh put it:

So long as white servants made up most of the labor force, English work customs tended to prevail . . . . But once slaves came to dominate the bound labor force late in the seventeenth century, the experiences of slaves and servants diverged. Slaves had no claim to English workers' customary rights [to barely adequate food, shelter, rest, and so on].[88]

And that's even before we come to the matter of bodily autonomy for African and Africa-descended females.

It's time to return to sugar. With the rise of that industry among the British (and, to a lesser extent, tobacco cultivation), colonists wanted a labor force so completely under their thumb that it would perform excruciating labor or face nearly unlimited retribution.

Indentured servants were still people; and, for the new sugar-growing industrialists, the new capitalists, that was a problem. There were vast fortunes to be made for sugar growers and their investors in London, Amsterdam, or Edinburgh. Sometime after the middle of the seventeenth century, the sugar exports of Barbados alone were worth more than all the silver and gold exported from Spain's New World mines.[89] Yet indentured workers from England or Scotland wouldn't do the excruciating work, or wouldn't do it at a price low enough for growers.[90]

It was body-breaking, even killing, work. To grow sugar, laborers slashed and burned the land to clear it. They then planted shoots, "cane stems," by hand, in long, shallow furrows. To be clear: planting wasn't about casting seeds, it was about men, women, and children bending over under the subtropical sun to place shoots in the earth, at least several thousand per acre. The threat of violence or even torture might very well enforce captives' rate of work. After planting, the enslaved workers had to weed, cull bad shoots, and work against vermin.[91] Harvesting and processing the tall plants was even worse and, because fields matured at different periods, went on continually for half the year. Anthropologist Georgia L. Fox, who painstakingly uncovered English sugar operations on the island of Antigua, wrote:

> To avoid spoilage, extracting the juice from cane stalks quickly was critical. Crushing the cane in the mill . . . was dangerous work that required skilled hands and calm minds. The powerful jaws of the iron rollers might mangle hands

and arms, while the rapidly spinning sails could sever human heads. In the boiling room, stirring and monitoring kettles of molten sugar could result in third-degree burns. Packing the sugar into large hogsheads and loading them onto wagons required strong backs and alert drivers to haul cargo over gutted dirt roads.[92]

Work went on for at least twelve hours a day, or during all subtropical daylight. Writing of a later era of cotton slave-labor operations, historian Edward Baptist's words capture something that was already developing in this earlier era. He called it "calibrated torture": slaveholders fine-tuned the maximum labor they could wring out of their victims, while minimizing their allocation of food and sleep, and while injuring, but not breaking, their bodies.[93]

At certain points, the high prices for sugar meant it made balance-book "sense" to work people to death. Yes, in the new system of slavery-from-birth, slaveholders got a "free" slave from a captive infant. But the churning machine of the sugar operation didn't allow for trafficking more women or keeping them or their children healthy. Instead, sugar capitalists kept feeding young Black men's lives into the sugar mill in the Caribbean (and, later, the Louisiana area) before the end of the trans-Atlantic trade. Put another way, there was a "natural decrease" in the numbers of the enslaved. But nature, in the form of disease and few births, played only a part. It's clear that owners chose work-to-death over keeping humans alive, too.[94]

For women in particular, their transformation from unfree laborers to property in the eyes of the law meant horrors. Indentured women were supposed to retain the right to their bodies. They were poor and vulnerable, so those rights were often on paper only, practically few or nil. But the record shows that, if they were lucky or connected to free and privileged people, indentured women could and did appeal to the law in cases of rape or its threat, sometimes successfully.[95] The threat of court and social norms provided *some* protection, at least. Not so when slavery replaced indenture and when a race-basis evolved to justify and protect slavery. Colonial laws tended to be silent on the topic of slaveholders' *right* to rape enslaved women; on the other hand, they were explicit on the slaveholders' right to violence against their captives who, in the law's words, "resisted" them. Masters' rights were total, including the right over life and death.[96]

Fear of Revolt as a Driver of Race-Based Slavery

Besides the desire for a captive labor force, the English were motivated by their fear of uprisings. The English had no precedent for their developing slave societies in the New World, colonies in which the enslaved locally outnumbered enslavers, where the essence of the colony itself depended on slave labor. For example, by the 1670s, there were 44,000 Africa-descended people, compared with 21,000 English and other Europeans in Bermuda.[97] Most resistance by captives was quiet, daily, meant to hamper their captors, not result in a lethal response.[98] But while it meant taking a desperate, maybe even hopeless, risk, captive people did rise to attack the slave societies around them. You'll recall that the very first Africans trafficked to the North American eastern seaboard set a fire to cover their escape. And the fire and flight never stopped down the generations, with very roughly one uprising – or the bloody repression of a rumored uprising – each year on average over three centuries in the English-colonized Americas.[99] For example, in 1712, there was a large uprising in New York, where the enslaved were around 20 percent of the population. The list goes on and on.

The famous Bacon's Rebellion of 1676–1677 saw the English Crown briefly lose control of its Virginia colony at the hands of a large, successful rebel body. It centered on animosity toward Virginia's Royal Governor and his pro-landlord policies. They also charged that he was too soft on Indigenous peoples, even though he favored attacking and enslaving some of them.[100] But, although it wasn't much of a justice movement, indentured English and enslaved (or indentured) Africans united in an uprising that saw Jamestown largely burned down. The English put the rebellion down quickly after Nathaniel Bacon died of disease, but colonial leaders took its lesson to heart. In the classic tactic of the British Empire, they would divide and conquer, passing piecemeal laws that would separate and stratify poor Englishmen and Africans.[101]

Perhaps just as frightening to slaveholders were rumors of conspiracies; for example, in 1690 there was a panic in Massachusetts over a supposed conspiracy among an Englishman named Isaac Morill, an enslaved African named James, and an enslaved Indigenous man named Joseph. Rumor had it that they were planning on running to a French colony and returning in force to free the enslaved population.[102]

A slightly different way of expressing "fear of uprising" might be "an awareness that slaveholders were persecuting their fellow humans who *quite naturally* would resist and were capable of doing so." (James Baldwin wrote "the people who settled the country had a fatal flaw. They could recognize a man when they saw one. . . . the only way to justify the role this chattel was playing in one's life was to say that he was not a man. For if he wasn't, then no crime had been committed."[103]) Historian Kay Lewis emphasized that slaveholders were quite aware that their West African and Amerindian captives were very often capable fighters who'd had the misfortune of being taken captive in war. Far from thinking that they were "lesser" or "docile" or naturally subservient to some kind of master race, English observers expected able, strong resistance.[104] As Thomas Jefferson wrote, the enslaved were "at least as brave" as whites.[105]

Thus, English enslavers passed new laws or "slave codes" out of fear. Indeed, the first, the Barbados slave code of 1661, justified itself by claiming that the enslaved – Native American and African – were "uncertaine, dangerous kinde of people."[106] The rules, which largely provided a model for other colonies' laws, demanded severe, public punishments, including mutilations, to make an example of captives who physically resisted.[107] They also absolved captors of severe liability if they maimed or killed their victims. Not surprisingly, the rules demanded public, horrific beatings and torture of African captives suspected of planning revolts or "guilty" of the like, too. For similar reasons, laws like Jamaica's 1696 slave code demanded that those Africans who'd successfully escaped but were later caught be sensationally maimed. To stop conspiracies, real or imagined, later codes barred public gatherings of the enslaved, limited their movement, and banned teaching captives to read. The laws effectively warned that "Free Blacks" must be watched by officials, too, for signs of conspiracy. Thus, new laws in the middle of the eighteenth century in places like New York and Philadelphia restricted Free Blacks' movements and other activities.[108] Over-policing of Black people in America is an old tradition.

Denying formerly enslaved men the vote was also meant to teach them their place: Virginia's governor wrote that the Black freeman "looks on himself . . . to be as good a man as the best of his neighbours," which couldn't be allowed to stand.[109] Virginia denied voting rights to freemen in 1723, suspecting that they'd use their votes to help the cause of the enslaved. Laws declaring that children born to enslaved mothers were also slaves were certainly opportunistic – slavers simply wanted more laborers, and there was no one to stop them; but fear of a population of Free Blacks in the English/British midst was also part of that transition.[110] That fear led to savage, public torture and murder of the enslaved for reasons ranging from aiding escapes to minor breaches of social rules, part of the prehistory of the lynching you'll read about in Chapter 7.[111]

These trends made early modern slavery in the New World unlike any before.[112] Slavery transformed in the eyes of free English/British people. Once, it had been an unfortunate status that the victim suffered temporarily; but, as 1700 approached, it became synonymous with flesh tone.[113] As one Barbados missionary, Morgan Godwyn, wrote in 1680, "these two words, Negro and slave, [are] by custom grown homogeneous and convertible."[114] The new slave codes were practical – malevolently useful – tools to terrorize and keep captive large new populations of enslaved people engaged in what was essentially brutal factory-farming. Englishmen wanted their victims not only afraid, but also easily recognizable by color, which practically turned brown-hued people into a slave race, which was unprecedented in English, Welsh, and Scottish history. As historian Alejandro de la Fuente wrote of the new laws, they "made blackness, rather than enslavement, the mark of degradation."[115] In turn, this made light-hued people the race from which masters were drawn, too.

The rise of "black" and "white" reflected back on England, as well. Earlier, you read how skin tone was hardly worthy of comment in England prior to this period. What mattered was religion. Historian Richard Maguire shows the evidence that New World race-making now came home, so to speak, with Africa-descended people in East Anglia starting to be labeled "black" in the same 1600s period. And it's little surprise: the new capitalists whose investment wealth flowed from a slave labor system on the other side of the Atlantic were invested in a permanent, "life-captive" slave race.[116]

From the 1670s, the English human trafficking industry started ramping up. In 1672, King Charles II gave a royal charter and monopoly on the West African trade to the Royal African Company. Within a decade, the company was kidnapping around 5,000 people a year, landing them in the Caribbean. And, in the next

50 years, the publicly held joint stock company trafficked at least 150,000 victims.[117]

I should state directly what you've already deduced: capitalism and whiteness developed alongside each other.[118] Or, more than "alongside": capitalism as we know it emerged in the 1600s and 1700s with the rise of new kinds of wealth and new kinds of wealthy. The stockholder and early industrialist emerged. And, with sugar the best industrial investment, directly or indirectly capitalism encouraged the invention of master and slave races.

Final Thoughts

To repeat: while all of these circumstances transformed slavery into a thing of color and a new slave-race, people never stopped resisting or decrying it. First, as always, was the perpetual opposition of the captives themselves in a variety of forms, which was particularly heroic because so often it came at the cost of life or limb. Second, certain English colonizers called it an evil, even in the years during which "legal race-making" was triumphant. For example, Puritan writer Richard Baxter stated in 1673 that slaveholders were "the common enemies of mankind . . . fitter to be called incarnate Devils, than Christians."[119] And a splinter Quaker organization opposed the Quaker majority's complacency and participation in human trafficking, distributing a pamphlet in 1693 condemning "these evil Practices of Man-stealing [that] transgresseth that Golden Rule and Law, To do to others what we would have others do to us."[120]

Others knew that it was unnatural to brutally abuse their fellow humans, but did so anyway. In 1734, an English slaver captain named William Snelgrave didn't deny that the people he trafficked were his fellow humans. It was just that slaving money was too good. "Objections," he wrote, "have often been raised against the lawfulness of the trade. . . . I shall only observe in general that tho' to traffic in human creatures may at first sight appear barbarous, inhuman, and unnatural, yet the traders herein have as much to plead in their own excuse . . . namely, the *advantage* of it."[121]

So, no, not every "man of his time" supported slavery or believed in a slave race. If a subset of Quakers were on the social fringe, others who spoke out were not. A Massachusetts judge, Samuel Sewall, published a pamphlet against slavery in 1700, in which he argued that "all men, as they are the sons of Adam, are coheirs; and have equal right unto liberty. ... That which God has joined together men do boldly rend asunder; men from their country, husbands from their wives, parents from their children."[122]

What of the native peoples of the Americas during this transition? They didn't become slaves-by-color in this process. In part, that was for the practical reason that by the 1700s there were far fewer enslaved Indians on the eastern seaboard of North America than Africans or Africa-descended people. And yet, in later chapters, we'll see how Native Americans became "nonwhite" in additional ways.

***

The extraordinary changes leading to whiteness in this era were:

- The very particular history of the **Spanish laying the groundwork** for transatlantic trafficking and the way the English followed in their wake. To avoid the trap of thinking it was inevitable or natural that Englishmen would traffic human beings, it's important to look at the highly specific developments **that made it profitable and politically beneficial** for them to do so.
- Another misstep is to think that the mere color of West Africans led to the English declaring them a slave race. In fact, **the English overwhelmingly began with enslaving and trafficking the native peoples.** And while the English never really enslaved the Irish, the English experience of stealing the land of a people who resisted them, citing "just cause," was key for the things to come in the New World.
- There was a vast change in the status of slavery in the decades around 1700. Although it had existed all over Europe for POWs and criminals for eons, **slavery rapidly became a lifelong status** in English colonies. That was because of evil opportunism. There was no local community, and no foreign court, to advocate for their human treatment. And, eager for sugar's incredible profits, the slavers were desperate for laborers who would do the terrible work of harvesting and processing sugarcane. And they wanted more: they wanted the children of the enslaved to be enslaved, **making slavery a condition of blood.** And, out of fear of revolt,

the English did not want a population of freed Blacks in their midst.

- And **resist they did**. Whether by sabotage or escape or uprising or abolitionist campaigning, Africans and native peoples never stopped resisting – even the Pequot people whom the colonists tried to erase from the face of the Earth.

3 DEFINING WHITENESS THROUGH THE "ENLIGHTENMENT," 1600-1800

The story isn't over just because we've seen the rise of a perpetual "slave race" in the eyes of colonial American law in this period. Far from it. White supremacy came to cover the globe and has survived centuries. It took more than legal race-making in American colonies to create and reinforce it. White supremacy isn't just a situation in which pale-skinned people deem themselves superior solely to sub-Saharan African people, solely in one context. And we'll see that white supremacy didn't end with the piecemeal end of slaveholding in English-speaking lands; so, there's more to it than slavery. Furthermore, a great many white people who opposed slavery still held assumptions of white superiority. Something made whiteness (and nonwhiteness) more universal, more broad, more long-lasting. Those roots – while they certainly can't be extracted from colonization or slavery – in part lay deep in something we call "the Enlightenment."

First, a too-brief, too-reduced definition of "the Enlightenment." The term was coined in the 1800s to describe an international movement of elite thinkers of 1600 to the early 1800s who believed they were "bringing light to," or enlightening, the world.[1] These individuals, mostly men, tended to make self-aggrandizing claims that they were rejecting former sources of authority, seeking new knowledge, or using new methods of discovery. They also told themselves they were working toward progress, benevolently using their discoveries to raise human societies to new standards of reason and well-being. John Locke (writing around 1690) argued that rulers' authority came from the consent of the governed – not God – whose rights were spelled out by natural law; David Hume (writing around 1740) said that he was creating a new "science of man"; and Immanuel Kant (around 1797) proposed universal moral laws based on "practical reason." These all may sound humane in the abstract. However, in practice, not only were the key Enlightenment writers silent on slavery and related matters, but also each of the men I name above, and far more "Enlightenment" figures besides, either benefited from the slave trade or argued that non-Europeans were innately inferior.

Therefore, in this chapter, we'll see several things. We'll watch how early Enlightenment scholarship was connected to colonization (and all of its cruelties) and exploration. They were mutually dependent and reinforcing. Profits from New World slave-labor operations supported natural philosophy that justified New World slave-labor operations. Slavery and a new imagined "slave race" told the English/British that *they* were a uniquely free race and their homeland a uniquely free place. Connected to this, we'll observe how Enlightenment writers tended to place Western Europeans – themselves – atop a hierarchy of humankind. At their most extreme, some separated light-skinned Western Europeans as one *species* and darker-hued people as other species. In sum, white supremacy as we know it would have been impossible without the contributions of these elite thinkers who justified, and were justified by, colonization and slavery.

Enlightenment Writers Classifying and Ordering Humans

Chapter 1 showed how the Greeks and Romans thought about different *genuses* or families of peoples. They developed climatic or environmental theories to explain surface differences – hair and skin – and some inner differences – fiery, frigid, or depressed, for example. Chapter 2 showed how medieval English people were far more concerned with who was and was not a Christian in ways that led to an idea of Christendom or Europe. These ancient and medieval trends, though, were not the same as modern race-thinking.

It's no surprise that these longstanding patterns of dividing the world and peoples continued during the time of the Enlightenment. In fact, Enlightenment writers were explicitly writing in conversation with the ancient sources they were translating in this period. Those ancient sources tended to say that environment shaped peoples, difference was skin deep, and the important question to ask was whether a stranger was civilized or not. But, more and more, early Enlightenment observers wrote in an expanding global context that suggested *theirs* was a slave-master race while others were slave races (with gradations in between). So, say around the turn of 1600, English/British thinkers and writers often saw differences in "peoples" as being changeable; sometime in the 1700s, they more often saw differences as deep, essential, and unchanging.[2]

With greater interaction with distant peoples, Europeans carried on their centuries-old habit of classifying and, though some didn't admit it, ranking them. Such classifiers were simply following the example of those like Carl Linnaeus (1707–1778), who put Swedish flora in order, or George Cuvier (1769–1832), who put newly observed Egyptian species in ranks.[3] For some natural philosophers, the examples of the plant and animal world supported an argument that God had created several different "species" of humankind around the Earth, an idea called "polygenism."[4] Others viewed such ideas as blasphemous, as Christians' holy text stated that God created just one family line of humanity, descended from Adam and Eve, an idea called "monogenism."[5] (And, indeed, the previous chapter showed how advocates, for example some Quakers, used this sort of reasoning against the cruelty of human sibling against human sibling.) It's easy to see how polygenism was, for centuries, a convenient theory for those who wanted to justify a higher-ranking, "master" white race. In fact, a later chapter will show how arguments for separate, unequal human species grew most important in the decades around the demise of slaveholding in English-speaking lands. Those who benefited from inequality, put simply, needed new justifications and proofs. But I'm getting ahead of myself.

And yet I mean to. I'm talking about the distant forebears of post-Civil War classic scientific racism, and the Enlightenment writers who started classifying humans in ways that broke from Greek tradition were absolutely necessary to that development. There was, for example, Frenchman François Bernier (1625–1688), who strongly influenced his acquaintance John Locke.[6] Bernier traveled to Egypt for a year and Indian lands for twelve in the 1650s–1660s. A few years after his return to France, he published *A New Division of the Earth*, in which he wrote that there were "four or five

Species or Races of men so notably differing from each other that this may serve as the just foundation of a new division of the world." He labeled them "Africans," "East and Northeast Asians," "Lapps" (meaning "savages" of the far north), and a conglomeration of everyone else – people we might call "white" today, including South Asians – which he called the "first" race.[7] (Bernier came close to the line of blasphemy, of course, with his suggestions; but he avoided it by not denying the Biblical account of creation. He simply said nothing explicit about this.) According to Bernier scholars, what's important about him and those who built on his proto-anthropology is that he switched focus from Greek climatic–environmental concerns to a concept of fundamentally different human "species." The debate was far from over in 1684 when he published his book, but Bernier helped mark a switch from observations of religion, morals, customs, language, and so on to fixed characteristics we'd today call "racial."[8]

But, again, for many generations, key writings combined Greek-style environmental explanations for human categories with newer ideas of human divisions.[9] One of the most well-read naturalists, the French Comte de Buffon (1707–1788), while believing in the surface-level superiority of Europeans, was monogenicist, argued for environmental determinism in shaping humanity, and believed in the permeability of the races.

Still, by twists and turns, stronger and more ambivalent arguments, the new field of "natural history" hardened and hardened again the lines between newly defined human categories – new "races." And Enlightenment authority after authority distinguished whiteness in the century or two after Bernier. Between Bernier's death in 1688 and 1800, Carl Linnaeus designated whites as *Homo europaeus*, Buffon spoke of "white Europeans," and Kant write about the "white race."[10]

Of course, Europeans didn't leave these terms and categories of whiteness empty – they filled them in, listing their qualities in just the same way as they listed the qualities of, say, orders of birds. To begin with, Europeans had the "highest" qualities. William Petty (1623–1687) wrote that "Europeans do not only differ from ... Africans in color ... they differ also in their natural manners and in the internal qualities of their minds."[11] David Hume (1711–1776) wrote that whites were essentially the polar opposites of Africans, and explained, "I am apt to suspect the negroes, and in general all the other species of men (for there are four or five different kinds) to be naturally inferior to the whites."[12] Immanuel Kant (1724–1804) wrote that "humanity is at its greatest perfection in the race of whites," for instance. So, the opposite was supposed to be true, too; the darker the skin, the inherently lesser was the mind.[13] Such words were ignorant, vile prejudice. But they didn't spring from a mere sense of superiority, mere xenophobia or arrogance. They emerged in a new historical situation that provided – at least what these men seized on as – "evidence" of white superiority. To see that, let's back up a little.

Colonialism, Slavery, and Enlightenment Activity Reinforced Each Other

Notice how we date the Enlightenment to roughly the same generation that saw an explosion of new wealth from sugar processed by kidnapped forced labor. There's not much mystery in this: Enlightenment had to be paid for; the money came from the new trade that was directly or indirectly dependent on human trafficking. That is, the class of people who actually did the thinking and writing we call "the Enlightenment" had to be supported – sheltered, fed, given time and space to think deep thoughts – by new income and, in turn, by new institutions. (French and German contributors often had university posts or wealthy patrons, too. Note also that significant figures got their support from the Catholic Church; of course, that institution certainly profited from the slave trade through its donors at all ranks. That important story, though, is outside the bounds of this book.)

Enlightenment thinkers sitting in London, Edinburgh, or Paris were, in fact, not quite so far from the violence and cruelty of emerging white supremacy as the reader might think. Don't think of ivory-tower philosophizers sitting in comfortable Cambridge or Edinburgh studies, on the one hand, and the people physically brutally abusing other people in Jamaica or Tasmania, on the other. The worlds were linked; in fact, they were one. Scholars have dug up those very immediate connections between slaving wealth derived from colonization and the time, security, books, and other essentials that it bought for Enlightenment philosophers.[14] That ivory-tower philosophizer was sometimes scribbling justifications for investors, sometimes telling them *it's okay to brutally abuse that sort of human because it's good for them. They're not quite human; or, if they are, they're not as human as you.*

Take, for example, Enlightenment figure Hans Sloane, whose vast collections formed the basis of the British Museum, founded in 1759. (Literally, the museum mainly amounted to a display of his things, at first.[15]) Sloane's life and work connected science, slavery, and concepts of whiteness. (Some historians of science discourage us from using the word "science" to describe eighteenth-century activities because it suggests the wrong things: it hints that those activities resembled the science of the later nineteenth and twentieth centuries. The term "natural philosophy" would be more appropriate. But those considerations are beyond this book, so I'll use "science" as a simple shorthand for practices that eventually changed into something we recognize today.) Sloane arose from a modest background in Protestant Ireland to become a physician in London. A collector and explorer by inclination, he jumped at the opportunity to serve as doctor to the governor of Jamaica in 1687. There, he found himself in a slave society, which would soon count 40,000 enslaved people, compared with 7,000 free. And he made a study of his fellow human beings who were enslaved as if they were just another detail of the exotic flora and fauna of the island.[16]

In sum, he went looking for the essential, eternal differences between "black" and "white," turning away from the Greek-derived learning that said place and climate shaped body and spirit. Instead, he said, West Africans were closer to brute animals than they were to men. They lacked the same thoughts and feelings as Englishmen, being instead ruled by animal passions and motivations. What little good was in them – say, a mother's love for her child – was simply that of a bear for her cub, the stuff of mammal instinct. They appeared, he wrote, almost non-verbal, favoring shrieks and howls. And they needed brutal punishments because they were "perverse," meaning "unreasonably contrary." Applying these lines of thought, Sloane personally injured at least one enslaved person. Convinced they were shirking, Sloane invented fake "treatments" to torture slaves who said they were in pain or were nearly catatonic to drive them back into the fields.[17] Sloane, meanwhile, started a collection of human skulls around this period to locate deep-set differences in races he already "knew" were there.

And why did someone like Sloane do this? Because he was simply making what he thought was an honest observation, perhaps under the influence of new natural history trends? Perhaps. But Sloane clearly depended on the friendship and trust of slaveholders not only for his job in Jamaica, but also for travels around that island to collect and observe. If he was kept in his post and supported in his exploration, it was at least partly because his natural philosophy, his science, was *useful* to the slaveholders around him, the men whose labor supply and wealth depended, in turn, on the Royal African Company of human traffickers. Simply put, Sloane justified slave-holders' kidnapping, even their torture, of West Africans.[18]

When, back in England, he married the widowed heiress of a Jamaican slaveholder and sugar baron, Sloane's life of collecting and writing was even more directly dependent on promoting the idea of West Africans as a natural slave race. Like Britain's science academy, the Royal Society, itself, Sloane personally invested in Royal African Company shares in 1704, probably making a tidy profit.[19] Cruelty, the profit from cruelty, and reassurances that the cruelty was justified by science all reinforced each other.

Or take the early Enlightenment figure John Locke (1632–1704), a physician and philosopher supported by one of the most powerful men in England, the Earl of Shaftesbury, in the 1670s. Shaftesbury's wealth came from many sources, but they included slave-labor operations in the Bahamas and the Royal African Company. (John Locke, too, was a founding shareholder.[20]) But, far more directly, Locke helped draw up rules for Shaftesbury's biggest project, the new Carolina Colony around 1669.[21] Those rules more than accepted slaveholding; they spelled out, literally in Locke's own hand, how each Englishman would have "absolute power and Authority over his Negro Slaves."[22] And, within two years of its foundation in 1670, about one-fourth or one-third of the colony's inhabitants were enslaved.[23]

Meanwhile, Locke described how the "wild Indian" haunted "the vacant places of America," "insolent and injurious in the woods." The natives didn't improve the land and therefore had no right to it. Scholar Anthony Pagden wrote that Locke's "intention was to provide settlers . . . with a powerful argument based in natural law rather than legislative decree to justify their depredations."[24] In other words, Locke argued that it was natural to dominate or destroy Indigenous peoples.

Locke hardly completes the list.[25] For two more examples, early Enlightenment figures Thomas Hobbes (1588–1679) and John Donne (1572–1631) promoted the Virginia Company by, sometimes literally, preaching *Terra Nullius* doctrine. That doctrine suggested that North American lands were empty, or empty of people worthy of respecting, and so the English had a right to take those lands. Scholar Patricia Springborg argues that Hobbes's famous line about "savage" life being "nasty, brutish, and short" was in fact a particular reference to Indigenous peoples of what today is Virginia. The significance is that Hobbes was, by extension, justifying English invasion because it was based on a right governmental basis and, supposedly, the opposite of "nasty, brutish, and short."[26]

Natural philosopher – we might even say "chemist" to jump the gun a bit – Robert Boyle (1627–1691) was another who represented the reciprocal relationship between Enlightenment learning and slavery and colonization. Boyle prided himself on experimenting for the purpose of finding useful, profitable substances and processes. Thus, he spent years experimenting with the chemical qualities of that world-changing substance, sugar. He also supported "Praying Indian Towns," or a kind of workhouse-colony to "civilize" Indigenous people in English colonies. In other words, he aided settlements where Indigenous converts to Anglican Christianity could learn to assimilate and be "useful." Meanwhile, Boyle sought out natural history data – information about plants and such – from slaver captains. Some of this data he turned toward finding things like antidotes for tropical ailments for white colonists much like Sloane.[27]

Setting aside the slave blood-money that funded figures like John Locke and others in England, Caribbean slaveholders themselves funded Enlightenment art, architecture, and science in the Caribbean itself. Historian James Robertson uncovered how West Indian sugar barons didn't just read the latest natural philosophy printed in Edinburgh, but also funded it or encouraged it in their backyards. They created botanical gardens, supported the latest music, and imported antiquities. Meanwhile, as ever, the relationship extended back across the Atlantic, with sugar moguls' beneficiaries publishing articles in scholarly journals printed in London or sending specimens to Scottish universities and museums. A common focus of such natural philosophy was how to keep European bodies alive and well in the subtropics; in other words, new Enlightenment science sometimes explicitly aimed at maintaining colonization.[28]

The Enlightenment was built on the backs of the enslaved more directly still. Colin Campbell was an astronomer, whose 1730 admission to the Royal Society was sponsored by Edmond Halley, after whom the comet is named. Campbell also owned a slave-labor operation in Jamaica. A University of Edinburgh graduate, he used that slavery-derived wealth to import state-of-the-art telescopes for an observatory at his home in Kingston. Campbell also used that wealth to support a second natural philosopher as his assistant in studying magnetism and chronometers. And the two sent their research back to Britain for the discussion of natural philosophers there.[29] When Campbell died in 1752, he bequeathed his captive victims to his wife and son.[30]

When enslavers like Campbell spent their windfall profits on scientific equipment, they sometimes donated instruments to English or Scottish institutions. A fellow sugar baron, Alexander Macfarlane, bought Colin Campbell's precious telescopes and sent his observations back to London and the Royal Society. When he died shortly after Campbell, his will bequeathed those instruments to his old university in Edinburgh, which, in turn, created the Macfarlane Observatory around them. There's no record telling us to whom Macfarlane bequeathed his 791 enslaved victims.[31]

Enlightenment Calls for – Very Specific Kinds of – Liberty

Yet readers might be confused because many will have come across the message that the Enlightenment was an age that rejected superstition in favor of rational, liberating humanism, that questioned the rights of kings and promoted liberties and rights for all. That confusion may lie in the fact that *later* advocates used the words of Locke, Hobbes, or even Jefferson to demand rights for women, rights for non-British people, and rights for the poor. Men like Jefferson and Rousseau – even more so – were surrounded by those calling for abolition and equal treatment. These ranged from kidnapped people themselves to certain Quakers to Mary Wollstonecraft and many in between. So, if Locke or Jefferson and the others had wanted to advocate for true liberty and justice for all, they could have.[32] They didn't, even if we do – sometimes – with their words.

Men like Locke or Hobbes believed that women were lesser, that Indian prisoners were justifiably enslaved, and that whole orders of foreign races weren't capable of European-level reason. Their writings, like the writings of Jefferson, didn't *have to* clarify that "We, the People" didn't include Black folks or Indians. Obviously, they weren't included. It was "self-evident" that "all men, created equal" were white men.[33]

And these arguments for greater rights for a new kind of man were connected to English colonization and slaving in North America.[34] It was no accident that this was the same period in which wealthier Englishmen made claims to greater freedom against the Crown. Two big moments in that period were, first, the Civil War between king and Parliament in the 1640s, ending with a headless crown and an empty throne for almost a decade; and second, a generation later in 1689, when Parliament won its most important – in some ways, final – victory over the monarchy. This is called the "Glorious Revolution," when, though it's a broad generalization, the Crown rapidly became subservient to Parliament.

In sum, from the 1640s to about the 1690s, on the eve of the Enlightenment's heyday, Englishmen argued that they ought to be "free" from what they called monarchical tyranny. And, yes, wealthy members of Parliament suggested that they were in peril of becoming little better than slaves. They said they were like the Anglo-Saxons of England in 1066, strapped into the "Norman yoke" of William the Conqueror. When he'd crossed from Normandy centuries before, he trampled, they said, their timeless, inalienable, constitutional rights and made them serfs.[35] It had been tyranny in 1066; it was still tyranny in 1640 or 1688. As a Puritan pamphleteer wrote in mid-century, they'd beheaded Charles for his "oppressing Norman laws, whereby he enslaved us . . . we have recovered ourselves from under that Norman yoke."[36] (Thomas Jefferson embraced the "Norman yoke" mythology, too, in order to justify his fight against the imperial center of London.[37])

Enlightenment calls for liberty were, in large part, calls by members of the newly emerging "master" race, who argued that they were, or *should* be, the furthest thing from the people they were enslaving.[38] English/British people got a greater and greater sense that a man – and, again, we're talking about men, here – should own his body and labor with great independence. *They* were individuals. Meanwhile, the old forms of serfdom or bonded labor were outsourced, so to speak, to the colonies. We might put it this way: scholars see the idea was developing in the mid and later 1600s that, in England, every man had the heart of a master – or, at least those men of sufficiently high class, as it was a rigidly classist society. In the colonies – that is, among the enslaved – this was not so.[39] Historian Michael Guasco shows that more and more slavery in the midst of English colonists, and greater contact with it by observers or investors on the home island, made them more conscious of Englishmen's individual rights. "Our lives will be as cheap as those negroes," warned those campaigning for greater rights in court and Parliament.[40] By the way, something similar influenced French Enlightenment assumptions that Frenchmen, as distinct from the people they were trafficking and enslaving, were inherently freeborn and due rights. For example, Rousseau, and by extension his many British readers, acknowledged the existence of enslaved people and that slavery was a thing – yes, an ugly, even shameful thing – that was going on across the sea; but the "true" horror was the lack of political rights that "enslaved" Frenchmen.[41]

So, the emerging idea of slave races – and its corollary, the concept of free races – contributed to Enlightenment calls for – "free" – peoples' self-determination; but we should also get down to the brass tacks of power: money. From 1650–1750 or so, slave-labor operations in the colonies created a whole new category of early capitalists.[42] Meanwhile, new sources of investment in things like sugar made older wealthy families – formerly rich on landlordism – rich, instead, thanks to sugar or other wealth connected to colonialism and slavery. (We can add, here, those growing rich off of expansion in India of the spice trade, but that story will have to wait until the next chapter.)

Thus, England and Britain's most powerful families, who could make trouble for the Crown and whose members sat in key offices, demanded more and more rights. They wanted protection against the sort of arbitrary power that could take their property or nullify their contracts. They wanted guarantees of jury trials and protection from the law equal to that enjoyed by the old landed aristocracy. They wanted a free press so that they could print pamphlets and broadsheets in order to make their cases in public. They wanted these things whether they were in Barbados, Boston, or

Bristol. Parliament passed mercantilist laws to maintain a favorable balance of trade and increase, according to theories of the time, the kingdom's total wealth. And, practically, they demanded that English, Welsh, and Scottish traders purchase certain products from London and not foreign ports or merchants, which not only kept money and resources within the colonial system, but also created tax revenue. And it's easy to see how, when a man's slavery-derived wealth was threatened by mercantilist Navigation Acts locking him into trade with London, his loyalty to Crown and Parliament got a bit shaky.

Replacing States Built around Dynastic Crowns with States Built around Races

This is no small thing. Because, when European kingdoms threw off royal or imperial rule, either through gradual fights for rights for wealthy men or through revolutions, they justified new organizations – new states – as natural unifications of races. We use one of the contemporary synonyms of "race" for these: "nations." Put differently, by the later 1700s, wealthy men proposed replacing crown-states with states organized and justified by race – race-states. Race provided a basis for new states and then, as scholars put it, in turn, "states made race."[43]

So, did the promoters of a "free" America say they were creating a "white state"? Not exactly, but Enlightenment writers of their day gave them new race categories with which to think. While some Enlightenment figures were classing whites together – as superior, many also distinguished between sub-categories or "varieties" of whites – just as they might with flora and fauna. After all, natural philosophers didn't stop their natural taxonomies with groups or classes, but kept dividing things into orders and families. As one such classifier wrote in 1789, when the trend was already decades old:

> the Author of nature, as he formed great varieties in the same species of plants, and of animals, so he also gave various races of men . . .: a Tartar, a Negro, an American [Indian], &c. &c., differ as much from a German, as a bull-dog, or lap-dog, or a shepherd's cur, from a pointer. The differences are radical, and such as no climate or chance would produce . . .[44]

Depending on the author, these subcategories were things like Nordic, Frank, Gaul, Briton, Celt, and so on. (These were more or less mythical; we can see when and how people invented them.[45])

Already by the late 1700s, natural philosophers started collecting things like skulls to confirm the (false) deep physiological differences they already believed were there. The heyday of cranial study and similar race science was still to come, though, as shown later in this book.[46]

Enlightenment figures not only divided European races, but also made claims about which were most rational, which had higher qualities, which were best. For the Englishman Hume, the Irish tended to be liars – no surprise.[47] The German Immanuel Kant, also no surprise, discovered that Germans were the highest order of Europeans, possessing all the best traits of other Europeans in excellent balance.[48] In the later 1600s, the English started in earnest proclaiming the myth that they were a people called "Anglo-Saxon." This was in part to proclaim their special freedom-loving essence, which in turn justified things like the break with Rome and got put to use in Parliament's fights with the Crown.[49] The American colonists, naturally, took this up, with Thomas Jefferson, for example, suggesting that they inherited Anglo-Saxon liberty.[50] Benjamin Franklin thought the English and the Saxons – or Germans – were best. He wrote of his concern that "swarthy" or "black and tawny" races would soon outnumber "lovely white" people in the Pennsylvania colony in 1751:

> Why should Pennsylvania, founded by the English, become a colony of Aliens, who ... will never adopt our language or customs, any more than they can acquire our complexion? ... The number of purely white people in the world is proportionately very small. ... the Saxons ... with the English make the principal body of white people on the face of the earth. I could wish their numbers were increased. Why increase the sons of Africa, by planting them in America, where we have so far an opportunity, by excluding all black and tawneys, of increasing the lovely white and red?[51]

Meanwhile, a German philosopher shortly after 1800 developed the theory that the best Europeans shared a branch with superior ancient Indians, a human family he called the "Aryans."[52] Here, obviously, we've arrived at a moment of foreboding about the twentieth century.

But the importance of natural philosophers' dividing Europeans into various new sub-groups didn't await the twentieth century; it was key to the development of new ideas in the 1700s and thereafter. The Greek idea of the *genus*, the human tribe, had been around for millennia; whereas in the new English language of 1611, peoples were called "nations" after the Latin *natio*. In sum, people were familiar with the idea of lumping people of common language and real or imagined history into the idea of a nation.[53] But that wasn't all that important when a king or emperor ruled over lands as his personal property. King Charles II, for example, ruled over nations of Scots, Englishmen, Welshmen, and Irishmen, in his eyes; the various Habsburg emperors of Europe, many more.

What happened in the late 1700s through the 1800s was an explosive alchemical mixture of all these trends: a combination of these very old ideas of the nation-as-historical/mythical-group, infant proto-race-science ideas of the distinct racial branches, and the rise of a new class of wealthy men, connected to colonialism and capitalism.[54] When these wealthy men, drawing on ideas like those of Locke or Rousseau, threw off the power of kings (or gutted it, as the British did), it made perfect sense for them to argue that their unifying factor was a historical race. In the wreckage of kingdoms, they formed nation-states, what scholars tell us should more appropriately be called race-states.[55]

"We the People," the old text went, "do ordain" a state over *ourselves*. It should be clear by now that "the People" did not include the enslaved and was obscure at best about Africa-descended freemen and Indigenous people. And not only did the new constitution of the land of freedom *not* free those held captive, but also the 1787 Constitutional Convention forbade any law against the slave trade for twenty years. Slavery, then, was built into the US Constitution. Securing "the Blessings of Liberty" was obviously for one race and not others.

Which came first: the concept of the Anglo-Saxon, which then provided a logical unifier? Or the needs of revolutionaries, with racial subdivisions invented to serve them? It's probably impossible to unravel.

(Meanwhile, there's no doubt that nineteenth-century nation-state movements in places like Italy and Germany coincided with the full maturing of European race science and "race is all" thinking in those decades.[56])

Speaking of race-as-unifier, one so-called "founding father" explicitly used race to argue for that new constitution to unite the successful American rebels in 1787. In a series of pamphlets called *The Federalist Papers* that he wrote with James Madison and Alexander Hamilton, diplomat John Jay made the case for a singular race that needed its own federal state:

> Providence has been pleased to give this one connected country to one united people – a people descended from the same ancestors, speaking the same language, professing the same religion, attached to the same principles of government, very similar in their manners and customs, and who ... have nobly established general liberty and independence.[57]

This new Providential American race – and the new state for that race – were not new in the sense that it was a racial mixture of various hues of flesh. On the contrary, it was quite clearly a race descended from the British – and perhaps the Germans and Dutch and any other pale Protestant, whatever Ben Franklin's complaints. (Tom Paine, for example, argued that the new American race was an amalgam of European races; in short, "the persecuted lovers of civil and religious liberty from every part of Europe."[58]) As historian Kathleen Wilson writes, the colonists argued that they should have equal rights to the British precisely because "they were not 'a compound mongrel mixture of English, Indian and Negro, but ... freeborn British white subjects' and so deserving of the same liberties and privileges as Englishmen at home."[59]

Finally, it will therefore surprise no one that the new USA started passing laws making whiteness equivalent to citizenship from its very first years. The classic example is the Naturalization Act of 1790, which reserved citizenship opportunities to "free White" immigrants. Laws against mixed marriage quickly followed. And, while individual states could grant citizenship to "free Blacks," the federal government tended not to grant passports to Black people.[60] The so-called Founding Fathers envisioned a white America, with nonwhites present – on sufferance – at the margins.[61]

What about the status of Jews in the new country for freeborn men? Were they welcome? Were they white? Research suggests they existed in a hazy middle-ground during the era of roughly 1700 to the later 1800s. On the one hand, they were outsiders in a Protestant Christian environment, and subject to ages-old stereotyping and xenophobia, being the butt of slights and epithets.[62] Still, a 1774 *History of Jamaica*, describing the growth of the island's population, speaks of the increase in the "number of Whites, exclusive of Jews," suggesting that in those early days of whiteness, Jews were in a sub-category thereof.[63] In other words, if the *History of Jamaica*'s author had to explicitly state that he was placing them in a sub-category of whites instead of lumping them together, that's telling. On the other hand, in places where public office required swearing an oath on the Christian Bible or where higher offices were expressly reserved for Protestants, Jews were effectively barred from juries and important civic posts. And yet experts generally place their status higher than that of Catholics in this period, with local exceptions.[64] There was a fashion, historian Frederic Cople Jaher showed, among self-styled enlightened elites to learn ancient Hebrew and express admiration – paternalistic, of course – for the Jews as "a people."[65] And, compared with Indigenous people or Black freemen, there's no contest: Jews were of far higher status. Jews were a tiny minority, and thus an even greater minority of them were slavers in the West Indies and America.[66] And yet they fell on one side of the slaver/enslaved divide.[67]

This relatively near-white status would come to an end with the rise of more scientific racism in the second half of the 1800s, a story we'll get to later. Then, Jewishness transformed from a religion – changeable – into a race – indelible, a thing of blood. This is a moment to point out why this book is a history of whiteness in the English-speaking world, specifically; Chapter 1 showed that concepts of Judaism residing in the blood were, for centuries, far more significant in the Spanish-speaking world than among the English.

***

It's easy to see, after all this, the grim paradox. Men writing about freedom and natural rights, engaging in learning and wrestling with new ideas, drew their writing time from the blood of their fellow humans being tormented, at best; at worst they reinforced the slavery-and-murder system in a reciprocal relationship. As scholar

Cristina Malcolmson writes, "extensively intertwined institutions of government, colonialism, the slave trade, and science were collaborating to usher [new ideas about race] into public view."[68]

And yet it's not a paradox. Enlightenment figures like Locke or Kant *did* believe in certain concepts of freedom and justice. It's *we* who have to understand from their historical context that they meant freedom and justice for "real" people who belonged in the state: the highest, white, men.

As with every time and place, of course, there were those who rejected Enlightenment suggestions that flesh tone revealed essential "truths" about people's nature. For example, Lady Margaret Cavendish (1623–1673) – playwright, poet, and natural philosopher – implicitly mocked natural philosophers' race-reductionism in her semi-utopia *The Blazing World*.[69] Soon after, Jonathan Swift (1667–1745) did much the same thing in his satire, with Lemuel Gulliver tying himself in knots to prove to himself that he was superior to the "brutish" Yahoo race – yet ultimately failing.[70] Or take the example of Dutch-German anatomist, member of the English Royal Society, Johann Nicolas Pechlin, writing around the 1680s. In the face of great counter-pressure, Pechlin argued that his research showed flesh tone to be a simple, utterly superficial, difference, and not a mark of a deeper distinction of some kind of human subspecies. But it's easy to see how that counter-argument wasn't profitable for those in power.[71]

And, yes, if it strikes the reader that the clamoring of American colonists for "self-evident" human rights was a bit hypocritical when they denied rights to their fellow humans, the reader is not just a "person-of-*their*-time," they're like a "man of the eighteenth century," Nathaniel Appleton (1693–1784). As a young man, he was a slaveowner. But, repentant, in 1767 he published a pamphlet calling out his Boston neighbors:

> Oh! ye sons of liberty, pause a moment, give me your ear, Is your conduct consistent? can you review our late struggles for liberty, and think of the slave-trade at the same time, and not blush? ... How should we have been ... struck dumb, had Great Britain thrown this inconsistency in our faces? how justly might they, and all mankind have laughed at our pretensions ...?[72]

Final Thoughts

Jamaican philosopher Charles W. Mills (1951–2021) was one of the first to really dig into the connections between the Enlightenment and the evolution of white supremacy. He asked:

> Where is . . . Locke's stirring *Letter concerning the Treatment of the Indians*, Kant's moving *On the Personhood of Negroes*, Mill's famous condemnatory *Implications of Utilitarianism for English Colonialism*, Karl Marx and Frederick Engels's outraged *Political Economy of Slavery*? Intellectuals write about what interests them, what they find important . . .[73]

The so-called Enlightenment's call for liberty was not for all.

***

- Drawn to overseas lands by the prospect of riches, Europeans encountered new peoples. Natural philosophers added them to their taxonomies, their classifying systems, as if they were exotic plants. In this way, they contributed to **the creation of new races.** Participants in the Enlightenment also helped fashion white supremacy **by placing races in a hierarchy.** By doing so, they served colonization. There was **a reciprocal relationship** between natural philosophers, who argued that whites were superior and Black and Indigenous people inferior, and their wealthy patrons who profited from colonization and slavery.
- The grim paradox is that the very people benefiting from the displacement of peoples and the new chattel slavery get credited for espousing liberty for all. In part, this was because they had **new ideas about contrasting themselves – as "freeborn Englishmen" – and the peoples they were enslaving, supposedly "slave races."** This was also the outcome of burgeoning capitalism and new wealth: it gave some men pretensions of equality with traditional aristocrats. They demanded new rights for themselves.
- In Britain (slowly) and in the American colonies (abruptly), wealthy white men took this even further. They argued that a country was comprised of a race; it wasn't a king or emperor's property. They created the first nation-states, **which meant ancestry- or racial states. In doing this, they defined which race was the**

"true" people of the country and which races were not. Whites were the sole legitimate racial stock of the land. In our world of nation-states, this fact remains perhaps the most powerful force maintaining white supremacy.

- These were particular circumstances. A colonizing race became something new: white. The societies whose lands were invaded became a new race: "Indian." And the people actually doing the planting and processing of the colonies' most valuable commodity became a new race: Black. Race is written all over the story of the founding of the USA. If you tried to extract it from the story, you'd end up with nonsense and lies. French Enlightenment figure Voltaire (1694–1778) made a witty observation about the regimented, pugnacious Prussians (of today's northern Germany): "where some states have an army, the Prussian Army has a state." We might say, "where some states have race problems, the USA is a race problem with a state."

Part II

Redefining the "Master" and Inventing the White Man's Burden

Before turning to Part II, let me introduce one of its main themes. In the post-slavery age, white supremacy could wear a softer guise and repress through bloodless means. There could be no better expresser of this than the nineteenth-century champion of white imperialism Rudyard Kipling (1865–1936), perhaps the most popular author in English of his time, who wrote at the end of the British imperial century:

> Take up the White Man's burden –
> The savage wars of peace –
> Fill full the mouth of Famine
> And bid the sickness cease;
> And when your goal is nearest
> The end for others sought,
> Watch Sloth and heathen Folly
> Bring all your hope to nought.[1]

In this stanza of this 1899 poem meant to encourage Americans to join Britain in an "Anglo-Saxon," imperial project, Kipling sketched the two main concepts of *both* whiteness and imperialism that took root in this period before the mid 1800s. His talk of "savage wars of peace" and "filling mouths" was more than idle rhetoric. These two things – war-making and trade across the world – were what shaped and spread whiteness in this timeframe. These factors, then, explain how the British, who lost their largest set of colonies – slave-holding colonies – went on to build an empire that created, and was reinforced by, whiteness across the globe in the next 100 years.

How did things get to a point where Kipling wrote this classic expression of both white supremacy and imperialism by the end of the 1800s?

4 THE EMPIRE OF WHITENESS, 1600–1830S

In the previous chapter, we saw how whiteness emerged, in part, *amid* colonialism, rather than colonialism coming *from* a new idea of whiteness. After the loss of the American colonies, British imperialism was far more actively encouraged and justified by the developing, evolving ideas of whiteness and supremacy. As the 1800s went on, English-speaking imperialists not only thought whiteness best, but even believed that white global ascendancy was inevitable, so that it was supposed to be natural that whiteness eliminate non-whiteness. "White-might" made "white-right." That threat or justification of ethnic cleansing and genocide – that whiteness should scour others out of existence – shows its sinister kernel in this chapter.

On the other hand, as this period reveals, white supremacy also started to wear sheep's clothing. It could dominate via indirect, neutral, or even benign-seeming means. In this chapter, you'll see how commerce and the birth of capitalism contributed to whiteness-making in India and beyond. You'll see how white and Black abolitionists' victories in ending the overseas trade by the British, and the institution of slavery in the empire, did not end white supremacy. Instead, these victories forced white supremacy to shift from the iron manacle to gentler constraints. And you'll see how, even after owning humans was made illegal in the empire, colonists still demanded to dominate Indigenous people wherever they found them. Through control and sometimes even elimination, self-styled whites reinforced their faith in their superiority and others' innate inferiority. And following the flag, the leading edge of colonization and domination, were early race scientists, the early forebears of eugenicists and Nazis. Under the sheep's clothing of scholarly neutrality and utmost fairness, they continued to promote racial hierarchy.

Whiteness wasn't made only by the invention of slavery-by-blood in the New World, nor only by the creation of a state for a race/nation that considered itself the (exclusive) home for the "sons of liberty." The British Empire, not the new USA, was the largest and longest-lived entity that spread the ideas and power of white superiority. And not only did the empire outlive the loss of its North American colonies, but also it practically surged afterward, like a Royal Navy ship freed from a snarled anchor. Its wealth, territory, and influence essentially multiplied many times over during what historians term the "Second British Empire" and its "imperial century," the 1800s.

Creating Whiteness in India and Beyond

Did white supremacy *cause* imperialism? Is that what propelled English-speakers onto ships and out into the world to conquer or meddle in the late 1700s–1800s? Yes; but understanding that history is not as simple as imagining explorer Captain James Cook (1728–1779) or Governor Robert Clive (1725–1774) departing England for distant points motivated by, or aiming to assert, white racial domination, in so many words. (That sort of more bald-faced assertion of whiteness-as-motive had its heyday in the second half of the 1800s, as Chapter 5 will show.) Instead, the concept of whiteness, its compulsion, often acted through different pathways. Whiteness – or "civilization," its basic equivalent – retroactively justified naked violence in the name of outpacing or fighting European rivals, as was the case with Cook and Clive. And the principles and effects of whiteness were often called simple profit-seeking. Put a different way, the far-flung activities of British imperialists, *learning* to see themselves as white and superior, molded and reinforced the notion of whiteness.

First, an inadvisably fast survey of the empire up to roughly 1865. The English landed in Surat, a busy port in the Indian Mughal Empire in 1608; by 1775, the British controlled or coerced over half the subcontinent; and, by 1860, most of today's Pakistan, India, Burma/Myanmar, and Sri Lanka. From around 1760, the British expanded their Canadian footholds by taking territory from the

French, and then pushing westward with economic and settler imposition. From 1788, the British inserted settler colonies amid the peoples in what is today Australia, closely followed by Tasmania and New Zealand. From 1806, the British colonized southern Africa from a base in Cape Town. And the British claimed more lands, including Indian Ocean colonies, from Napoleon's France in the 1810s. This list is far from exhaustive.

Why did the British sail off over the horizon in the 1700s to explore and create an empire? Plenty of other kingdoms with the same technology didn't do so. The mighty Qing emperors in China, the Marathas, and the Ottomans didn't. The answer clearly involves the fact that not every empire that has the wealth or ships to do so makes that choice.[1] The other answers have to do with very specific historical trends and events that were going on in Europe that were different or absent elsewhere. This is why Chapter 1 introduced King Henry VIII and his problems with the Pope: there were life-or-death religious–political rivalries that forced the English into a race of arms and colonies. Further, in Europe, kings' accountants told them that power was based on how much silver each kingdom had in its treasury. Silver bought armies, after all. So, it was good to go out into the world to find silver mines, yes; but it was also critical that English merchants *not* leave their silver coins in the marketplaces of Lisbon or Antwerp. Far better to go direct to the source for pepper, silk, or tea and then welcome foreigners – and *their* silver coins – in London. Overseas exploration by certain Europeans, and the absence thereof by others, was the practical consequence of specific goals and historical circumstances, not of something superior in European races or cultures – or even their guns and sails.

The first voyage of the newly incorporated East India Company (EIC) departed London in 1601, with a mighty thirty-eight-gun ship, originally built to fight the Spanish, leading four others. A group of London merchants purchased and outfitted the little fleet simply to make money. They wanted to cut out foreign – Catholic – middlemen in their quest for spices. Queen Elizabeth heartily approved and, to encourage them, granted the corporation a monopoly on English trade beyond southern Africa's Cape of Good Hope.

On the flagship leading the others out of the English Channel, in the safekeeping of its captain, was a letter from the queen herself addressed to "the Kinges of Sumatra and other places in the East Indies." In it, she said that her subjects came in friendship for mutual benefit; she humbly suggested her English subjects could provide excellent goods at least as well as the Portuguese; she asked that the merchants be allowed to leave a trader in their ports and under their protection where they would "apply themselves to learn the language, and direct themselves according to the fashions of his country."[2] These were not the words of someone who envisioned innate white superiority. Those words, that vision, would come later.

The ships made it to the islands of what today is Indonesia (imagine if they'd run into a killer cyclone), where the rival Portuguese were already trading for cloves, nutmeg, and other spices. But the people of the warm islands naturally had little interest in what the English had to offer in trade: warm wool. What were they to do? The leaders of the expedition stumbled upon the answer: they played pirate against a Portuguese ship, stealing its Indian luxuries and other wealth. Now the English had something valuable to trade. This set the tone for the next several centuries of EIC trade: whenever possible, they traded *between* ports in search of attractive tradegoods and to limit the export of English silver coins. One of the most destructive forms of this was the eventual inter-trade in opium between India and China. (It's beyond the scope of this book; but, briefly, a popular early modern "theory of state" said that a kingdom needed to amass as large a treasury of silver as possible in order to outfit an army in times of trouble. Thus, sending all the silver in the land to the East Indies was supposed to be bad policy. Another theory said that the kingdom should encourage and maintain as large a population as possible, also for war-readiness.)

The fleet returned to London and fantastic profits, each investor getting a share of the windfall in proportion to how much silver they'd invested to outfit the fleet. In a few short years, the company started sending out annual fleets. It began leaving more and more agents in ports abroad to arrange deals in advance of the next fleet's arrival. By 1613, the company had a permanent agent in Surat and several posted on Indonesian islands. By midcentury, they had almost twenty agents' bases circling the Indian Ocean and points east. By making deals with local rulers, these agents got favorable trade agreements over rival Europeans, sometimes by offering their naval "muscle" against rulers' rivals. They also won permission to build secure warehouses, and eventually powerful forts, to protect their personnel and tradegoods. From these bases, the company's direct and indirect force grew.[3]

Because of the regularity of the ventures and the terrific wealth, more and more merchants and aristocrats wanted a piece of the action. Soon, the company issued permanent stock, borrowing that idea from the Dutch, who may have invented it, so that, instead of "paying-up" or settling accounts upon each fleet's return, the company paid annual dividends. The market value of the paper stock went up, as well. The company could issue stock, then, to finance greater and greater operations. This was a revolutionary new form of wealth and investment opportunity that was a key harbinger of capitalism.[4] Again, capitalism and white supremacy cut their teeth together because, with this new kind of attractive wealth, more and more people in England, Scotland, and elsewhere became – literally – invested in the success of imperialism and, by extension, slavery. Banks had an interest; the Crown (which taxed the company's imports and demanded loans from it) had an interest; Members of Parliament had an interest. And, speaking of interest, the company regularly paid 7–8 percent, and occasionally 12 percent.[5] This parallels the story of those who had an interest in supporting American colonization and slave-processed sugar.

And, yes, though the volume paled in comparison with the Atlantic horror, the EIC did commit human trafficking across the Indian Ocean from almost its earliest years. In 1622, at almost the same time as the first West Africans were trafficked to Jamestown, the EIC carried twenty-two enslaved people from India to their foothold in Batavia (today's Jakarta), Java. It's important to remember that the EIC was not a settler company like, say, the Massachusetts Bay Company; that is, it didn't want to take British settlers to its distant bases. That, simply put, wasn't a good way to make fast money. But, as the company negotiated more grants from local princes for its bases, as it invested in things like clove and nutmeg operations, it grew more and more interested in captive labor. The company wanted enslaved people for domestic and warehouse labor, too. So, from 1622 to the British prohibition of the trade two centuries later, the EIC trafficked around 5,700 people, according to expert Richard B. Allen.[6] So, yes, as in the Americas, slave trafficking *did* tell EIC personnel and perhaps the company's investors that *they* were a master race and East Africans, the Malagasy of Madagascar, and the other Indian Ocean peoples were *slave* races.

But more influential to the story of the EIC creating whiteness was its long history of domination. At the beginning of its century-and-a-half lifetime, from 1601 to 1857, it controlled little more than beachheads of territory: places like the island of Bombay (today's Mumbai), for example, or a narrow, 300-mile strip of land called "Bencoolen" on the west coast of Sumatra. But all that started changing during the global Seven Years' War (1756–1763), which included the French and Indian War in America. In those years, the British and the French in India battled to drive each other out. Or, more precisely, the Indian allies of the small British company contingent battled the Indian allies of the small French company contingent. When, in 1757, the Mughal governor of the rich territory of Bengal allied with the French in the hope of driving out the British, he bet wrong. Through treachery and bribery, the EIC managed to undermine the Bengali governor's armies, and the company's sepoys (native foot soldiers) won handily. Suddenly, the trading corporation was the effective government of a vast province of millions. This set a pattern of similar conquests in the coming years and decades. Other times, the company purchased influence or created puppet princes as they picked apart the Mughal Empire and the Maratha Empire.

By the end of the Seven Years' War, the EIC controlled an area in India approaching the same size as England and with a far greater population. Just after the turn of the 1800s, the EIC dominated a far greater area, roughly double that. And just after midcentury, the British dominated, directly or indirectly, the vast majority of the subcontinent.[7] And they did it with a relatively minuscule number of pale-hued men. At that time, there were around 40,000 British civilians (and twice as many soldiers) in a land that approached 300 million souls.[8]

Therefore, from the second half of the 1700s, the British – at least those with an interest in doing so – could tell themselves that they were a stronger strain of man, nation, and race than the various Indians under them. Like those investors in the slave-labor operations in the West Indies, perhaps more so, the EIC and its investors were making terrific profits through violence and domination. And so, they sought self-serving justifications for themselves (and arguments against British critics of their rather obvious greed and ambition). They argued, as Governor Warren Hastings and others did, that the British would be better, more enlightened, rulers than the old Mughals. "Our power in India," argued a Scottish EIC officer, "rests on the general opinion of the natives of our comparative superiority ... to their own rulers."[9] The British must display it.

Besides, the Indians needed a strong hand poised over them: the British were a minority in the country, after all. "If we do not make them feel that they are servants, they will soon be masters," an Englishman in Calcutta wrote in 1786.[10]

All of this self-concept and projected image depended at least in part on certain British concepts of the Indians as malleable, docile, willing to be dominated, and more devoted to their "superstitions" than to their freedom.[11] In the early period of company rule, the British weren't entirely dismissive of the various subcontinent cultures they encountered. And so they wanted to, as historians Bose and Jalal put it, conduct "cultural bribery," to convince a powerful majority to accede to minority English rule.[12] But that didn't mean they didn't indulge in stereotyping that eventually built the implacable set of malicious assumptions we call "Orientalism":[13] that people of "the Orient" were "sleepy" or lethargic;[14] lacked the rational, ordered mind of the European;[15] indulged their senses too much rather than deploying their reason or engaging in physical work; accepted tyrants over themselves;[16] and were crafty, "subtle," or dishonest.[17] And, from awareness of the monuments and ruins of bygone South Asian civilizations, British observers couldn't deny that the Indians had spectacular bygone ancient forebears; but today they had fallen from that glorious past, now decayed.[18] Or they had failed to make progress from the ancient days of gods and magic to the modern days marked by ... well, all the things the British told themselves *they* were: industrious, aggressive, forward-looking. Like they were doing over the Atlantic at the same time, the British were inventing an elevated "white" at the same time they were inventing a lesser, degraded "Oriental."

Indeed, as the decades of the nineteenth century passed, British ruling culture in India tended more and more to emphasize separateness; that is, the British told themselves they were a race apart and should reject the older ways of being simply white "nawabs," that is, Mughal governors in different dress. As scholar Partha Chatterjee wrote, towards the mid 1800s, the British administration was far more likely to "premise its power" on "difference," on the "alienness of the ruling group."[19] So demonstrating alien-ness came to mean, in part, demonstrating whiteness. (It naturally followed that the British in India were very sensitive to displays of poor, ill-behaved whiteness. Historian Aravind Ganachari showed how embarrassed British officials in 1860s Bombay [today Mumbai] tried to deport British "vagrants," essentially to keep up the appearance of superiority.[20])

There was a broad pattern in the British approach to domination in India. Whereas in the years up to around the mid 1800s, they self-servingly justified themselves as Enlightened replacements of the old imperial regime who needed to prove themselves, after that period, they were more arrogant and forceful: they were going to correct Indians and "modernize" them. This new program reads essentially like a program for spreading the benefits of "whiteness," but the program should not, could not ever turn Indians white. So, toward the 1800s, British commenters wrote that the Indian inherently required the Englishman over them to spread "his juster laws, his purer morals, [and] his truer faith."[21]

The program, as laid out by people like Thomas Macaulay (1800–1859) and John Stuart Mill (1806–1873) and adapted from thinkers like Jeremy Bentham (1774–1832), emphasized new initiatives for "better" court procedures and criminal law, more "rational" land/property regulations, and English education.[22] Indeed, this active program was supposed to be suitable for reforming Indians while being explicitly too paternalistic, too interventionist for British subjects. Again, this harkens back to the old idea that British people, from high to low, were naturally inclined to freedom and independence, whereas other races were not. John Stuart Mill, son of an EIC agent and several decades an administrator in India himself, wrote that the British must improve societies like India's on behalf of those societies, since freedom wasn't suitable, or even safe, for "backward states of society in which the race itself might be considered in its nonage [childhood, minority]."[23] Meanwhile, officials like Thomas Macaulay argued that Indians (at least what he deemed high-caste Indians capable of learning) must be lifted from the backwardness of their native literatures:

> I have no knowledge of either Sanskrit or Arabic. But I have done what I could to form a correct estimate of their value. I have read translations of the most celebrated Arabic and Sanskrit works. I have conversed both here and at home with men distinguished by their proficiency in the Eastern tongues. ... I have never found one among them who could deny that a single shelf of a good European library was worth the whole native literature of India and Arabia.[24]

And the British told themselves that the new imperial craft of managing "intransigent" races had been difficult since the early days of domination in Ireland. Like the Irish, the Indians often "resisted their good example" in the century after the British capture of Bengal, the subcontinent's richest province. And their complaints about the Indians sounded almost exactly like their complaints about the Catholic Irish. They clung to "superstition" and refused to adopt the right religion. They were insolent: the lowest servant was so insolent as to refuse to touch dishes on which their bosses had eaten pork.[25] One observer complained how, despite himself, "an English gentleman stoop[ed] to the basest tyranny over his servants."[26] Something about them supposedly dragged good, civilized British men and women down to Indians' level.

Native Peoples as Obstacles

If the mid 1800s mark the ascendance of a more bloodless, indirect domination, that doesn't mean that it was all bloodless, that there were no more chains. After the loss of the American colonies, in some corners of the Second Empire, the British enslaved people in ways that were similar. And this persisted after Parliament's ban on British subjects' participation in the slave trade in 1807. The main differences between slavery in these places and America were in scale and the level of systematic brutality. The West Indies and southern American colonies had large industrial-style slave-labor "machines," while Australian or southern African environments did not.

But don't let that confuse things; Indigenous people kidnapped and held captive in those places, for example, were treated like property and a slave race. In the Cape Colony of southern Africa, the enslaved, both Indigenous and trafficked, marginally outnumbered the free.[27] And their status was essentially the same as that of the enslaved in American colonies. For example, an enslaved woman in the Cape Colony could not choose her husband, and her children were born enslaved. She was coerced into Christian conversion because it was her only chance for marrying, as scholar Cecilia Morgan wrote, and conversion made it illegal for her children to be sold away from her.[28] Still, she was subject to legal rape, as elsewhere. In Australia, the English forbade slavery, so traffickers hid their trade in First Peoples (they used the word "Aboriginal") children as "servants," and, later in the 1800s, kidnapped or deceived Pacific Islanders for sugar operations and pearl diving.[29]

But, yes, in the Second British Empire, without large slave-labor industries, more often, the British treated the native peoples they encroached upon as obstacles rather than property. The world over, in fact, British colonists – or American, or Canadian, or others – spoke in a common vocabulary, scholars tell us. They wrote and spoke about the "Aboriginal Problem," the "Native Question," or the like.[30] The problem was that native people were present, occupying the land in ways inexpedient for the newcomers, resisting, sometimes pricking the conscience of self-styled enlightened colonial governments.

Australia was the largest new realm in the British Empire after the Americans broke off (Canada, vast and lightly populated by settlers, remained). And, measured in scale, Australia was the main new site of sweeping violence and displacement toward the people who lived there. When attempts to plant convicts in penal colonies in West or Southwest Africa failed, the British looked for an alternative place to unload "undesirables" and perhaps plant the flag to obstruct colonial rivals such as the Dutch and French. And, tremendously distant though they were, the British targeted new coasts mapped by Captain James Cook. The first 1,000 British convicts, guards, and sailors landed in 1788. Unlike in the previous century in the North American colonies, the British did *not* make treaties or trade for land with the various Australian First Peoples who watched the curious foreigners stumbling around on their sea legs as they poured out of their ships.

The British simply claimed their Australian footholds as theirs because, they said, while there were *inhabitants* in the land, those inhabitants did not farm it. The British didn't deny the existence of "the Aborigines," yet it was "terra nullius," they said, "nobody's land."[31] Was this simply opportunistic? Surely, it was for some; but it wasn't simply that. They embraced the doctrine of "nobody's land" so that they could be assured of a clean title when they bought and sold their stolen property. They worried there'd be rivals who'd make more legitimate, documented trades with First Peoples. It wasn't merely that the British saw that Australian First Peoples were dark-hued, and thus their land was forfeit. Again, surely "Aborigines'" flesh tones, dress, and habits marked them as lesser in many minds; but British imperial agents and officials made many deals with peoples they believed lesser. It was easier just to deny land rights to nonwhites. (Within just a few decades, prominent British officials and observers argued, without much success, that Indigenous displacement should be compensated or that large areas of the map should be reserved for the native peoples.[32])

British colonists were often violent, their animals ravaged First Nations' managed landscapes, and isolated run-ins sparked larger-scale fighting or massacres of native people.[33] British claims that they had more right to the land than the people who lived there certainly promoted British expansion and violence.

A certain 1830 episode of early ethnic cleansing offers a horrifying sign of things to come in the history of race. The British started colonizing Tasmania (then called Van Diemen's Land), an island off the coast of southeast Australia, in 1803, largely to forestall French colonization. Before that, they hunted seals and, repeating the old sinister pattern, abducted and enslaved Indigenous women and children from coastal areas.[34] The turmoil from such kidnappings, newly introduced diseases, and the ecological mayhem from sheep spread far deeper than the shoreline, so that, when British intrusion began in earnest in the 1810s and 1820s, the native First Peoples population was more than halved, perhaps 2,000 or 3,000 only.[35] Naturally, this small population sought to resist invasion; but there was little they could do against a British settler population approaching 23,000 on the eve of 1830. First Peoples raided farms for food and animals, sometimes killing the colonists who'd driven them from their former hunting lands; but their limited numbers and other factors meant they couldn't mount a pitched battle or truly threaten British encroachment across the island.

Still, the native people, naturally, resisted displacement and violence mainly on an individual, case-by-case, basis. Tasmania's British governor responded in the mid 1820s by declaring any "Aboriginal" in the hinterland a potential "enemy combatant," so to speak. This spurred the army and vigilantes to raid native camps or shoot people on sight.[36] (A British observer in the 1830s went so far as to write that the British in Tasmania in the 1820s were even *worse* toward the native people than the Spaniards – traditionally held up as the unenlightened opposite of the British – had been in the Americas.[37]) Pressured by settlers who called for the "extirpation" of the native people, the British governor essentially declared all native people an enemy army, declared martial law, and declared general conscription of all British men.[38] In 1830, the colonial government directed over 2,000 men to assemble at various starting points, where they formed human chains and started walking toward the coast to drive all hinterland Indigenous people onto a peninsula. There, the native people were supposed to be rounded up and shipped to a nearby island. This, of course, was a perfect exemplar of ethnic cleansing. In fact, since the so-called "Black Line" was expressly intent on the elimination of a people as a people, it was attempted genocide. (White Tasmanian colonists frequently called Indigenous Tasmanians "black," thus the "Black Line.") For understanding the evolution of white supremacy, it matters little that the Indigenous people overwhelmingly managed to slip through the lines of hunters. Within a few years, nearly all First People had been exiled offshore by the local colonial government.

Did the Black Line *begin* with British views that Tasmanian native people were subhuman – like animals driven before hunting dogs? Or did the Black Line *end* with that, result in that? Both, surely. But the British didn't undertake it starting from the position that the native "black" race must vanish. They didn't usually murder Tasmanians who served them; there were native guides leading the Black Line, after all. The British did it because, like various Indigenous peoples of the Americas, the Tasmanians were in the way, daring to resist. And yet the British didn't cleanse to the last man, woman, and child any group that resisted their conquest – not even the enemy Irish. So, there *was* something fundamentally lesser about Tasmanian First People as a race.

These factors must have reinforced each other, so that Britishness – and thus whiteness – meant "being the one who pushes through any resistance," and non-Britishness – nonwhiteness – came to mean, in British eyes, "being the one who gets pushed through or out if they resist." They told themselves that whites were takers, whereas native peoples were retreaters. Or, as scholar Kathleen Wilson has argued of the era of Captain Cook and other eastward voyagers, the British were uniquely scientific, showed manly virtue, and were natural explorers. The races of "the East" were the ones explored.[39]

The Black Line wasn't an isolated incident in the period of English-speakers' colonization – the number of Indigenous people in Australia massacred in the 1830s alone was around 1,170 – it was simply a shockingly obvious exemplar.[40] It should call to mind the

Pequot War of 1636–1638 and the English attempt to wipe the Pequots from the face of the earth – even from memory – described in Chapter 2. And the next chapter will show how it had parallels at the same time – with colonizers and officials using the same vocabulary of "extirpation" – in the new United States.

New Sciences That Expanded and Reinforced Whiteness

Finally, the dominance and displacement of settler colonialism was far from the only thing that invented and recreated whiteness in the empire in this period. Whiteness also emerged with the quill and press. In this century spanning roughly 1750–1850, the British conducted more and more observation and documentation of non-European peoples, going hand-in-hand with exploration and expansion – and wrapped up with the so-called Enlightenment's emerging "natural history of man." One wouldn't call these observers "ethnographers" or "anthropologists," at first; that'd come about during the 1830s–1840s. (Ethnography is the study of human custom and cultures, the term dating from 1811, according to the *Oxford English Dictionary* [OED]; "anthropology" is an older idea, but the OED suggests that its modern meaning, which can be defined as the study of humans and their cultures, dates from roughly the middle of the nineteenth century and was rooted in colonial observations of Indigenous bodies and societies.[41]) So who were they?

At first, they were the very officials spreading out across the face of new "conquests." They were district officers sending reports back to colonial capitals and beachheads or to London. They were missionaries or Anglican priests. They were EIC agents, penal colony officers in Australia, or officials who'd replaced Dutch counterparts in the Cape Colony. Sometimes they were primarily motivated by discovery – perhaps they were physicians whose training at Edinburgh had taught them to observe and order the world around them. But, as Chapter 3's story of Sloane and others already showed, the motives of profit, patron, and expansion combined to encourage the scrutiny (and effective ranking) of foreign, non-British "human species."

And, yes, this scrutiny sprang in part from run-of-the-mill cultural arrogance as it had since time immemorial; foreigners and non-Christians had long been curiosities. But the research and writings of the new proto-ethnographers went further than describing human idiosyncrasy, because they did it in the context of emerging whiteness and new dominance.

And the ultimate consequences of colonial ethnography were vastly grimmer than mere arrogance and insult; this colonial description led to human ordering of a kind far more profound, and ultimately vastly more deadly, than that of Herodotus, which began this book. It led to a mature race science in the later 1800s, which, coupled with the new Social Darwinism to be introduced in Chapter 6, paved the way for the worst scenes in humanity's history.

Enlightenment classification and proto-anthropology were supposed to aid the British and other European colonizers in governing the "lesser" peoples beneath them.[42] The colonizers themselves needed, after all, to understand things like the ancient hierarchies that they at least appeared to find in India; or they needed to break through "inscrutable Oriental" foibles. As scholar Shruti Kapila put it speaking of India, the British Empire sought "the reduction of its peoples to measurable objects."[43] In fact, the documents show, colonial officials of various kinds competed with each other to claim expertise about the peoples they dominated or with whom they traded.[44] And they made little division between the physical expressions of the races they described/invented and their cultural expressions or religion. Put simply, proto-anthropologists argued that culture stemmed from race. So, again, race was *essential*: "inner" race explained "outward" features.[45]

Colonial proto-ethnography of Native Americans came together out of many strands. Begging forgiveness for another deep backtrack, it's clear that these sorts of "cultural studies" were inseparable from the earliest exploration. Take the early, powerful influence of Richard Hakluyt (1553–1616), who promoted English colonization in North America as a chief advisor to Queen Elizabeth I (ruled 1558–1603) and King James I (ruled 1603–1625). He gathered and translated Portuguese and Spanish accounts of the New World and its peoples, portraying them generally as friendly, generous, inventive, and "as mannerly, and civil, as any in Europe."[46] His object was clear: he wanted the English to join other European kingdoms in exploiting the resources and trade opportunities of the New World, and his depiction of the native peoples there followed from that. (He was soon a director of the Virginia Company and later an advisor to the EIC.) Hakluyt invented an accommodating "Indian," for certain; but at the same time, he did *not* report that the land was "empty," *terra nullius*; nor that the inhabitants were "not white," given that the idea was lacking; nor that the English should conquer or remove the people who lived there. All of these things developed across a few generations.

Many varieties of English/British proto-ethnology followed for many – generally self-serving – reasons. Missionaries, for example, studied native peoples and their languages for the purpose of conversion.[47] People wanted to know (or, really, define) which tribes were "friendly" or "cruel," for the purposes of trading with or living near them.[48] People sometimes told tales of "noble savages," amounting to critiques of British or American culture rather than portraying Indigenous peoples on their own terms.[49]

Another kind of race-organizing or race-theorizing was in vogue about the same time. Around the turn of the 1800s and after, Anglo-American writers invented theories about the distant origins of native North American peoples. This fit into the growing European trend for "the classification of human beings according to the primordial 'seat' of their race," as one scholar put it.[50] Thus, British and early American observers studied Indian artifacts (which often meant looting graves) to argue that Native Americans might really be transmigrated Hebrews or Persians, for example.[51] British observers following in the wake of Captain Cook in the Pacific theorized that the Māori of what's today called New Zealand may have been distant relatives of the ancient Hebrews or Egyptians.[52] These and countless other theories – called "diffusionist" – appear so far-fetched today that the reader might laugh them off. But, if they were aimed at finding the roots of things, they equally identified deep, lasting differences. They isolated (purified?) lines of descent – including the newly theorized Caucasian or Aryan branches of humanity.

***

In the same years, by the 1820s, British craniologists (or "proto-phrenologists") were collecting thousands of Indian skulls on the other side of the globe in their quest to identify and order South Asian races. They were working under the influence of Johann

Friedrich Blumenbach, who, while German, had extensive contact and exchange with King George's court and British explorers. Blumenbach studied skulls and other features to argue that there were five human races: the first, "Caucasian," race, and the four others supposedly devolved from it – Mongolian, Ethiopian, Malayan, and (Native) American. Consequently, Blumenbach and his British counterparts wanted to know how Indians of the subcontinent fit in this scheme. The theory was that the Indians were devolved from Caucasians on a transitional path (decline, really) to Mongolians.[53] Meanwhile, an EIC surgeon, for example, measured and amassed skulls in his search for purely descended Hindus and Brahmins, thus creating a "Hindu race" and its supreme subdivision.[54]

Again, Greek-tradition environmental theories of race still held significant power; but these decades leading to the middle 1800s saw the rise of race science with its more indelible – that is, unchanging, essential, blood-locked – race theories.[55] In those decades, a Europe-wide scientific network was busy dividing races and linking physical features to who was intelligent, masterful, and civilized. In France, Georges Cuvier (1769–1832) reported to fellow scientists that "a flat visage" was an indicator of "Mongolian" essence, an essence which in turn explained such peoples' "stationary" civilizations.[56] (Again, this was a major theme of the Orientalist worldview, that Asian lands were frozen in time or fallen – unlike energetic Europe.) In Sweden, Anders Retzius (1796–1860) crossed Scandinavia and Finland with calipers to measure skulls, and by extension brains (supposedly), to prove that Swedes were a conquering race over the Finns, who were supposed to be an Indigenous, subject race. Retzius, in turn, drew on Danish correspondents' similar work.[57] In sum, scientists across Europe collaborated on a system of physical metrics to measure their racial superiority and others' inferiority in the early to mid 1800s.

These weren't arcane musings locked behind the doors of scholarly societies. People put them to use to justify and expand their domination. In Australia and Tasmania, British executions of First People supplied a "steady flow of Aboriginal heads, crania, and skeletons [to] metropolitan anatomists," in one scholar's words. These were supposed to reveal First Peoples' extraordinary savagery and predict their quick demise.[58] Meanwhile, white Americans, no surprise, took up the new craniometry discipline to justify their slave society and dispossession of native peoples – all under the guise of disinterested pure science, of course.[59] For example, a Philadelphia anatomy professor, Samuel George Morton (1791–1851), measured the volume of skulls to argue that the "American [Indian]" race was "slow in acquiring knowledge" and "revengeful," and thus "incapable of servitude."[60] While the "Ethiopian" race was "the lowest grade of humanity," it was "pliant," "yielding," and could wield a "heavy burden."[61] As for whites, Morton argued that they were from the same racial stock as ancient Egyptians, arguing from the supposed evidence of depictions on relics and monuments. Thus, American slavery was natural: the inevitable outcome of timeless physical predestination at the level of blood and bone across 100 generations. (We're far, now, from the Greeks' environmental, situational race concepts.) Slavery's supporters gladly embraced Morton's message.[62]

Did Halting the Slave Trade, Then Slavery, End Concepts of Nonwhite Inferiority?

To keep tracing white supremacy's changes in the early 1800s, we now need to make a jump in topic, though not in timeframe. We have to examine why white supremacy didn't die in its childhood with the ban on the slave trade and the institution of slavery in the first few years of the 1800s. While they were wonderful developments that saved countless lives, the bans didn't end white supremacy; they themselves weren't even free of white supremacy in their roots and legacy.

So, if white supremacy was alive and well in the first decades of the 1800s, why did Parliament vote for the gradual abolition of slavery in 1833? In large part, because of centuries of resistance by the enslaved all around the world. They were never the slave races many British people imagined they were. Such people fled their captors, stole what they could, slowed or stopped work, insisted on their humanity, and – despite the odds – rebelled en masse when they could. As historian Manisha Sinha wrote, slave resistance itself led the way to abolition.[63]

Beyond these brave acts, the record shows key moments in that centuries-long story when the enslaved carried the abolition struggle. For example, an uprising by the Jamaican enslaved, 60,000 strong, contributed one final push to get Britain's 1833

Slavery Abolition Act done.[64] It started as a Christmas Day strike led by Black preacher Samuel Sharpe, when the enslaved refused to work until they received modest wages and more rights. And had Jamaica's enslavers met their terms, acknowledged just a little of their captives' humanity, they may have preserved their slave profits longer. Instead, the slaver elite attacked the strikers, turned the strike into an armed conflict, crushed the Black "rebels" in eleven days, then tortured and killed anyone suspected of organizing or leading the uprising, around 300–350 people. They also assaulted white missionaries, whom they blamed for encouraging the uprising.[65] When news of these cruelties reached Britain, abolitionists successfully used it as leverage. These included Mary Prince. Brought to England from Antigua by her enslavers in 1829, she dictated a brutal life story to a woman who, with the Anti-Slavery Society, published it in 1831. The autobiography went through three printings in the years before the 1833 Act.[66]

For just one other example of a Black abolitionist, Robert Wedderburn (1763–c. 1835, Figure 2) was born to a Jamaican enslaved woman and her Scottish captor.[67] Sold by his father, his new owners emancipated him at age ten, roughly. After serving in the Royal Navy, he settled in London as a tailor. Around 1805 or so, he became a Unitarian preacher and fiery, uncompromising abolitionist. No incrementalism for him: he called for immediate liberty for all – Black and poor white together – and railed at the hypocrisy of

Figure 2 Robert Wedderburn, from *The Horrors of Slavery* (1824).

British claims that their country was the land of liberty. He called for rebellion in Jamaica and hinted at it so strongly for England, as well, that he was arrested and briefly imprisoned.[68]

Yet, trafficked and captive people and Black abolitionists couldn't do it on their own. By 1807, the white supremacist conceptual framework was too deep and broad; too much slavery-wealth – in the Caribbean, among Members of Parliament, and beyond – arrayed its weapons against the abolition of trafficking and the institution of slavery itself. So how and why did white Britons defeat interests who trafficked roughly 200,000 people in the 5 years before the 1807 Act, making, according to the historical record, at least 10 percent return on investment?[69] The answers are many, and historians have worked long and hard to uncover them. Some categories of explanation certainly emerge and, instead of pointing to one cause, the evidence shows several at play. Extrapolating a bit, these motivations could be labeled "basic, human sympathy," the practical, economic effect that the wealth and power of slave-sugar growers was on the decline in the late 1700s, "religious/moral indignation at injustice and wrong-doers," and "a longstanding sense that the British constitution was outraged."

Some were simply appalled by the conditions of the trade itself and the brutal treatment of kidnapped people. They called it "evil," plain and simple, like Scottish Enlightenment philosopher James Beattie (1735–1803), who battled in print with craniologists (skull-measurers) and others who argued that Africans were sub-human. Appealing to the Greeks, Beattie took the ages-old position that sub-Saharan Africans' physical traits were surface-level outcomes of environment, and meant nothing essential. "All men on Earth, whatever be their color, are our brethren, and . . . it is our duty to love them, and to do unto them as we would that they do unto us," he concluded, as slavery's opponents had for almost two centuries.[70]

And there were always those who spoke out against the idea of a hierarchy of imagined human species. Writing around 1813, English physician James Cowles Pritchard (1786–1848) argued that, while there were different races, there weren't different human species, and they were equal in all important, essential aspects. And he argued against slavery and Native American repression on that very basis.[71]

Additionally, declining profits from blood-stained sugar might have helped bring about the end of Caribbean slavery.

Trinidadian historian Eric Williams's famous *Capitalism and Slavery* (1944) encouraged scholars to explore how wealth made from the broken bodies of the enslaved got infused into the home British economy and transformed into things like factories and canals and industry.[72] At some point, *that* secondary wealth was more important, made more powerful people rich, than direct slave-sugar wealth. At that point, MPs could abandon West Indian slave-masters. Similarly, if their sugar investments were paying less in an emerging era of freer trade and competition with the new USA, wealthy MPs might quiet their headaches from abolitionist rabble-rousers by giving in in 1807 and 1833.[73] Indeed, humanitarian agitators used these economic arguments to great effect.[74] Put simply, slave sugar wasn't paying so well anymore and other industries closer to home were.

There's no question that abolition was a popular humanitarian movement. And the reformist, evangelical Christian sects in Britain partly led the way. People like William Wilberforce (1759–1833) and Hannah More (1745–1833) appealed to Golden Rule sympathy, while people like Thomas Clarkson (1760–1846) publicized the bloody brutality of the trade.[75] Also, as they'd done since the earliest court cases by enslaved people fleeing their Spanish or other captors, white abolitionists argued on the eve of 1807 and 1833 that slavery was unconstitutional in Britain. Abolition scholarship suggests that this was another key: that British self-conception as a uniquely freedom-loving people in a uniquely free land helped make the fight against the trade and institution an inherently "national cause" for many.[76] Poet William Cowper (1731–1800) neatly put it this way:

> We have no slaves at home – then why abroad?
> . . . Slaves cannot breathe in England; if their lungs
> Receive our air, that moment they are free,
> They touch our country and their shackles fall.
> That's noble, and bespeaks a nation proud.[77]

The banning of the trade and later banning of slavery were tremendous victories for people like captive resisters, formerly enslaved abolitionists like Olaudah Equiano (c. 1745–1797) and their British allies in Parliament. But that did not end white supremacy. The bans weren't even entirely divorced from white supremacy. And you can see that by peering into the details of what "liberation" looked like. For example, in British southern Africa, the formerly enslaved very frequently stayed in exactly the same position after emancipation, having few other options to survive. As historian Samuel North wrote, new laws gave masters, now called employers, extraordinary powers of physical dominance over the formerly enslaved.[78] Laws, for example, dictated that, in most places in the British Empire, the law required the formerly "owned" to be unpaid "apprentices," essentially indentured servants, for a period of usually four to six years. Flogging, sexual violence, and other abuses followed; the formerly enslaved didn't become worthy of full human dignity in the eyes of their white former owners; we might say, the "race" of the formerly enslaved didn't change.[79]

Thankfully, so-called "apprenticed" people resisted, some publicizing their vicious abuse in print and, acting together with sympathizers in Britain, a movement against the apprenticeship gambit arose.[80] It worked. "The country is ... in convulsions," of outcry, in the words of one paper. Parliament passed a law canceling forced apprenticeship in 1838.[81] Still, Britain was far from the Caribbean, and the farmer elite there held bitterly to power, excluding as many rights from the newly freed laborers as they could.[82] It's easy to see how owners' profit-interest aligned with disempowering the "race of people" who outnumbered them.

Speaking of profit, Parliament's 1833 Act that heralded the end of slavery in the British Empire called for a mammoth cash payout to slavers and their beneficiaries. The British government paid over £20 million pounds to slaveowners, money which, measured as a relative cost to its budget, we might gauge at £218.3 billion today.[83] Besides many thousands of slaveholders around the world, over 3,000 families in Britain, absentee slavers, made claims against the payout fund. (The record shows they sometimes kept quiet about their slave-derived wealth, suggesting that they knew it was wrong or at least distasteful in the public eye.[84]) A team of scholars have tracked down which families in Britain drew their wealth from enslaved people and sometimes where the buyout money got invested in new British industries.[85] Put plainly, the 1833 Slavery Abolition Act was *not* a rejection of the principle of property-in-humans; it didn't demand justice for captives and punishment for their captors as many would have done. It set things to right for those who "lost their property," while leaving the formerly enslaved – whose labor continued to grow British wealth – with none of their own. It was, practically speaking, a ransom payment to kidnappers and also a statement that property rights trumped the rights of humans with African heritage. Historian Kris Manjapra found that the British state finally completed servicing the debt from the Slavery Abolition Act in 2015.[86]

Final Thoughts

Looking past the USA in this period shows that white supremacy didn't only grow amid the enslavement of African and Indigenous peoples; if that were the case, we might expect it to have ended with abolitions in the British Empire in the mid 1830s and the United States in 1865, effectively. Instead, white supremacy adapted and grew, and covered the world wherever English-speaking people went (and beyond), from Africa to Australia to India and many points beyond and between. Such was the path to Kipling's perfect statement of benign white supremacy, of the "white man's burden," that opened Part II.

***

- The **British Empire in India was a key place**, after the loss of the American colonies, where the English invented new ways of claiming superiority based on their race. At first, they weren't richer or more powerful than the Mughal rulers they encountered in the 1600s. However, drawn by great profits and driven by grasping greed, the English/British outlasted the Mughal Empire to become politically dominant. They took from this "success" the false lesson that their race was better, more advanced.
- In places like Australia and Tasmania, white people deemed native people obstacles. Motivated by the desire to expand their property, whites told themselves that Indigenous peoples had no right to a land they supposedly "didn't use" in the proper British manner. They also exaggerated and took advantage of isolated instances of native resistance as justifications for war and ethnic cleansing. As they had in India, whites took the false lesson that **theirs was a race of inevitable expansion**, whereas nonwhites would naturally disappear in the face of white advancement.
- In those ships and on those frontiers with the colonizers were proto-anthropologists. Missionaries, natural philosophers, or government agents, they catalogued – invented – more nonwhite

races inferior to themselves. With skull-measuring and other physical metrics, they continued to destroy ancient notions that humans were roughly the same under the skin, and that only environmental and other circumstances changed them. More and more, new "sciences" **suggested that there were very different human species.**

- The efforts, sometimes the mortal sacrifices, of Black and white abolitionists paved the way to the end of the seagoing trade and the end of slavery itself in the British Empire in the early 1800s and around 1830, respectively. But **the way the British ended slavery did not acknowledge the trade as a criminal outrage against humans.**

5 BETWEEN WHITE FATHER AND ELIMINATION, 1800–1865

Whiteness and white superiority always evolved, so what form did they take in the decades before the US Civil War, very roughly 1800–1865?

First and foremost, their core was the belief – reinforced by laws, customs, violence, and 100 other things – that whiteness and blackness (and Indian-ness, Irish-ness, "oriental-ness," and so on) were separate, and distinguishing between the two was all-important.[1] And making those distinctions wouldn't have been important if it hadn't been a stark matter of power. Generally, people judged "white" were supposed to be inherently better; specifically, they were supposed to be members of an expanding, conquering, innovative, masterful race. They believed history showed themselves to be natural rulers, while clues from nature – head and face shape and so on – supposedly revealed their greater intelligence and civilized disposition. In practice, commentators left these concepts ill-defined for tactical reasons: the better-defined, the easier to disprove, after all.

As ever, countless people, ranging from the enslaved to the colonized to the many decent people observing the Golden Rule, rejected these assumptions and behaviors.

These broad concepts of whites as intelligent/conqueror/master sat in tension with another definition of whiteness: the idea that whites were uniquely freedom-minded people. That is, white people supposedly descended from "freeborn Englishmen" had an inborn instinct for personal liberty, which they contrasted with so-called "Orientals" or people deemed Black. (In fact, as Chapter 3 showed, the rise of that freedom concept was connected to

Englishmen becoming slavers.) Those "freedom-loving" Englishmen also told themselves that they were reasonable and lawful in their colonization, unlike the Spanish, whose "slavish" Catholicism and perhaps inborn bloodthirst made them arbitrary, cruel, and tyrannical.[2] And yet the tension arose because British slave societies in the West Indies were hardly secret, nor was anyone confused about where the delightful sugar in their tea came from. Good and brave people – people called "radicals" by the more "moderate" – railing against these things helped end the British trade after 1807 and slave status in the years after 1833.

What about the new USA, though? How did the master-race concept coexist with the idea that America was supposed to be the supreme land of freedom? The USA, after all, was going to be a new state precisely *for* a new race, essentially called the "sons of liberty."

The answer, as this chapter shows, is that it sat somewhat poorly. That's not because leaders like Jefferson (president 1801–1809) really meant that "*all* men are created equal" or that James Monroe (president 1817–1825) intended to respect the land of native peoples who'd tended them for millennia. But it did mean that a land that promised freedom for some and captivity or displacement for others did not rest easy. It was like a sheet of American cotton cloth being pulled hard in multiple directions. Cotton capital in the South anchored the textile hard; the question of white western expansion and the various Indigenous societies there provided its own strain; the northern states' interests didn't align with the southern slave societies; while people like Black Abolitionists applied their own hardy pressure. Meanwhile, a significant middle ground of white America was satisfied to "wait and see"; perhaps they were effectively a patch poorly holding the shredding fabric together.

Indeed, that's what white supremacy has most resembled over its lifetime of several centuries: a makeshift, shredding, constantly reinforced patch holding the status quo together. When it's failed, a self-interested majority has always had to re-stitch it with new patches.

Whiteness as Paternalism

As in Britain, American political elites tended to fancy themselves enlightened on the subject of race. In the new USA, in the decade after the revolution, there were about 900,000 people held in captivity. That's almost one in five people in the country. Roughly 300,000 people were enslaved in the USA's biggest slaveholding state alone, Virginia. And, in the decades around 1800, some American statesmen characterized this as "a problem." As historian Nicholas Guyatt showed in his *Bind Us Apart*, people like John Adams, Thomas Jefferson, and James Madison were consistent in what they said publicly about American slavery: the trade was dishonorable at best and the institution of slavery strained the cohesion of the new republic.[3] Yet, except for two, the first dozen US presidents held people captive. Guyatt showed that men who styled themselves Enlightenment devotees attempted to square the circle of their claims to freedom by arguing publicly that they'd inherited the "problem" of slavery from British slaving profiteers of an earlier age or from unenlightened investors in an unscrupulous, cruel trade. At root, it wasn't really their fault.

Did slavers like Washington, who hunted endlessly for those who escaped him, or Jefferson, who fathered children on his captives, justify themselves by writing that their enslaved were lesser by blood?[4] In Washington's case, no; in Jefferson's, he kept quiet on that question in public. In fact, Guyatt showed that arguments for Black inferiority went against enlightened self-image: such arguments would've been "prejudiced," would've been hate – and those were supposed to be unenlightened things.[5] So, instead, these men tended to offer two reasons for enslaving people: the threat of societal violence should captives be freed and the argument that the enslaved had been "degraded" by slavery and now must be treated like children. (Mind, as we've seen, those who didn't style themselves enlightened thinkers simply claimed that Black people were an inferior slave race.)

We've already read about the old argument that the enslaved would strike out at their captors unless physically held down. Then, in the 1790s, world circumstances sharply renewed this old fear for whites. In that decade, the enslaved population of 500,000 on the island of Saint-Domingue/Haiti joined with its Free Blacks to throw off their captivity under the French. When the British, Spanish, and French landed to crush the revolution, the self-liberated Haitians defeated or outlasted each, one-by-one. Of course, if the USA had truly been devoted to equality, this would have been the moment to intervene on the side of the revolutionaries. Many Americans, instead, used the Haitian rebellion to justify clamping down on their own population in chains. And, although a decent few Americans loudly called on their young country to support Haiti, President Jefferson worked to embargo the new republic economically and diplomatically.[6]

The other main argument that self-styled "enlightened" leaders used to justify inaction on slavery was that Africa-descended people had been degraded by years or generations of captivity. That is, the enslaved person may have descended from Adam and Eve just like the whites, but generations of enslavement had reduced their whole race at a deep, deep level. This was consistent with that old, Greek-influenced idea with which you're now quite familiar: races get created by environmental circumstances. In this case, that "environment" was supposed to be slavery itself – being severely mistreated, working incessantly, kept from learning, having families broken up. This theory suggested that someone freed from slavery would be hapless, hopeless, and brutal. Therefore, any plan for emancipation must include a vast program for lifting emancipated people from this essential degradation. (One can see how such transatlantic ideas influenced the British scheme for forced West Indies "apprenticeship" after 1833.)

Could the formerly enslaved ever rise to equality with whites, given enough schooling or apprenticeship or other programs of upliftment? Elite views varied. Thomas Jefferson placed Africans on a lower rung either because they were a different species or because they had degenerated over the generations. Meanwhile, a Massachusetts official believed they could *almost* rise to equality, that enslaved children should receive a public education, "raising the blacks ... nearly to the same grade as whites."[7] Then there were those who rejected theories of fixed inferiority and argued for genuine equality, like Irish American David Warden, who published a translation of Henri Grégoire's *De la littérature des nègres* in 1810 in New York.[8] That book argued that "systems" for ranking humans were corrupt, created "by men, who, interested in colonial culture, seek, in the supposed want of the moral faculties of the negro, another reason for treating him, with impunity, like a beast of burden."[9] Black abolitionists cited Grégoire's many examples of African genius. And, as ever, enslaved and Free Blacks might have had something to say about their degeneracy to those who cared to ask.[10]

The degradation idea was, as Grégoire and his readers understood at the time, self-serving for those who profited from slavery, some of whom argued that captivity was "infinitely better" than "degraded freedom."[11] More subtly, it was self-serving for those who believed matters of slavery and abolition stressed the union of southern states and northern. Time and again, leaders who chose to weld together slave societies in the south with northern parts made the expedient choice: leave it alone.[12] Enslavers like George Washington expressed private doubts about the justice of slavery, stating plainly – behind closed doors – that it tore apart families.[13] In private, too, slaveholder James Madison admitted that holding people against their will was incompatible with the sentiments of the Declaration of Independence, yet he'd eventually bring his own captives to the White House with him.[14] Even John Adams, who never enslaved anyone and claimed he was personally against slavery, wrote to Quaker abolitionists that emancipation might "produce greater violations of Justice and Humanity, than the continuance of the practice," given, he said to the Quakers, the "degraded State of the blacks."[15] Adams, then, endorsed the expansion of slavery into the new Mississippi territory in the late 1790s as a practical means of expanding American farming into Indian lands.[16]

And this is key to the development of white supremacy: even many of those whites – American and British – who promoted abolition in the years between the revolution and the Civil War embraced the theory of the essential racial degradation of the enslaved. Put simply, they advocated for relief, fairness, and an end to brutality, but very often *not* for the sort of equality people like Grégoire or Black Abolitionists advocated. And this is key: this strain of paternalism has, while it's changed this way and that, never left the genes of white supremacy since. That is, so-called "enlightened" whites throughout the English-speaking world did not suggest taking captive Africans, Indians, or Australian First Peoples and making them equal citizens. They were supposed to be childlike, and "white father" knew best for them, would have to protect them, in fact.

Removing People from the Spaces of Whiteness

Nor did abolitionist whites want them as neighbors, very often. Yes, many thought Africa-descended folk "degraded," but they also believed there'd be violence between Free Blacks and whites. Even liberal-minded or sympathetic white abolitionists imagined old wounds of captivity would lead to resentment. They went so far as to imagine Free Blacks would be animalistic, bloody avengers on their new neighbors – the age-old fear of uprising because, as 1820s Secretary of State Henry Clay said, "we are enemies of each other. They know well the wrongs which their ancestors suffered."[17] Connected to this bloody vision of mass uprising, American and British leaders justified inaction on slavery by saying that poor, unenlightened whites in particular would resent and possibly put down a newly freed Black population competing with them.[18] This concept persisted up to and through the US Civil War. As even a sympathetic anti-slavery newspaper stated in 1842, after a white mob burned the church of Black free men in Philadelphia, "degraded whites, most of them low foreigners, could not endure that the black population should rise above them and therefore conspired to trample them into the dust."[19] That is, better-off whites blamed "low" poor whites for their inaction.

Clay and other members of the national elite led the very popular movement for an American colony of Free Blacks in West Africa.[20] Yes, this was essentially the idea, which circulated before the turn of 1800 onward for decades, and was championed by the likes of Jefferson,[21] to send people – most of whom knew no homeland but Virginia or Georgia – "back" to Africa. (The movement got its first real start under a British project, in fact: an ill-fated attempt to settle Black Britons and Black American refugees in Sierra Leone in the 1780s.)

From 1816, the American Colonization Society proposed that voluntary deportation to what they named "Liberia" would provide an argument against slaveholders who insisted they *mustn't* release their captives owing to the risk of violence. And, yes, a small number of slaveholders released their victims on the condition that they be deported to Liberia; but the argument that there'd be violence or that integration was impossible was surely self-serving. (Other slavers opposed the Colonization Society precisely because its success *could* provide an argument for emancipation; and they used positions in Congress to limit federal support.) On the other hand, for northern white abolitionists, colonization appealed because, in the words of scholar Nicholas Guyatt, for "white reformers, colonization provided easy relief from the moral and political challenges of integration."[22] The organization honored slaveholding President James Monroe for his support of the scheme by naming their main settlement in Liberia "Monrovia."[23] Unfortunately for its relatively few settlers, Monrovia proved a miserable place of endemic malaria and conflict with the people of the region. Still, as late as 1862, President Abraham Lincoln (in office 1861–1865) believed emancipated people should be sent to colonize Panama or perhaps Haiti, in part because he doubted there could be happy coexistence, and in part on the basis of the old Greek environmental theory: they'd supposedly thrive in the torrid climate.[24]

Did Free Blacks support colonization? Some. It seemed some despairing Black abolitionists feared it was the only way to get support for emancipation among fearful whites or those who insisted the USA could only be "Anglo-Saxon." Better free in a strange land than chained, raped, and tortured in their birthplace. But they were in a vast minority.[25] By contrast, Frederick Douglass (c. 1817–1895), perhaps the most powerful Black abolitionist voice of all, saw clearly that colonization schemes were a way to avoid providing true, restorative justice, "to correct the injustice and wrong" of the enslaved and Free Blacks, in the words of his newspaper.[26] There were also suggestions that freed Blacks be settled on the American western frontier. The clear-eyed Douglass foresaw that proposed colonies there might meet the fate of Indigenous communities on the frontier; in the sinister logic of colonization, it might be far easier for settlers to gun down or force away Black settlers just beyond the border than to gun down their Black neighbors in Georgia.[27] Meanwhile, Douglass's white allies like William Lloyd Garrison (1805–1879) turned on colonization fiercely from the 1830s, writing that "it stigmatises our colored citizens as being natives of Africa, and talks of sending them to their native land; when they are no more related to Africa than we are to Great Britain."[28]

Like Garrison, there were plenty of people – prominent people – who rejected things like liberals' expedient hopelessness, colonization, degradation theory, and so on. And the pre-Civil War decades saw new kinds of multi-hued coalitions of such people against white supremacy. When a young Frederick Douglass went to Ireland in 1845 to speak (and avoid the predators threatening to return him to the South and slavery), he was bowled over by being among people he thought, at first, were white, but who didn't look down on him. But he was too smart to be confused for long – he soon learned they weren't *really* white, or, more precisely, were not *as* white as the British and Americans.[29] Douglass proceeded to think comparatively about Irish and Black subjugation.

His ally in this, the man Douglass said was an inspiration, was the great Irish Catholic reformer Daniel O'Connell, whose movement won a range of civil rights for Catholics in British-dominated Ireland with a landmark Act in 1829. But O'Connell also argued that the cause of Irish rights was the same as native rights throughout the empire, from India to Australia to New Zealand.[30] And despite the fact that friends warned him that the ongoing freedom movement in Ireland depended on Irish-American support, O'Connell was utterly fiery about American slavery, even using his speeches to denounce the sainted George Washington's slave-holding hypocrisy. And he rejected gradualist schemes in favor of immediate freedom for his fellow human beings.[31]

Another cause that united people across the color spectrum was forced removal of Indigenous societies from their southeastern homelands to windswept plains west of the Mississippi and Missouri Rivers. Black abolitionist and white worked together to campaign against President Andrew Jackson's (in office 1829–1837) forced expulsions.[32] And women, including Black women, especially, took up the cause in ways that laid firm building blocks for female political activism in the generations before women got the vote.[33] As ever, though, the oppressed minority themselves were the first resisters: Cherokee women were the first and most implacable foes of removal. They gathered in 1818 to organize their resistance, then petitioned US officials and pressured Cherokee men who'd lost hope or planned to expand their property by taking the poisoned chalice of promised new lands.[34] In the end, though, Jackson and Martin Van Buren (in office 1837–1841) were going to have Cherokee land regardless of property rights, legitimacy, or justice. "Established in the midst of a . . . superior race," Jackson said in a speech before Congress, "they must necessarily yield to the force of circumstances."[35] Thousands of Cherokees died in the course of their forced march west, as did thousands of Choctaw, Creek, Seminoles, and others forcibly removed in the same period.

Today, we'd call it ethnic cleansing, this series of campaigns in the first decades of the 1800s and peaking in the 1830s and 1840s to remove people, *as peoples*, from southeastern lands desired by white settlers and their government leaders, especially for expanding the cotton industry. This, of course, was an old process, one endlessly repeated across the frontiers of English-speaking colonies the world over. Settlers, profit-seekers, and officials desired more and better lands. When they met resistance – as, naturally, they did – colonists deemed it cause for war, or saw opportunity.

Frontier removals in the USA were reflected elsewhere. For example, in Canada in the 1880s, the government removed and isolated mobile Plains Metis peoples so that white settlers could have land.[36] And in mid-1800s Australia, there were many Native Police preserves or "Aboriginal Stations" and government-supported religious missions where First People were taken off the land "for their own good."[37]

Both in the USA and in Canada, Indigenous peoples pushed onto reservations needed passes to leave, a kind of segregation, and a severe limit to native peoples' opportunities and prosperity. "Notify the several tribes or bands of Indians under your supervision," ordered the US Commissioner for Indian Affairs in 1873, "that under no pretext must they leave [their reservations] without a special permit in writing."[38] Fifty years later, the South African government established the same pass rules for Indigenous peoples confined to "Native Reserves."

But removals and wars were not solely local responses to local conflict. From around 1830, especially, whether in interior areas of the USA or Canada or Australia, they appeared like the fulfillment of racial prophecy, so to speak. To frontier governors or central officials or newspaper editors, such eliminations seemed to confirm two related concepts that were becoming central to the idea of whiteness versus nonwhiteness. The first was the trend among elites, even self-identifying liberal-minded ones, that the encounter between Englishmen or white men and Indigenous people would – even though the "enlightened" found it unsavory – end in nonwhite "extirpation" inevitably, almost as a law of nature. The second connected idea was that Indigenous peoples of the American frontier or other interiors were dying out, anyway, through natural processes. English speakers' armed victories, in sum, seemed to confirm these foregoing ideas; or, perhaps as often, created the ideas.

"Extirpation": in the period around the turn of the 1800s, writers often used it in a medical context, referring to the "extirpation of tumors," for example, or injured parts of the body.[39] In its Latin origins, the word was about rooting something out, literally pulling a plant out by its roots, and in the early 1800s writers often used it to mean "weeding," too.[40] It was also the word of choice for various observers or officials writing about "weeding out" Indigenous people on the edge of white expansion.[41] It seemed a less ugly way of talking about elimination – extinction through weeding.[42] For white writers who imagined themselves enlightened, extinction or extirpation was supposed to be "lamentable," according to scholars like Jean O'Brien and Jeffrey Ostler.[43]

Still, white critics of white frontier brutality could use the word stripped of its euphemism. That is, some called out "extirpation" for what it really was – and it wasn't just "weeding." A Methodist missionary in southeastern Australia, Reverend Lancelot Threlkeld (1788–1859), made no bones about calling his neighbors' assaults on "Aborigines" a "war of extirpation." In reports to his Church superiors, Threlkeld detailed murders while mocking white pretensions to superiority held by "monsters boasting of superior intellect to that possessed by the wretched Blacks!" Such pretenses were only "convenient assumptions," in his words, to justify killing.[44] There's a clue to the ever-evolving character of whiteness in Threlkeld's story. Threlkeld wasn't alone in calling out murderous whites on the colonial frontier, but he didn't stop at charging "low-class" whites; he accused higher-class landowners and some officials. This seemed to make "respectable" white Australia unify against him and violently repudiate him.[45] He was a race traitor.

Again, some officials and writers argued that nonwhites would die out of their own accord. This was even before the era of Darwin's *On the Origin of Species* (1859) and its message about competition between organisms, with species coming into and out of existence. It fit into early ideas about degradation – that races could decline – just taken to the extreme. And these ideas about racial extinction could serve paternalistic white supremacy.[46] For example, a promoter of greater colonization in New Zealand wrote in 1842 that the British, with "justice and benevolence," uplifted the Māori, "who would otherwise continue to be debased and savage till they perished in misery and extinction."[47] Or take Australia, where British colonists eased their consciences by saying that their destruction of First Peoples was the simple, if regrettable, consequence of natural dynamics. The ascendant race and culture, they said, will simply displace the "fragile" race, the "dying race."[48] On these grounds, "philanthropic" whites in the mid 1800s encouraged removing native Australian children from their parents to mission schools or sometimes to adoptive families. From the 1880s, the Australian government became more and more aggressive in this, until it made itself the legal guardian of all First People or First People-related children and, by the early twentieth century, removed roughly two-thirds of such children from their parents.[49] This story of elimination by assimilation was already old by that time.

On the other hand, extinction, according to observers in the first half of the 1800s, might come at the hands of grasping, illiberal whites; that is, "poor whites." Indeed, the idea that poor or "degraded whites" stirred up violence – whatever the law, or despite enlightened governance by their betters – was a common one from Canada to Australia. Now, there can be no doubt that in this period of frontier colonization in the 1800s, whiteness was getting more entrenched and more one-dimensional. And that's for a simple reason: white elites *had to know* who was white and who was not, so they knew who had rights and who didn't. And they didn't like fine distinctions; indeed, "mixed-race" people caused them no end of confusion and consternation when elites wanted whiteness, linked to superiority, to be rock solid. There was, however, one main division within whiteness, related to class: on the one hand, respectable whites; on the other, "bad," degraded, poor whites. These were the whites who didn't show all the marks of civilization like whites were supposed to do.[50]

And why do historians point this out? Because this category of "degraded whites" was a very expedient, convenient tool for white supremacy. White leaders told themselves that degraded whites' proclivity to violence against native peoples demanded their intervention: namely, the removal of native peoples. In other words, the stories elites told about poor whites on the frontier causing conflict and mayhem justified ever greater paternalism over Indigenous peoples.[51] In a manner of speaking, officials in Washington, Ottawa, or Sydney told themselves that those uncivil frontier whites were *forcing them* to intervene to violently remove Indigenous people or push them into "protective" reservations – for their own good.[52] In the extreme, that justified things like ethnic cleansing. People like "Indian Affairs" agents of the USA could thus justify colonialism or ethnic cleansing as *in the interest of* the dispossessed. "If the benevolent designs of the government … are to be carried forward to a successful issue," reported one such official, "there appears but one path open – a home remote from the settle-ments must be selected for them. There they must be guarded from the pestiferous influence of degraded whitemen."[53] Those degraded whites on the frontier could even spread their degradation to Indigenous people heretofore "unspoiled," in a manner of speaking, from their noble savagery.[54] Such midcentury ideas, whether in the USA, Canada, or elsewhere, helped lead to an alternative theory of white paternalism in the 1900s: that it was best to isolate "non-whites" from whites within an empire. The brains and "constitu-tions" of nonwhites were too delicate to accommodate modernity and would only be ruined by it. Best leave them in their "backward-ness." This, as you might guess, was partly at the root of systematic underdevelopment in colonies.[55]

When Paternalism "Failed," Whiteness as Elimination

Genocide marks this mid-1800s period, though it didn't end in the 1800s by any stretch. Genocide is a relatively recent term for something that's very old. It means a group's intent to destroy a people – down to the last individual, if possible – through violence, through things like education or cultural erasure, or through dispos-session and attrition until none remain.[56] The point to the definition is that the goal is elimination, either piecemeal or at once. Whether it's successful or not has no bearing on the definition. In earlier pages, we've seen ethnic cleansing. Genocide is ethnic cleansing, but not all ethnic cleansing is genocide. Ethnic cleansing means "cleansing" a region of a people; the perpetrator is concerned primarily with the removing, not *necessarily* with total erasure, of a people. In its spirit, it's no less horrific than genocide; and the label "ethnic cleans-ing" is not a "gentler" one. Genocide and ethnic cleansing mainly differ in scale: total versus regional elimination. They both existed and exist because the perpetrator identifies an inferior race unworthy of the same right to life and land as them.[57]

The USA, Australia, Canada, and other white settler empires attempted genocide in one form or another in this period. Take the California genocide of around 1846 to the mid 1870s, during which around 120,000 Indigenous people died due to US government or white settler violence and dispossession. On the one hand, there were many thousands shot by the federal army, California militia, or vigilante killers, estimates ranging from 16,000 to 100,000.[58]

Sometimes, the army or others justified slaughter because some Indigenous group defended itself or stole livestock to survive; but, as scholar Ben Madley showed so well, the violence was overwhelmingly one-sided, with whites effectively creating "an unwritten doctrine of collective, mass reprisal. . . . indiscriminate killing and great losses of life that cannot be separated from the larger pattern of genocidal killing."[59] But it wasn't really "unwritten." Various officials in the new state, its senator, its governor, officials of the army, and more, *did* document, in many forms, a desire for collective punishment and piecemeal extermination, even if there wasn't some kind of sole genocide protocol.[60] As one California senator said in 1852, California's native people, "will be exterminated before the onward march of the white man." "Humanity may forbid," he went on, "but the interest of the white man demands their extinction."[61]

As was ongoing for centuries across white settler frontiers, murder killed more than those shot in the back. The children of the murdered went unfed or uncared for; the same went for elderly community members; agriculture or industry went untended; leaders vanished, along with knowledge. Many thousands of native Californians were practically enslaved, and children were sent to mission schools or made "apprentices," which the reader will understand from Chapter 4.[62]

In about the same timeframe, the story of California mirrored Australian horrors. There was the eliminationist Black Line in Tasmania in 1830, described in Chapter 4. But, wider than that, the mid 1800s was a time of particular violence by Australian frontier police, colonial vigilantes, and others against First People communities.[63] The number will never be known precisely, but violence and expulsion, together with the upheaval of newly introduced diseases, combined to kill around 80–95 percent of First Peoples between 1788 and 1850. That left perhaps 60,000 survivors in 1850.[64] To take just one example of murder, in 1847, a Scottish settler gave a native Australian community poisoned flour for the purpose of mass murder, killing about fifty.[65] Historian Timothy Bottoms documents case after case of communities being surrounded by police and gunned down to the last individual for, say, stealing a bull or hunted by death squads as if for sport for supposedly spearing sheep.[66] All of this, while white observers *tsk-tsked* that it seemed Providence was allowing the lesser race to "fade away" before the advance of "European civilization."[67] Of course, besides the resistance of the First Peoples themselves, decent white people, like one Edward Wilson in 1856, called out such self-serving claims: "there is too great a readiness in recognizing, as 'the Hand of Providence,' that which is directly traceable to our own notorious neglect and wickedness. … We have shot them down like dogs."[68]

And, while there were always such voices opposing white supremacist arguments, historians Ann Curthoys and Jessie Mitchell clearly show that there was a midcentury movement in colonial circles to make Australia a sort of "white preserve." In the words of one high-level Colonial Office administrator in 1841, whites should take care to make Australia a "place where the English race shall be spread from sea to sea unmixed by any lower caste."[69] This official, James Stephen, wasn't writing about eliminating the native population in this context – people of his position tended to believe they were a dying race, after all – he was writing about immigrants. He was supporting an Australian movement to block South and East Asian people from migrating to Australia for work. And the next chapter will highlight anti-immigration as central to preserving white supremacy roughly from 1850 to 1940.

While it was common in Australia, too, Canada offers a prime example of elimination through schooling, or what they called "Indian Residential Schools." Those words put too neat a veneer on it, though; perhaps "reprogramming" or forced cultural destruction through purpose-built institutions is better. There, from the earlier 1800s but accelerating in the 1870s, Christian organizations, funded by the Canadian government, taught children to abandon their language, culture, and communities.[70] Canada's first prime minister, John A. Macdonald (1815–1891), was a strong supporter of removing Indigenous children from their families to send them to "Residential Schools." He said:

> When the school is on the reserve the child lives with its parents, who are savages; he is surrounded by savages, and though he may learn to read and write, his habits and training and mode of thought are Indian. He is simply a savage who can read or write.[71]

As one Canadian official wrote, "the North American Indian cannot be civilized or preserved in a state of civilization (including habits of industry and sobriety) except in connection with … religious instruction and sentiment."[72] Besides being culturally eliminationist in intent, the schools tended to be horrific places, with malnutrition, abuse, and illness rampant. Naturally, white Canadians didn't carefully record how many native children died in their institution, but several tens of thousands is probably a conservative estimate out of around 130,000 Indigenous children who entered the system.[73]

In the USA, they tended to be called "Indian Boarding Schools," and they were quite consistent in intent and results.[74] Holding perhaps one in five native American children in around 1900, they were intended to eliminate Indigenous culture, and the results were horrific (Figure 3). In recent years, Indigenous people have stepped forward to attest to the great extent of sexual abuse by Catholic church staff at the schools.[75] The other result? Failure. Indigenous people and their cultures remain, despite the efforts to erase them as peoples.

Besides these, there were acts of military ethnic cleansing and race-motivated colonial slaughter in this period, too. In 1857, the British tried to kill every last man, woman, and child in the Indian

Figure 3 J. N. Choate, "Carlisle Indian School student body around 1885, with the Superintendent's House in background" (1880–1889). Dickinson College Archives & Special Collections.

village of Mahua Dabar for supporting the attempt to throw off British colonial rule sometimes called the Sepoy Rebellion. The British erased the village from the face of the Earth as well as from maps and forbade its reconstruction.[76] In Jamaica a few years later, there was a protest movement of poor Black tenant farmers who pleaded for the right to cultivate unused fields to relieve their poverty. Over 100 poor petitioners wrote to Queen Victoria in early 1865 asking for changes so they could farm and work. "We beg ... with submission, to inform our Queen that we are in great want at the moment," they began. In a response published and circulated across the island, Victoria wrote back that "the Prosperity of the Labouring ... Classes depends, in Jamaica ... upon their working for Wages, not uncertainly, or capriciously, but steadily and continuously."[77] This argument sprang from the theory that non-whites lacked a work ethic as well as from the common Victorian view that the poor – of any skin tone – were poor due to laziness. When police arrested squatters on abandoned fields, protestors went to the trial to interrupt it. When police arrested the protestors in turn, the crowd freed them. This resulted in limited tit-for-tat violence. But then British police and proto-military militiamen went on a rampage, murdering 439 – "man or woman or child," in the words of one militiaman – in response to the uprising.[78] Back in England, decent people like Charles Darwin protested the arbitrary slaughter, while others like Charles Dickens defended the Jamaican government's actions as necessary "law and order."[79]

Final Thoughts

The USA was fighting a civil war in the same years that saw Americans, Australians, and Canadians trying to eliminate indigenous peoples. That civil war evolved into a contest of whether the federal union of states would make Black men citizens or not. And it was a conflict that had been brewing for many decades, indeed from the moment of the writing of the Constitution itself, with all of its accommodations for slavery. In a way, the war was a test of whether whites were, as stated at the beginning of the chapter, a uniquely freedom-minded race or a conquering, dominating race. Was the white race so freedom-loving that it couldn't tolerate a subject race living in chains in its midst? Or was it a conquering master race that must "parent" lesser races or watch them die out as destined by nature?

In the USA, the war settled the question of whether Black men were citizens with, at least, rudimentary rights. Although the US Civil War didn't start as a war to make Black men citizens, in a way, it ended as one, with a constitutional amendment establishing birthright citizenship passing soon after the South's defeat. But that did not mark the end of white supremacy. Far from it. Roughly a decade after the war, US state governments in the South and beyond began passing laws to restrict citizenship rights sharply. Meanwhile, those interested in preserving white supremacy built a regime of racial terror and systematically turned capitalism against nonwhites. White supremacy didn't end; it just shifted the grounds on which it battled to preserve itself.

***

- This chapter showed the incredible range of white supremacy's faces in the early and mid 1800s. On the one hand, it could look like a perverse sort of caring. Cosmopolitan, "enlightened," John Adams, for example, could shake his head at the "degraded State of the blacks," and use that as an excuse to conclude that they were better off enslaved. Meanwhile, paternalistic white abolitionists cared enough to oppose the institution of slavery, but envisioned deporting people to Africa or reservations on the American frontier.
- On the other hand, white supremacy also manifested itself as murder, ethnic cleansing, and genocide. Sometimes liberal, better-off whites blamed violence on degraded whites. And sometimes they said that expelling Indigenous people from their homes was necessary for their protection. Other times, forced removals in places like the USA or Canada were government policy, blamed on the violence of resisting peoples.
- Sometimes the elimination of peoples as peoples took a softer form than the volleys of frontier rifles. In Canada and Australia, especially, the state employed the tool of removing children from their parents and communities for cultural reprogramming in government or missionary schools.

6 CREATING THE WHITE MAN'S BURDEN, 1865-1930S

The US Civil War appeared to settle the old question of whether Black people were citizens of the nation-state, the race-state. Black men (and I write strictly of men, here) joined white men as citizens. But time would soon tell that this citizenship was only in name, only on paper. Why? Because, even if some vast portion of American northerners still believed themselves superior to nonwhites, this was still a blow to the security of whites' superiority. Thus, those invested in white supremacy – those who believed that their wealth and position depended on repressing rival races – needed to buttress their defenses using new tools. Remember: fear that whites *aren't* supreme, or won't easily *stay* supreme, is woven through white supremacy's history from its first days until now.

This chapter shows how this extended beyond the USA to the rest of the English-speaking world. After grudgingly freeing their captives from the mid 1830s, colonizers and white-nation-builders in the British Empire also needed to reinforce and justify their power over nonwhites in new ways. If the "master race" could no longer show their mastery by arbitrarily controlling and violating the bodies of the "slave race," if there ceased even to be a slave race, then whites from Australia to Canada needed new ways to deny nonwhites power, while absolving themselves. And these pages show their methods of monopolizing power and wealth while whitewashing or vindicating themselves.

They drew from long-developing and new race sciences to do so. They adopted worldviews like Social Darwinism and new practices like eugenics. They invented new races. And, across the English-speaking world, they employed new techniques like immigration restrictions to quash nonwhite power.

Ethnocracy – rule by one race – and the white state needed defending. One of the leading white race-theorists of the 1920s was recommended reading by US President Warren Harding (in office 1921–1923).[1] A 1929 quote from Lothrop Stoddard works like a sort of equation – you can read it forward and backward:

> We know that our America is a White America. ... The overwhelming weight of both historical and scientific evidence shows that only so long as the American people remain white will its institutions, ideals and culture continue to fit the temperament of its inhabitants – and hence continue to endure.[2]

He also meant the reverse: as long as whites invented historical and scientific evidence, and as long its institutions and culture remained in the hands of whites, America – and he could've been saying the same thing in Australia or Canada – would remain a white race-state.

Race Science and Social Science in Defense of Whiteness

For white supremacy, modern race science came to the rescue. If slavery-by-blood and physical chains no longer asserted who was supposedly slave and who was master, stories about slavishness and mastery *in the blood* would have to do the work. You've already read about the early skull-measurers of the 1700s like Hans Sloane and Johann Friedrich Blumenbach. They spent generations separating and classifying "the races," which they were, of course, inventing along the way. Claiming to be dispassionate men of science, they tended to insist that they were *not* ranking better or worse races. (They simply seemed to find themselves in the best, most advanced race – and shrug at their good luck.)

From these beginnings, the later mid 1800s saw some important changes in race science. In part, this was an outgrowth of changes in universities and the solidifying science and social science professions themselves. That is, the Enlightenment "gentleman natural philosopher" was fast being replaced by the "modern" university-credentialed "scientist." Where wealthy patrons supported natural philosophers in different ways during the so-called

Enlightenment, now they more often endowed positions, or "chairs," in universities. The scientist was becoming a formally trained professional, who tended to be on a faculty and belong to a professional scholarly association. He (and, sometimes, she[3]) was not supposed to have interests that were broad and shifting interests, but was expected to study one thing only and exhaustively.

But it's not just that race-science went along for the ride of science professionalization: race scientists like Francis Galton (1822–1911) *led* the way.[4] Speaking of the new medical science profession, meanwhile, historian Christopher Willoughby argued that "nascent ... medical professionals campaign[ed] to market themselves as scientific masters of racial difference."[5]

And, for the new medical scientists, racial difference usually meant racial superiority and inferiority. As scholars Evelyn Hammonds and Rebecca Herzog wrote, later-1800s medical scientists, for example, argued that the kinds and rates of diseases suffered by nonwhite races revealed "intrinsic racial characteristics." Their medical science revealed that whites were noble and nonwhites debased. Depending on the "disease in question, vulnerability might be ennobling or debasing, a sign of civilization or degeneracy."[6] Of course, white scientists kept proving what they already believed. For another example, the President of the American Association for the Advancement of Science published research sponsored by the US Government in 1869 that showed "lung capacity in blacks ... to be deficient [and] a salient racial characteristic."[7] Meanwhile, the *Medical and Surgical Reporter* offered its opinion that the "Saxon" (white American of northern European descent) body was the world's strongest, which accounted for the successful "westward march of civilization."[8] And in 1887, to name one more among countless examples, *The New York Medical Journal* published a study arguing that Native American bodies were terribly prone to tuberculosis, but that hope lay with race-mixing: "white blood, which is already adapted to a higher plane of civilization, will certainly improve the Indian."[9]

It wasn't just that scholars across the English-speaking world published medical science tracts on the topic of race difference and hierarchy. Scholars in all kinds of fields, in all kinds of publications, disparaged or reduced nonwhite and elevated white from the vantage of new professions. Take sociology: Yale's first Professor of Sociology, William Graham Sumner (1840–1910), wrote that, if Africans had been enslaved in the USA, that was just the natural order of things.[10] He also argued that British colonizers did "a service to our race" by taking over lessers' lands.[11] Or take anthropology – truly, the roots of modern anthropology in the mid 1800s overwhelmingly lay in the task of separating and hierarchizing races. Oxford's first Professor of Anthropology, Edward Burnett Tylor (1832–1917), was influenced enough by Charles Darwin (1809–1882) that he thought all humans evolved from a common ancestor; yet he wrote in 1871 that "the superior intellect of the progressive races has raised their nations to the heights of culture." Of course, he distinguished such "progressive races" from "American savages" and "African barbarians."[12]

The name "Darwin" has popped up in our story and it's an important one, because clearly white supremacists cited him in their proofs. Charles Darwin was a university-trained geologist, and his observations of how the Earth changed over inconceivably long periods helped inspire his ideas of how living species did so, as well. With great clarity, he presented ideas about how slight variations in species' individuals would occasionally give them an advantage in surviving over their less lucky cousins. Accumulated over countless generations, those advantageous variations would eventually constitute a new species, since that family line, "better fitted" to its environment, outproduced those on a different branch of the family tree. The "struggle for existence" was a harsh battle in which inter-species variations created victors and the vanquished.[13]

Darwin, by the way, was a strict abolitionist, and believed that all humans were descended from the same forebears; he rejected the idea that whites and nonwhites were separate species. On the other hand, he believed that many or most nonwhites were lesser than most whites. There were, in the words of his *Descent of Man* (1871), differences or "gradations" in "intellect" and "moral disposition" "between the highest men of the highest races and the lowest savages."[14] At least Darwin believed (mistakenly) that education achieved by a parent could pass down finer qualities to offspring through particles called "gemmules." That meant Darwin believed that the "lowest" races could improve. As historian of science Jessica Riskin put it:

> Darwin considered that Black children might learn less well than white children from a certain age owing to differences they'd inherited from their parents. But he also thought that

if this turned out to be the case, it meant that the children's education would improve not only their own abilities but those of their children and grandchildren.

Race science, again, could cloak white supremacy in softer words and practices than the slave-driver used.

In *The Descent of Man*, Darwin embraced a kind of linear model which ordered the world's races along a single timeline and scale of civilizational progress.[15] All races were supposed to move along the same line from an ancient past of savagery to modern-day advanced civilization, with several stages in between.[16] Darwin wasn't alone in using this scale, and anthropologists ran with it, believing they could study "primitive" (nonwhite) peoples for clues about what the ancient Britons were like, for example (Figure 4). They were supposed to be a kind of human time capsule or, as historian Peter J. Bowler wrote, like "living fossils left behind by the march of progress."[17] Take American Lewis Henry Morgan (1818–1881), who studied (or at least *held forth* on) the Iroquois and read about the Australian native people for this purpose. The "Aborigines" were supposed, in his words, to let the anthropologist "look down the incipient stages" of humanity, offering a "glimpse at society when it verged on the primitive."[18]

This certainly helped put the last nail in the coffin of the ancient environmental explanations for race difference. Again, on the surface, it was a "softer" kind of prejudice, because the Social Darwinists who subscribed to the theory of evolutionary stages sometimes said that all humans were the same, but that different races of humanity found themselves at different points along the timeline. In other words, while the theory of a social evolutionary timeline continued to "prove" that whites were superior, just as the

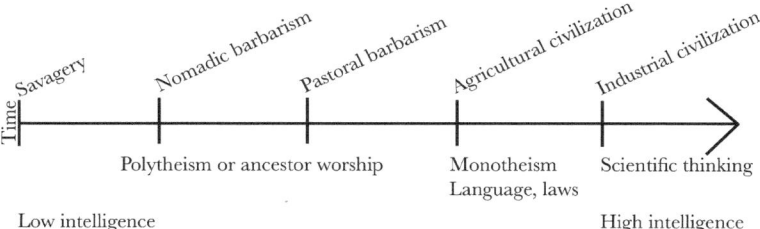

Figure 4 Scale of societal evolution, a synthesis of many thinkers' ideas.

natural philosophers had, it let the race scientist appear judgment-free. Lesser races were simply stuck in an ancient past, and whites had nothing to do with it.

Social Darwinism

It's past time to dig into the topic of Social Darwinism, because it was a dominating idea that inspired the thinking of social scientists (and their students: future presidents and prime ministers) from the Ivy League to Oxford. Social Darwinism was (and is) the belief that human races or nations competed against one another in a global contest for the "survival of the fittest," a term coined by Darwin's contemporary Herbert Spencer (1820–1903). Yes, races were supposed to compete via war-making, so that a technologically advanced race defeating a less-advanced race was excused as natural, if not good.[19] "Warfare among men, like warfare among animals, has had a large share in raising their organisations to a higher stage," wrote Spencer in his *Study of Sociology* in 1873, "it has had the effect of continually extirpating races which, for some reason or other, were least fitted to cope."[20] (But Social Darwinists tended to focus on the "advanced" part, not the war-making part. The most advanced, white civilizations, those supposed to be at the far end of an evolutionary spectrum, should outgrow war-making but still out-compete their lessers.)

This "survival of the fittest" idea was very attractive to white imperialists. Take Cecil Rhodes (1853–1902), infamous even in his day as a colonial opportunist and warmonger, who said at the beginning of his career as a diamond miner in southern Africa, "I contend that we are the finest race in the world and that the more of the world we inhabit the better it is for the human race. ... more territory simply means more of the Anglo-Saxon race, more of the best, the most human, most honourable race the world possesses."[21] Or take Rhodes's contemporary, famous British explorer and author Richard Burton (1821–1890), who believed it was right for "higher" races to displace lower, telling his vast reading audience that "a race either progresses or retrogrades, either increases or diminishes."[22] And, in parallel with British colonizers' justifications, white southerners in the late-1800s USA liked the "survival of the fittest" model and the social evolution timeline, too. It let them argue that, with two races in the same space, the one more advanced in "the grade of race evolution . . . must . . . assume control and determine the policy of the community." That would be "the best result for both races, especially for the lower race."[23] In the 1930s, speaking with approval of the Palestinians being displaced by Jewish settlers, Winston Churchill joined in:

> I do not admit for instance, that a great wrong has been done to the Red Indians of America or the black people of Australia. I do not admit that a wrong has been done to these people by the fact that a stronger race, a higher-grade race, a more worldly wise race to put it that way, has come in and taken their place.[24]

Despite Spencer's and others' confidence that competition raised whites and kept down or even "extirpated" nonwhites, white anxiety strongly latched onto Social Darwinist thinking. Much of this anxiety centered on the idea that, as superior as they were, whites might be outnumbered and overpowered by lesser races, either because they'd out-birth their white co-nationalists or because they generated greater foreign armies that could overrun a "white country." While US President Theodore Roosevelt (in office 1901–1909) believed whites superior – as evidenced by their spread across the globe – he worried that "bolder and stronger peoples will pass us by" and win "the domination of the world" if whites didn't prevail in contests of national strength.[25] And not just strength, but also baby-making; he said that a married woman who "refrains from having children, is in effect a criminal against the race."[26]

A favorite theme of anxious Social Darwinists was what they called the "Yellow Peril." According to this delusion, East Asians would soon pour out of China or Japan and invade "the West."[27] This sinister phrase takes just a little explaining. Before roughly the middle of the 1800s, observers weren't always sure of the "color" of peoples east of Africa. For example, speaking of South, Southeast, and East Asians, they were sometimes "white," sometimes "olive," or "swarthy," or "yellow." But, as Englishmen and other Europeans hardened the boundaries of whiteness, scholar Michael Keevak explained, they had to invent a new color for many Asians: yellow.[28] While there was plenty of race-hate directed at Chinese immigrants in places like California before 1900, the Yellow Peril trope seems to have flourished from the time of the 1899–1901 anti-colonial Boxer Rebellion in China.[29] In 1902,

Winston Churchill told an interviewer that China was growing too dangerous as a "great, barbaric nation" which might "menace civilized nations." Civilized nations might have to partition China like Africa: a hard task, but "the Aryan stock is bound to triumph."[30]

In those same years, the British were fighting the Dutch-descended Boers in southern Africa, and a popular white supremacist writer of the day lamented that "it is criminal for Englishmen and Dutchmen to go on murdering each other, for all sorts of sophisticated reasons, while the Great Yellow Danger overshadows us white men, and threatens destruction."[31] Yellow Peril fear only grew after Japanese successes in the Russo-Japanese War in 1905. Then, European observers imagined Japan might overrun China and there breed enormous numbers of soldiers who would take over the world.[32] During the First World War, powerful press magnate William Randolph Hearst took up the call, again. It was incredibly dangerous for the whites of Western Europe to kill each other when the real danger was in the East. "The Hun comes not, nor ever has come, from Germany," he wrote, "nor from any part of Europe, but will come ... in successive, almost irresistible tides of invasion from the interior of Asia."[33] You'll hear a distinct echo of this in the next chapter, as well, from the "America First" movement.

Fear was at the core of the Social Darwinism of the white elite, whether in Britain, the USA, or Canada.[34] And that generated a whole sub-genre of writing around the turn of the twentieth century describing the threat to the white race – not white countries, but the white race – and proposing solutions.[35] Take, for example, Yale historian George Burton Adams (1851–1925), who worried in 1896 that whites would not be able to maintain their supremacy over world affairs in the approaching twentieth century.[36] He argued that "it is by no means clear" that "the Anglo-Saxon race" could maintain its "foremost place in the world."[37] For him, the enemy was "the Oriental," who might surpass the Anglo-Saxon in terms of population numbers and economy. The "struggle," he warned, "would not be one for supremacy only, but for existence itself." The solution was supposed to be some kind of global union – or empire, or commonwealth, or "united states" – of white countries working together to thwart their race competition. Adams thought a global "Anglo-Saxondom" should be led by the USA; not surprisingly, British writers of the same day thought Britain should lead such a white union against the global race peril.[38]

Eugenics: Social Darwinism Applied within One State

Since "advanced civilizations" were supposed to outgrow war-making – that ancient method for raising more advanced civilizations and "extirpating" weak ones – Social Darwinists pondered how to defend and advance the white race without it. Karl Pearson (1857–1936), a British mathematician who heavily influenced anthropology and biology, wrote about the ongoing "struggle of race against race."[39] In the past, "it was a blind, unconscious struggle of barbaric tribes. At the present day, in the case of the civilized white man, it has become more and more the conscious, carefully directed attempt of the nation to fit itself to a continuously changing environment"[40] A new science, a new practice and profession, offered the solution: eugenics, sometimes called "racial hygiene." In a way, eugenics was Social Darwinism consciously applied *within* a race. That Social Darwinist spectrum of stages? It also existed *within* a race.[41] That is, the "best" white people – or the "whitest" – were at the far end of the spectrum of civilization; the worst white people were closer to the barbaric stage.

Eugenics tried to encourage births among the "advanced" and discourage births on the "savage" end of the spectrum. In eugenicists' own eyes, they were dispassionate scientists working for the betterment of humankind. Like benign gardeners, they imagined they were pruning the human tree of sickly branches to strengthen the best parts of the tree. Like the "Enlightenment" natural philosophers before them, they just happened to find themselves in the "best parts" and the lower classes and nonwhite races in the "sickly parts." They also wanted to prune out people we'd call neurodivergent, whom eugenicists tended to call "feeble-minded," "deranged," or "shiftless," among the white race through sterilization. Eugenicists, unsurprisingly, tended more often to find women "mentally deficient" than men.[42]

It's easy to see that eugenicists were more likely to "prune" nonwhites than white. They had their chance when nonwhite women, especially, were cast into state institutions like asylums. There, the eugenics-minded could enforce sterilization. Historian Alexandra Minna Stern has found that, in California, the state disproportionately sterilized women with Spanish surnames. She and other researchers have found the same for Asian immigrants confined to hospitals or prisons in the early twentieth century.[43] Meanwhile, in the same period, coercive sterilization of Indigenous women was part of Canada's eliminationist policy.[44]

Connected to imagined "degeneracy," French and US scientists developed intelligence testing in the later 1800s and early 1900s. After all, to weed out the "degenerate," eugenicists needed a means of measurement. And it almost goes without saying that such tests would usually find white test-takers more intelligent.[45] Some eugenicists then used the "evidence" that people other than Western Europeans were less intelligent to block the immigration of undesired races.[46] (More on anti-immigration in a moment.)

And the test actually taught the taker: white is supposed to be more beautiful. A page from the 1908 Binet–Simon intelligence test asks the test-taker to identify "which of the two faces" in each row "is the prettiest." If the test-taker considered a larger nose or more slanted eye ugly, they were supposed to be more intelligent[47] (Figure 5).

Figure 5 J. W. Wallace Wallin, "A Practical Guide for Administering the Binet–Simon Scale for Measuring Intelligence," *The Psychological Clinic* 5 (March 1911).

Anti-immigration across the English-Speaking World

So, if eugenics was Social Darwinism applied within the white race, its logical extension was the elimination of lesser races themselves or their exile from whites.[48] The main tactic for doing this was to block nonwhites and "bad whites" from entering the USA, Australia, or Canada. The example of one eugenicist, Harold Fantham, shows how white supremacy was a global network across the English-speaking world. Fantham was educated in London, after which he taught zoology at Cambridge, and then anatomy in South Africa. There, he took a leading role in promoting eugenics for "safeguarding our nation from racial deterioration."[49] He enthusiastically supported the USA's Immigration Restriction Act of 1924 for barring what he considered "idiots, feeble-minded, paupers." Meanwhile, he admired Germany's 1924 bill for compulsory sterilization in cases of things like so-called feeble-mindedness, alcoholism, and apparent criminal tendencies.[50] Historians Rebecca Hodes and Rodney Reznek describe his opposition to Jewish immigration to South Africa as president of the South African Association for the Advancement of Science in 1927, three years before the Immigration Quota Act of 1930.[51]

Or take another case: Australian politicians' pursuit of what they called their "programme of a white Australia." Australia passed a series of immigration acts from 1900 to the Second World War that largely barred people from East Asia, Eastern Europe, and Pacific Islands. This was supposed to be for, in the words of Australia's attorney general, "the purity of race" and the "unity of race." He cited all the usual Social Darwinist and race hygiene justifications for keeping nonwhites out and deporting some who were there.[52] In one Parliamentary debate, a member of the Australian House of Representatives pointed to the internal race peril of the USA as a warning for Australia:

> The black people there have increased to such an extent, and have gained such power, that the jurists and statesmen there pause and look with fear upon them. A repetition of the trouble will occur in this country if these servile and objectionable races are allowed to continue to invade our shores.[53]

Meanwhile, a young Winston Churchill embraced an Indiana state law that allowed forced sterilization of those deemed "mentally unfit." And he feared that a low birth rate "among all the thrifty, energetic and superior stocks, constitutes a national and race danger which it is impossible to exaggerate."[54]

Eugenics seemed to offer a solution to this threat of lesser races overrunning such "superior stocks." Eugenicists and their supporters imagined growing hordes of nonwhites (or sometimes degraded whites) defeating "good" whites in a race to make babies. British philosopher Bertrand Russell (1872–1970), for example, wrote in 1916 that "after generations of selection of those who have neither intelligence nor foresight" white Europeans risked "their subjugation by less civilized races" or degenerating down to "a much lower place of civilization."[55] There's that scale and time-line of civilization, again. But you can't extract eugenicists' focus on degenerate whites from their concern about hordes of nonwhites swamping them. In South Africa, for example, eugenics was sup-posed to improve the stock and fertility of whites to counter the imagined black horde threatening white power there.[56]

And the same fears motivated segregating lesser from higher races via immigration restriction. Influential Yale natural history professor Nathaniel Shaler (1841–1906) preached that permitting "inferior races" into the USA would threaten white culture and democracy itself. Democracy, after all, gave a voice to everyone, including the growing "lesser" masses. (More on that in the next chapter.) Unsurprisingly, then, Shaler's students founded Boston's Immigration Restriction League in 1894.[57] One of those students wrote that their anti-immigration movement was "in its essentials a eugenic measure."[58] It made a sinister sense: anti-immigration was a kind of social hygiene meant to keep "impurity" away from the pure people.

The Emergence of a Jewish Race amid Social Darwinism and Replacement Theory

This later-1800s era of race science transformed and nur-tured anti-Jewishness. Earlier, in the English-speaking world, Jews were on the white spectrum, while supposedly in grave error on religion. They weren't eternally lesser as a matter of blood. While the story in the Spanish-speaking world was different, in Britain, someone named Benjamin Disraeli (1804–1881) could, having converted to Christianity at age twelve, rise to become prime minister of deeply Christian Victorian Britain in 1868. While there were certainly horrible instances of hatred directed against them, there wasn't a systematic scientific theory of their natural inferiority, of their inherent threat, even. That was about to change.

White race commentators like early anthropologists needed to place the Jews, like all others, on the scale of "development" and identify (create) their race origins. The term "Semite" (and thus today's "antisemitic") comes from the late 1700s when German and French linguists invented the race to fit their ideas about an ancient language common to Hebrew and Arabic.[59] Thus, this new race was supposed to include Arabs, Jews, and other peoples of the Levant and the Arabian Peninsula. English physician James Cowles Pritchard (1786–1848) picked it up from these Continental originators.[60] Then Frenchman Joseph Arthur de Gobineau, around 1850, argued that Jews had declined or degenerated from white origins, perhaps through race-mixing with Africans.[61] In the same period, others declared Jews "Asiatics."[62] Meanwhile, having broken out their skull-measuring tools, late-1800s British anthropologists descended on London's poor East End to measure Jewish people's skulls and make indices of Jews' eye-shapes and so on.[63]

So things proceeded. And, by the turn of 1900, white writers charged Jews with being "inherent conspirators, sexual predators, rapacious capitalists, or Bolshevik revolutionaries." At the very same time, according to historian John Efron, they were also supposed to be "effete, delicate, and unmanly, lacking in valor and decidedly unathletic."[64] Don't look to white supremacists for consistency: you might just say they were supposed to be the opposite of the "real" white citizens around them. Whatever else they were, Jews were supposed to be alien to the *nation*; that is, since white nation-states have always been white race-states, and Jews lost their status as a flawed sub-category of whites in this era, the Jews supposedly didn't belong in the nation. As a wave of nation-inventing swept Europe in the mid 1800s, with the creation of new countries called Germany, Greece, Serbia, and more, white majorities once again asked who's a *true* member of the nation. Who belongs?

There was no single progenitor of the idea, which we might call early "replacement theory," but British writer Houston Stewart Chamberlain (1855–1927) certainly was an early and best-selling one. (This is the same idea as expressed by the torch-bearing Unite the Right fascists – note the literal fasces on their plywood shields – in Charlottesville, Virginia, who chanted alternatively "Jews will not replace us" and "You will not replace us." It is the same idea, expressed at a slightly lower volume, by Tucker Carlson.[65]) Like many around him, Chamberlain worried about "infiltration by lesser breeds" in white nations, which could poison the blood of "the people."[66] For him, the worst of the "infiltrating breeds" was the Jew. He wrote that when true "Indo-Europeans," whom he also called "Aryans," welcomed Jews to their states out of "foolish humanitarian day-dreams," "the Jew rushed in like an enemy, stormed all positions and planted the flag of his, to us, alien nature ... on the breaches of our genuine individuality."[67] From these breaks in the fortress of whiteness, the Jews, guided by their innate racial drives, "the law of blood," took over "science, commerce, and literature," manipulated, and financially "fettered" pure whites.[68] If their power were unchecked, they would intermarry with "true" Europeans until whites vanished and there was only "one single pure race, that of the Jews" and "all the rest ... a herd of pseudo-Hebraic mestizos, a people beyond all doubt degenerate."[69] While raised in Britain, Chamberlain moved to his beloved Germany in 1909; and by now you've guessed that Chamberlain had a fan in Adolf Hitler. The feeling was mutual.[70]

Speaking of Hitler's favorite reading, the highest scripture of white replacement theory and eugenics was written by Madison Grant (1865–1937), American lawyer and landscape preservationist. Preservation indeed: in his best-selling *Passing of the Great Race* (1916), Grant called for the preservation of the white race, the best of whom he categorized as "Nordic." They were an endangered species. "There is great danger," he wrote,

> of ... replacement of a higher by a lower type here in America unless the native [white or "Nordic"] American uses his superior intelligence to protect himself and his children from competition with intrusive peoples drained from the lowest races of eastern Europe and western Asia.

Among other standard tropes of white replacement, Grant decried how whites were killing each other in the First World War in Europe, while "Orientals" in the East increased and spilled into the West.[71] Jews were roughly as bad, displacing the high-quality "man of the old stock," in New York.[72] Like other eugenicists, he believed part of the answer was to sanitize society of bad blood. This passage from *The Passing of the Great Race* begins by sounding like any number of foregoing eugenicists. But watch where it ends:

> A rigid system of selection through the elimination [by sterilization] of those who are weak or unfit – in other words social failures – would solve the whole question. ... This is a practical, merciful, and inevitable solution of the whole problem, and can be applied to an ever widening circle of social discards ... extending gradually to types which may be called weaklings rather than defectives, and perhaps ultimately to worthless race types.

Sterilization might put an end to entire "worthless" races.

Grant was tremendously successful as a writer and anti-immigration activist in his day.[73] That's partly due to the fact that he was a correspondent of several presidents, the likes of Andrew Carnegie and John Rockefeller, and a friend of Teddy Roosevelt, besides.[74] A former president of my own university, which still honors him with a name on a building I see from my office, praised Grant and cited him to make his own arguments for white racial purity and the supremacy of the "race."[75] And Hitler? He reportedly said that *The Passing of the Great Race* was his Bible.[76]

The Age-Old Issue of Who Was a Citizen of the White Race-State

From Australia to South Africa to the USA, perhaps the most widespread tactic for preserving power for "Anglo-Saxons" was denying citizenship to nonwhites. This was, in part, an expression of that essential gene, the nation-state (or ancestry- or race-state). The nation-state's elites have always judged who was a *real* member of the nation. Put more simply, there's always been a racial basis for full citizenship in the nation-state. But, in most of the English-speaking world, rulers didn't simply declare nonwhites non-citizens. After all, the US Civil War ended, at least, as a campaign to extend citizenship to the enslaved. And, in places like Canada or New Zealand, white rulers sought to preserve a veneer of universal citizenship for all races, perhaps due to their self-image as a uniquely freedom-loving, rights-loving race. But, as historian David A. Bateman argued, granting the vote to some and denying it to others was an act of creation or construction: it was about "people-making," defining who were the true people of the nation and who were not.[77]

Instead of issuing blanket edicts against nonwhite citizenship, white rulers denied nonwhites the vote through a variety of tactics. Historian Julie Evans led a team of scholars who compared the ways in which English settler colonies across the globe denied citizenship to nonwhites in the years around 1900, finding that voter suppression was key. This assured nonwhites couldn't secure rights on par with whites; thus, whites preserved discriminatory laws and norms since Indigenous and Black subjects couldn't vote for legislators who'd represent them.[78]

Other tactics for suppressing nonwhite votes were quite similar across the English-speaking world. (Mind, full citizenship was only for males until women – mainly white women, given the suppression of nonwhite votes – got the vote in the English-speaking world in the decades between 1900 and 1930.) A main method was to test a voter's reading and writing abilities. Or, rather, the method was to test *nonwhite* voters' literacy. As one critical Canadian editorial writer pointed out, if whites were given the tests, too, only "one-fifth of the population could vote."[79] Prohibited from denying the vote on a race basis, specifically, by post-Civil War changes to the US Constitution, white majorities in US states needed work-arounds. So reading and writing tests were a favored tactic in Jim Crow USA, as well. ("Jim Crow" was a folk story character and a stock character of blackfaced minstrel performers in the first half of the 1800s. By the 1880s, "Jim Crow" was a derogatory name for an African American. Observers applied the phrase "Jim Crow laws" to the many laws suppressing votes, reducing rights, and expanding segregation passed from the 1880s to the middle of the twentieth century. These were very often in the southern states of the former Confederacy, but were absolutely *not* limited to the US South.) Plus, roughly half of US states used poll taxes – fees demanded usually at the moment of registration – to reduce the numbers of Black voters.[80] In Australia, in addition to literacy tests, white legislatures issued poll taxes aimed at suppressing the vote of Chinese immigrants.[81] And in turn-of-the-twentieth-century USA, states passed "grandfather clauses," that restricted the vote only to those whose ancestors could vote prior to the Civil War.[82] This was a tactic to allow poor whites – whom poll taxes had hurt – the right to vote while denying it to those whose ancestors had been enslaved. These tactics succeeded: for example, new restrictions reduced voter registration in Black-majority areas of Louisiana by 96 percent in 1900.[83] Meanwhile, in parts of Canada, First Nations people were denied the vote if they were exempt from property taxes, as many were. In the USA, Indigenous people became citizens on paper in 1924, but few states gave them the vote for another generation.[84] And Australia simply barred First Peoples from voting in its first Federal Election in 1901.[85]

Denying the vote was the most straightforward way that whites blocked the possibility of true citizenship for nonwhites; but nearly as simple was the ongoing effort to block nonwhite immigration. The previous chapter introduced anti-immigration's eugenicist and Social Darwinist underpinnings, so there's little need to revisit that. But another core element of anti-immigration in the twentieth century was the fear that democracy might be a weak point in the bulwark of white supremacy. More immigrants meant more nonwhite votes. That is, while democracy could be trusted so long as it was restricted to "real" Americans, Australians, or New Zealanders, it was a liability if too many nonwhites participated in it. Democracy was for white people, as future president Woodrow Wilson wrote in 1889. Only "races purged of barbaric passions and … servility," only "temperate" races, could be entrusted with it.[86]

In some cases, whites comprised a minority of voters among a larger population of nonwhite potential voters. There was no way they would allow themselves to be outvoted. In the second half of the 1800s, US Congressmen worried that, if given the vote, Indigenous peoples in the thinly populated US West might outvote whites.[87] In South Africa, where whites were always a minority repressing a nonwhite majority, white rulers were hardly going to grant the vote, and real citizenship, to native peoples. A British anti-women's suffrage activist, Violet Markham, thought South African anti-democracy was perfectly justified. She cast this not as power-hungry behavior, but rather the act of a responsible government. "No white race can be expected," she continued, to permit "the balance of electoral power … [to] pass from their hands into those of men only recently emerged from savagery." Writing in 1913, she also justified South African anti-democracy by pointing to the US

South, another place where whites "safeguard[ed]" their political institutions from those "unfit" to practice political responsibility.[88]

Finally, to some degree, the Irish received admission into American (and probably Canadian and Australian) whiteness in the context of labor competition. In the later 1800s, white capitalists used poor Irish laborers as leverage against Black or other immigrant laborers who dared demand respect or higher wages. This implicitly moved the Irish higher on the scale of whiteness.[89] Also, to some degree, the Irish diaspora, having escaped from British overlordship in their homeland, self-whitened, so to speak. In this argument, the Irish were never quite so nonwhite as some historians argue – and, assimilating by acquiring more capital, intermarrying, and other means, invented their own "Celtic" heritage in much the same way as people invented the Anglo-Saxon race. This Celtic race was supposed to be particularly brave, hardworking, and freedom-minded – especially committed to their freedom to be Catholic. The "Celts" then adopted anti-Jewishness and anti-Blackness as their identity as proper whites took hold.[90]

Segregation across the Globe

Segregation, the practice of denying nonwhites access to the same spaces and same opportunities, was another chief tactic for maintaining a distinct, superior whiteness from the turn of the twentieth century. Segregation in various forms – separating those of different religions, separating barbaric foreigners from native subjects – has been around for millennia, perhaps as long as cities. But it took on new justifications and forms during the 1900s defense of whiteness.

It's time to return to the history of the British in India: it's there that English-speakers first practiced a whiteness-based segregation. The British never made a settler colony of India. They were always a tiny, even microscopic minority there: probably not reaching 0.04 percent of the population in the mid 1800s. That was around 3,200 Indians for every Briton.[91] And those white minorities in the important ports of the subcontinent – like Calcutta (today's Kolkata) and Madras (today's Chennai) – built walled enclaves for themselves. Within these walls, British administrators and traders and officers lived, church steeples rose, and polo fields spread. A great many Indian cooks and cleaners and maidservants resided in their poor quarters within, as well. Far more Indians traveled into the British district daily to sell the food and countless other items on which the British depended, or to tailor uniforms, or repair furniture. By around 1700, in places like Madras, the British district became known as White Town, and the neighborhoods outside the walls, Black Town.[92]

That was roughly the same time the concept of white and Black took hold in the West Indies and southern American colonies; but the rise of whiteness there grew like a cancer from slave-labor operations, not cities. In other words, in India, cities and towns were the sites where whiteness and white supremacy emerged. Within the White Towns of Indian cities, the British controlled the space, policed native activity, built schools, enjoyed public health works, and preserved exclusive access to amenities.[93] Segregation – and the British used the word as we do from around 1860 – meant reserving space for some and isolating others; but it also meant limiting the sorts of interactions possible between "races" and purposefully creating psychological distance. That is, many British did not want to know their Indian neighbors and wanted to appear distant from them, elevated. As one British observer put it in India in 1880, physical segregation from Indians also helped "secure that segregation of the mind required for [rule]."[94] When whites looked upon their environs built by exploitation, and then looked at the neighboring Black Town, they reassured themselves that theirs was a superior race, while the Indians (on whom they depended for nearly everything) were inferior. And, outnumbered over 3,000 to 1, whites believed it was their essential qualities as white keeping the masses in check.

It had much of its start in India, but segregation became a global movement in the English-speaking world as the twentieth century approached. The leading expert in segregation history calls this turn-of-the-century period "segregation mania."[95] This mania was largely due to the growth of modern cities themselves; in part because, with growth, came urban diseases. In the late 1800s, white minority rulers in the British Empire looked on their nonwhite subjects with suspicion, fearing they generated or harbored illnesses like cholera, yellow fever, and malaria. Segregation based on health fears originated in India and spread, via colonial personnel, to West Africa, for instance. There, officials with experience in India called for isolating whites from native populations who supposedly threatened them with malaria.[96] Sometimes colonial elites razed what they called "slums" in the name of hygiene and removed poor people to the edges of cities.[97] And policies ricocheted back to India, to Hong Kong, and on to South Africa, where, for example, white South African rulers imposed restrictions on the spaces South Asian immigrants could occupy, convinced that they harbored cholera.[98] In 1900s America, whites looked fearfully upon nonwhite neighborhoods with endemic tuberculosis and other killer diseases and drew the wrong (but expedient) conclusion: lesser races, they told themselves, harbored diseases because they were degenerate or ignorant of hygiene.[99] The truth was that poverty and explicit rules limiting nonwhites to less healthy (for example, mosquito-ridden) areas were to blame.[100]

The leading scholar of segregation across the globe argued that US whites sought to be separate from nonwhites for much the same reason as the British in India: separateness reinforced the notion that they were more respectable and healthy than nonwhites.[101] This appealed to more "enlightened" or "liberal" whites, as well. They professed a distaste for white violence or threats to enforce this, arguing, as American philosopher Josiah Royce (1855–1916) did in 1908, that "trouble comes when you tell the other man, too stridently that you are his superior. [Rather] be [his] superior, quietly."[102] Royce essentially argued for British Indian-style segregation in the US South, essentially colonization.[103] Let the separateness speak for itself; let separateness convey superiority.

Indeed, Black observers in the USA made informed comparisons of British Empire segregation and US segregation as that mania swept America in the early twentieth century. In Baltimore, a Methodist clergyman who'd recently returned from Africa warned his congregation that plans for segregating Baltimore block-by-block were in the same spirit as British Africa's White Towns and Black Towns in places like Sierra Leone and South Africa.[104] Despite objections, Baltimore made it illegal for nonwhites to purchase homes on white-reserved blocks in 1910.

But white elites' segregation policies were not just about denying spaces; they were about denial of opportunity. In a strong sense, segregation was the ongoing effort to deny nonwhites full citizenship or full participation in a white supremacist society. That's because restricting nonwhites to certain corners of the city had the practical effect of keeping them out of hospitals, schools, workplaces, and civic buildings that were essentially reserved for whites. In the 1950s, in the New Zealand town of Pukekohe, Māori and South Asians were barred from some cinemas, pools, bars, and barbers, while the town's schools, too, were segregated.[105] In 1946, Black Canadian Viola Desmond was dragged from a cinema in New Glasgow, Nova Scotia and arrested for sitting in the whites-only floor section well before Rosa Parks's 1955 arrest in Alabama for refusing to vacate a whites-only bus seat.[106] And in the 1950s, following the migration of Black workers invited from the Caribbean to Britain, Jim Crow-style housing ads stating "White Tenants Only" proliferated in British cities, along with signs reading "No Coloured Applicants."[107]

Segregation meant segregated healthcare, with consequences nonwhite people live (and die) with today. In Canada's Yukon territory in the 1940s, enough white people refused to be admitted to hospital wards that included Indigenous people that hospitals began segregating nonwhites in outbuildings.[108] In the USA in the same period, segregated wards and hospitals led not only to lesser care and even abuse of nonwhites out of the public eye, but also to medical experimentation by white doctors on unsuspecting Black patients.[109] In the 1930s and 1940s, white Canadian doctors ran vaccine trials – human experiments without consent – on First Nations infants at the Fort Qu'Appelle Indian Hospital. Midcentury white public health agents performed nutritional experiments on Indian Residential School inmates without consent, as well.[110] The mistrust and imbedded inequality engendered by such a history continue to afflict the health of Indigenous people across the English-speaking world and of Black Americans, meaning they die from treatable illnesses at a higher rate than whites.[111]

The US federal government contributed to housing segregation, as well. As part of Franklin Roosevelt's (1882–1945) anti-Depression measures, the government sought to spur employment and homebuilding in the mid 1930s. Two measures, in turn, spurred segregation. First, the government subsidized suburban housing developers, and those developers wrote racially restrictive covenants into their contracts. Racially restrictive covenants were rules barring the sale or rent of homes to nonwhites, and sometimes Jews, as well. Perhaps with more impact, the federal government started a home loan program that refused to support loans in or near Black or Latin American neighborhoods.[112] Officials drew a red line around these neighborhoods in their planning maps, and the policy became known as "redlining." (Private bankers did the same thing.) Federal agencies also tended to refuse loans to nonwhite applicants to keep them from escaping redlined neighborhoods.

A Federal Housing Agency manual provided guidance to employees who redlined and ranked neighborhoods in order to rate the riskiness of loans. They should

> investigate areas surrounding the location to determine whether or not incompatible racial and social groups are present ... [given] the possibility or probability of the location being invaded by such groups. If a neighborhood is to retain stability it is necessary that properties shall continue to be occupied by the same social and racial classes. A change in social or racial occupancy generally leads to instability and a reduction in values.[113]

What that really meant was that the government was happy to issue or guarantee loans to white people in "white neighborhoods," but should be wary of issuing loans in integrated neighborhoods. (Redlining expert Richard Rothstein argued that, in reality, the opposite happened: when Black families managed to buy a home in a "white neighborhood," house prices went up because other Black families were willing to pay a premium to join them.[114])

For most homeowners, their house is their most valuable piece of capital. And racially restrictive covenants denied nonwhites their best opportunity to build that capital. Capitalism intersects with segregation in housing in another way: whites worked hard to keep nonwhites from buying in their neighborhoods, thinking that nonwhites threatened their home values. White supremacy, in other words, paid – or at least white homeowners thought so. In 1933, an economist who studied Chicago real estate created a table ranking "races and nationalities with respect to their beneficial effect upon land values." English, Germans, Scots, Irish, and Scandinavians were at the top, of course; Russian Jews, South Italians, Negroes, and Mexicans had the opposite effect.[115] There goes the neighborhood (Figure 6).[116]

Experts find that owning a house or other property confers advantages down a family history. It can be borrowed against; it provides a place of refuge for family members suffering a downturn; it provides for a prosperous retirement; it can be passed down to children. And houses have historically been an investment with

LOOK At These Homes NOW!
An entire block ruined by negro invasion. Every house marked "X" now occupied by negroes. ACTUAL PHOTOGRAPH OF 4300 WEST BELLE PLACE.
SAVE YOUR HOME! VOTE FOR SEGREGATION!

Figure 6 A 1915 Missouri postcard encouraging white homeowners to vote for segregation. Image from Wikimedia Commons.

tremendous growth.[117] Home ownership can also mean the difference between living in a neighborhood of poor renters that's over-policed and a neighborhood of owner-occupied homes that is not. And an owner-occupied house is likely to be of higher quality than one owned by a landlord and rented out for maximum return on minimum investment.[118] Those neighborhoods where landlords invested the bare minimum, or less, in upkeep were called "blighted" or ghettoes.

Beyond capital in a house, white supremacy kept capital from nonwhite business owners. Segregation meant that nonwhite business owners made less money because nonwhite establishments, barred from white-designated areas, had a smaller clientele. This effect was multiplied when that nonwhite clientele was barred from decent jobs by racial discrimination. In 1924, a Mexican immigrant in Chicago applied to open an integrated pool hall for Black, white, and Mexican customers. The city commission that reviewed such applications made no secret that they were denying it because the pool hall would encourage fraternization between races; in fact, they seemed proud of their "successes" in blocking integrated businesses. Indeed, as historian John Flores found, they'd recently closed a pool hall enjoyed by Black and Mexican patrons due to undefined "opposition" by neighbors. When the man reapplied to open his pool hall in a segregated Mexican neighborhood, the commission granted the license because, they said, he'd chosen a "location among his own people."[119] The same dynamic recurred across the English-speaking world. In the capital of Ontario, residents and aldermen tried to block Chinese laundries from operating in "white neighborhoods" in 1912. They wanted them confined to segregated areas, as were most Chinese-immigrant businesses of all kinds across Canada.[120]

Job discrimination was another kind of segregation and denial of opportunity that kept money from accruing in the hands of nonwhite families. In the US North and West, the most common hardship facing nonwhites was being banned from decent jobs, especially before the Second World War forced employers to take them on.[121] In the same period, supporters of the White New Zealand League warned of "coloured people" becoming "our next-door neighbor and intermarrying with our children." But their impetus seemed to be that South Asian immigrants were out-competing white businesses, while South and East Asian farmers were getting too much of the potato market[122] (Figure 7). When Woodrow Wilson infamously segregated the US federal government bureaucracy, he didn't shuffle Black and white workers into separate-but-equal (and equally paid) positions. No. The policy shoved Black employees into lower-paying jobs – and kept them there. Offices created segregated cafeterias and toilets; no Black manager was to oversee any white workers.[123] We'll return to this story in the final chapter.

Final Thoughts

The introduction to this half of the book featured Rudyard Kipling's infamous 1899 poem about the "white man's burden" because it raises themes we'll deal with for a while. Kipling was echoing what many in the "white world" believed: that race was no longer about who was slave or master; rather, it was about world destiny. It was the destiny of the white race to inherit the Earth. In that poem, Kipling called upon his American (what he'd call "Anglo-Saxon") cousins to do what the British had done in the previous century. And he thought it a good thing: a master Anglo-Saxon race uplifting the world's lesser races for their benefit. Americans, in sum, must embrace their white destiny.

Figure 7 A racist cartoon of 1919 in the *New Zealand Observer* stoking fear that the South Asian immigrants would "paint the country black."

As ever, certain "men of their time" thought that this was worse than a joke. Take Social Democratic activist Eugene Debs, who, a few years after Kipling published his poem, found himself in a train station in Texas.

> Leaving the depot with two grips in my hands, I passed four or five bearers of the white man's burden perched on a railing and decorating their environment with tobacco juice. One of them, addressing me, said: "There's a n– that'll carry your grips." A second one added: "That's what he's here for," and the third chimed in with "That's right, by God." Here was a savory bouquet of white superiority. . . .

They were ignorant, lazy, unclean, totally void of ambition, themselves the foul product of the capitalist system and held in lowest contempt by the master class, yet esteeming themselves immeasurably above the cleanest, most intelligent and self-respecting Negro.[124]

Besides poking fun at Kipling's presumptions, Debs observed something else: well after the USA had disavowed the idea of a slave race and had made its Black men citizens, even the poorest white man thought he was superior to those he deemed nonwhite. (They may have taken their inspiration from Teddy Roosevelt, who said, "I suppose I should be ashamed to say that I take the Western view of the Indian. I don't go so far as to think that the only good Indians are the dead Indians, but I believe nine out of every ten are, and I shouldn't like to inquire too closely into the case of the tenth. The most vicious cowboy has more moral principle than the average Indian."[125])

Meanwhile, other strong voices spoke out against scientific and social scientific racism. Black physician James McCune Smith (1811–1865), an American trained in Glasgow, wrote that the Black people of the USA were the equal of white. He drew on the Greeks' environmental model to argue that local circumstances, not unchangeable essence, shaped the bodies of a unitary humankind.[126] And Frederick Douglass called out early anthropologists by name – like Josiah Nott, George Glidden, and Louis Agassiz – saying that their false inventions of natural slave races justified slavers' crimes against humanity.[127] And that Stoddard quote at the beginning of this chapter? It came from a public debate between him and Black sociologist W. E. B. Du Bois. The sentiment in it no doubt appealed to President Harding, but Du Bois appears to have humiliated Stoddard in that debate, making his white supremacist theories look like the fairy tales they were to a laughing audience.[128] And when William Graham Sumner made Herbert Spencer's Social Darwinist logic central to his sociology, Yale's president and some faculty came out against him.[129] When the president of Stanford University promulgated the idea that Jews were alien, manipulative conspirators, contemporaries published strong rejoinders.[130] And, even at its height, there were plenty of critics of eugenics who saw it as dangerous.[131]

To take just one more example, when Canadian Prime Minister John A. Macdonald declared Canada for the Aryan race in 1885 and spewed racism toward Chinese immigrants in Parliament, a number of speakers rose to reject his ideas. The Chinese immigrant, said one member, if he "labors and spends his money . . . if he comes to make Canada his home, we ought to make Canada free enough to even include the Chinaman." Several others joined him, saying that Chinese immigrants were respectable, industrious, and endowed with rights as new subjects of the empire.[132]

But if, as always, there were righteous voices speaking out against the white supremacist men-of-their-time, people overpowered them from the bully pulpit. It wasn't just that cloistered social scientists preached Social Darwinism and eugenics to themselves in an ivory tower echo chamber. Presidents and colonial governors sat in their classrooms or read their books. Theodore Roosevelt (in office 1901–1909) seemed to owe his white supremacist thinking in part to his natural history professor at Harvard, who called whites a "superior race."[133] And eventual President Woodrow Wilson (in office 1913–1921) learned at the knee of a Johns Hopkins professor who wrote that "the negroes, . . . are for the most part grownup children."[134]

✳✳✳

From the vantage point of the 1940s looking backwards, it doesn't seem like slavery's ending was much of a blow to whiteness itself. Yes, supremacy was no longer demonstrated by who was holding the whip; but, with the whip gone, it seemed softer hands could take up the task of elevating whiteness and suppressing nonwhiteness.

- When the sciences moved from the natural philosophers' study to the university lab, centuries-old practices of race-making and race hierarchy moved seamlessly with it. The same goes for the **newly professionalized social sciences** like anthropology.
- After Darwin popularized the new evolutionary science, these figures and others saw opportunities **to justify and even celebrate white domination and Indigenous displacement using Social Darwinism.** Supposedly, Anglo-Saxons, Nordics, or Aryans weren't brutal colonizers; they were akin to Galápagos finches, out-competing Indigenous peoples in their niche because of their random luck in being better adapted.

- Related to this, a model that placed cultures (really, races) on **an evolutionary timeline** helped make Social Darwinism look scientific and therefore dispassionate, not prejudiced.
- But, even though Social Darwinism told whites they were the best and shouldn't apologize for their domination and displacement of peoples, the rise of **race perils** revealed the anxiety underlying white supremacy.
- In the hands of **the new field of eugenics**, the old problem of degraded whites reappeared. Eugenicists sought to inhibit bad whites by means of sterilization, while encouraging the increase in "good" whites. Also called racial hygiene, eugenics concerned itself with combating race-mixing in order to preserve the superior lines of the white race. Eugenics' most influential popularizer and anti-immigration activist hinted that sterilization might altogether eliminate "worthless" races.
- The main challenge whiteness had to meet in the first half of the twentieth century was democracy itself. Whiteness had to fight it. **Jim Crow voter restriction and ongoing anti-immigration** centered on this. The idea that citizenship, not race, endows rights is the circle that can't be squared; that is, the nation-state form, with its "real" people fighting to keep "unreal" or "parasitic" others from power, has thus far failed to cut white supremacy from its genes.
- Key to this was **denying people of color capital.** And the main tactics for this were denying nonwhites opportunity by the **segregation** of schools and other amenities, **job discrimination,** and **denying them access to valuable housing or businesses.**
- Still, people of many kinds **called out white supremacist science and theories** as false, cynical, even laughable. They were direct, clear, and categorical. Far from absent, far from silent, they were shouted down – or beaten down.

7 WHITE SUPREMACY'S DEATH-GRIP, 1930S-PRESENT

The period around the Second World War was a time of furious activity for supporters of white supremacy. In the USA, whites maintained their power by denying the vote to nonwhites. And, sometimes systematically and sometimes violently, they denied capital – money, property – to nonwhites. And whites barred their access to the places whites themselves enjoyed – a kind of white supremacy laid over space. Connected, white mobs sometimes persecuted nonwhites through terrorism: public murders and mutilation. Meanwhile, Americans erected the bulk of monuments to Confederate (slavery-defending) soldiers around and after 1900 as declarations of who owned public spaces, who owned the country.[1]

As much as a spotlight belongs on Jim Crow USA, there were similar trends across the English-speaking world. In South Africa, whites were busy erecting the eventual Apartheid system in those decades. As in the USA, a key was keeping voting rights from most nonwhites and segregating the country at all levels, from neighborhoods to public spaces, while strictly limiting the share of land nonwhites could possess. In Canada, white mobs destroyed the homes and businesses of East Asian immigrants; in Australia, they looted and burned Italian businesses.[2] Race terror and dispossession, denying real citizenship and votes to nonwhites, segregation: across the white-colonized world the pattern was similar.

Then, in the mid 1930s, white supremacy offered perhaps its quintessential expression in Nazi Germany. It was certainly born of homegrown race supremacy, but the links between white supremacy in the English-speaking world and Germany were many and iron-fast.

If these trends were so prevalent and persistent, if they reached a nightmarish height in 1930s–1940s Germany, ought I to characterize the middle of the twentieth century as the *height* of white supremacy? Perhaps it was at its most *visible*, with demonstrations of white terrorism, blatant segregation, white supremacist monuments, and an actual global race war in the Second World War. But that didn't mean that whiteness was secure. A secure regime doesn't have to put up memorials to show it's supreme; a secure system doesn't have to publicly humiliate those of "lesser races" to put them in their place. If everyone agreed that lower races were, and would stay, lower, no whites would have to "put them in their place." "If," as Toni Morrison said, "you can only be tall because somebody's on their knees then you have a serious problem."[3] That's why I started this introduction by calling the twentieth century an era of "furious activity," not dominance or success.

From the mid 1900s to today, white supremacy has behaved as insecurely as ever, while desperately reaching for ages-old techniques of anti-democracy and nativism, and stoking race peril fears. The apparent strength of whiteness in the hands of race-baiting leaders – Trumpism, Brexit, anti-immigration measures across the globe – may be just that: *apparent* only. They might be the self-inflicted wounds of a cornered, thrashing monster.

White Terrorism

White racial terrorism (the term "terrorism" is neither hyperbole nor figurative according to terrorism scholars[4]) in the USA peaked in the early century, with whites murdering over 3,000 nonwhites by lynching between 1880 and 1930.[5] One of the most recent and complete studies by sociologists reports that 97 percent of lynchings occurred in former slave states and that "lynchings appear to be most common in places with a larger slave population in 1860." Still, lynchings weren't completely confined to the South, with white Texans publicly murdering Mexican victims, especially in border counties, Chinese immigrants lynched in California, and Indigenous people lynched in Oklahoma and North Dakota.[6] Surely, lynchings, regular as they were, comprised only the extreme instances of physical violence that occurred with even greater regularity but didn't make the newspaper. You've read about constant violent demonstrations of white superiority over the centuries. In the twentieth century, that persisted, but it was perhaps more spectacular in the age of mass communication.

Across thousands of cases, across decades, the details of the savagery were largely the same. White accusers, very often women, would blame a nonwhite man for a crime like rape, real or not, and a white crowd would kidnap, sometimes torture, and hang or burn alive the victim.[7] Other times, the victim was a man who'd killed in self-defense. Sometimes white mobs dragged the man from a jail cell where he awaited a hearing that would never occur. These public murders were meant to be spectacles, even displays of white solidarity or community-building according to some sociologists.[8] As a southern novelist writing at the time put it, the lynch mob supposedly represented something *good* in the white race. Describing a fictional lynching, he wrote "in a moment the white race had fused into a homogeneous mass of love, sympathy, hate and revenge. The rich and the poor, the learned and the ignorant ... were all one now."[9] (The fact that local Black folk didn't join the righteous lynch mob only showed that they were a species apart.) In a way, then, it was a kind of ritual murder.[10] In front of mutilated bodies, people posed for pictures; they made postcards out of them; people took souvenirs.[11] But most of all, they were a message: "if we choose, this could be the fate of any nonwhite man we suspect; our law is higher than the courts'; we're in control; keep your place."

Having read Chapter 2, with some of the earliest American slave codes requiring public torture and murder, or Chapter 4, with its story of the public killings of Jamaican "rebels," you know that spectacles of violence were woven into the pattern of white supremacy from the earliest days.

In the age of scientific racism based on evolution, something new entered the white supremacist pedigree. Arguing from evolution, white social scientists and other observers explained away lynching by saying that it was natural for a Black man to want to access white women's "superior" genes, leading him to rape white women. They were, after all, stuck in the "savagery" phase on the evolutionary timeline. It was equally natural for "superior" white men to be hyper-protective of their superior mates. Meanwhile, according to Brown University sociologist Lester F. Ward (1841–1913), Black women desired intercourse with white men in hopes of accessing their higher racial qualities.[12]

Something needs to be said plainly here. When mobs of whites – often middle class – terrorized, murdered, and mutilated Black victims, police could have halted such scenes with a sole gunshot, but did not. When, extremely rarely, lynch mob leaders were prosecuted, they were acquitted by all-white juries. Newspaper editors, meanwhile, justified this. The reverse is *not* true: mobs of middle-class Black (or Mexican) folks *did not* terrorize, murder, and mutilate white victims – not even in local regions where they were in the majority over whites. Black police *did not* stand by. All-Black juries *did not* acquit the perpetrators. Black newspaper editors *did not* justify Black-on-white terror.

The point is that one race had the power – and one race felt its superior power threatened; the others did not. Remember one of the epigrams opening this book: Trinidadian American anti-colonial activist Kwame Ture said in a 1991 interview that, "if a white man wants to lynch me, that's his problem. If he's got the power to lynch me, that's my problem. Racism is not a question of attitude; it's a question of power."[13] The reason white people could lynch Black and not the other way around is because they had all the tools of power arrayed, united, to do so.

Meanwhile, in Australia, stories of whites massacring First Peoples, which continued into the early twentieth century, were meant to keep native people fearful and in line.[14] And Indigenous Australian laborers reported that "whitefellas" were quick to draw their guns if people didn't jump to whatever was demanded of them.[15] And, if reports of murder weren't enough, Australia passed a law in the 1870s specifically for the purpose of allowing public executions of "Aboriginals." Public executions of white criminals had ended, but continued for Indigenous people up to the twentieth century – as "exercises in terror specifically for Aboriginal people," according to historian Penelope Edmonds.[16] Whites publicly whipped native people because they believed the native Australian race too unintelligent to understand subtler forms of motivation.[17]

It might seem strange that South Africa, with a white minority holding onto power over a Black majority, didn't maintain control through lynching. But on a closer look, the evidence shows that a combination of factors channeled control through the state, not the lynch mob. The minority white government handled domination, in sum, via rigid segregation laws. From 1913, Black South Africans were largely confined to "native reserves," the only places they could buy or lease land, and could not travel freely between them without a government-issued pass. Indeed, scholar Elizabeth A. Herbin-Triant found that some Jim Crow-era whites in the USA looked to South Africa as a good example for better segregating the rural South. They wanted to ban the sale or lease of farmlands to African American farmers.[18] Still, South Africa was far from non-violent even if it didn't have a tradition of lynching; whites routinely attacked Black workers on farms and in mines and other industries when they "forgot their place."[19]

Sometimes whites lynched, burned, or bombed because they saw power growing in nonwhite hands: political, financial, or both. Speaking of capital, Black journalist Ida B. Wells (1862–1931) became an anti-lynching crusader when a lynch mob murdered a Black grocery-store owner, a friend. Although the inciting event was a fight between a white and Black child in front of his store, it ended in a large, general brawl. Soon after, a white man, a well-known rival for business on the same street, accused the grocer, Thomas Moss, of holding secret meetings of Black men, plotting violence against whites.[20] (This is a scenario you know well from Chapter 2, with the first American slave codes justifying unprecedented evils out of fear of uprising.) Police arrested Moss and an employee (for resisting arrest) and rounded-up around 100 other Black men for good measure (Figure 8). A white mob soon dragged Moss and two others from their cells and hanged them.[21] For Ida B. Wells, the hanging of a grocer sparked an idea: all those lynchings based on rape accusations – or at least many or most of them – must have actually been motivated by a desire by whites to crush Black wealth or influence.[22] As she put it in her autobiography:

> The mob took possession of [Moss's] People's Grocery Company, helping themselves to food and drink, and destroyed what they could not eat or steal. The creditors had the place closed and a few days later what remained of the stock was sold at an auction. Thus, with the aid of the city and county authorities and the daily papers, that white grocer had indeed put an end to this rival Negro grocer as well as to his business.[23]

She was right. In 1917, in East Saint Louis, police stood by and watched a white mob murder more than 100 Black people and burn entire Black neighborhoods. The white workers of the

THOMAS H. MOSS
MURDERED BY THE MEMPHIS MOB.

Figure 8 Portrait of Thomas Moss in *The Appeal*, March 26, 1892.

Aluminum Ore Company went on strike that spring, and the company owner hired Black workers to replace them. White workers took to the streets to beat and kill Black people days later. But there was another general cause: Black migrants to the city, having fled the deeper Jim Crow South, were getting ahead.[24] Similarly, the infamous Tulsa Race Massacre of 1921 started as an all-too-familiar story of Black people trying to defend a nineteen-year-old falsely accused of rape from being dragged from jail and lynched. But it ended with an almost-systematic looting and burning of Tulsa's affluent Black neighborhood, nick-named "Black Wall Street." The mob killed between 75 and 300 and left 35 square blocks of Black Tulsa in ruins.[25] In the countryside, meanwhile, white terrorists formed gangs across the South called "Whitecaps," which snuck about posting warnings that Black tenant farmers must either abandon their farms and work for whites or have their farms burned down.[26] When these warnings went unheeded, white gangs burned houses and fired shots into them by night.[27]

White attacks on Black property weren't just a matter of fire and looting and mobs of Southern men with nooses. From 1950s California to Pennsylvania, crowds of "respectable" middle-class whites emerged from their convertibles and Cadillacs and gathered by the hundreds to march on the homes of Black families that dared to move into housing developments that were "supposed to be white."[28] Key was that police refused to step in to stop harassment, window-breaking, and even sometimes dynamiting. In Chicago in 1951, the police led the effort to keep Black Second World War veteran Harvey Clark, Jr. from renting an apartment in a segregated white suburb, warning him to get out of town "and don't come back … or you'll get a bullet through you"[29] (Figure 9).

Even more than the awareness that nonwhites dared to move into the middle class, perhaps the largest cause of white terror was the feeling that they were gaining political power. Within just a few years from the end of the Civil War, in New Orleans and Camilla, Georgia, for example, white mobs killed hundreds of Black people who were organizing or simply voting.[30] On election day, 1920, a white mob murdered thirty to eighty Black people in Ocoee, Florida after a Black man, a well-off farmer, who'd helped lead a voter drive, attempted to vote but was turned away. Whites watching the polls said he'd threatened them and formed

Figure 9 Harvey Clark, Jr. and family. Image by Associated Press / John Lent via Alamy.

a vigilante mob, with the usual results. Nearly every remaining Black resident, around 175 of them, abandoned the town.[31]

This brings us to the Wilmington insurrection.[32] In 1890s Wilmington, North Carolina, Black residents outnumbered white by a few thousand and were quite prosperous. When white Republicans and Black folks formed a political coalition, they swept into power in the 1890s. In the 1898 election, despite systematic race terrorism and vote tampering to suppress the Black vote, Black officials and their white allies remained in power. Unable to win even by cheating, a white mob of 2,000 launched a coup, murdering uncountable scores or hundreds, and installed themselves in local government.[33] The Ku Klux Klan also focused its race terror on Black political organizers and their white (or Jewish) allies.[34] Let's return to the story of white terror targeting efforts to secure voting rights for nonwhites when we touch on the Civil Rights Movement below.

A Brief Diversion to Germany

Despite this being a book about whiteness in the *English-speaking* world, and despite my commitment to keeping it to about 200 pages, which are fast running out, it's important to make a brief digression. And yet the history of Nazism *isn't* really a digression from the history you've learned. For Nazism was (and is) the ultimate culmination of the largest trends of white supremacy. It was the vile fluorescence of white terrorism, anti-democracy, Nordic/Aryan supremacy, race nationalism, race perilism, eugenics, and Social Darwinism. Hitler and the Nazis' fundamental logic and motivations were all based on the idea that race was the key to everything. They didn't invent this idea, as a reader of this book knows well. After all, Scotsman Robert Knox, the popular race theorist, wrote in 1850 that "race was all."[35] Poet and playwright Langston Hughes (1901–1967) had an insight into the Nazis even before the Second World War, even before the Kristallnacht attacks. "We Negroes in America do not have to be told what fascism is in action," he wrote in 1937. "We know." Black Americans lived, he wrote, under "theories of Nordic supremacy," with freedom of movement hindered, schools, universities, and businesses barred, with the ever-present threat of arrest for "vagrancy," being sentenced to the chain gang digging ditches or worse.[36]

Indeed, the emerging Nazi regime of 1930s Germany approved of and studied American methods for excluding nonwhites from white spaces and rights just as they intended to separate Jews and other undesirables from the rights and privileges due "real Germans." They had to make a quick study: the Jim Crow South and North developed their segregation laws over a generation, whereas the Nazis wanted to establish anti-Jewish segregation and make them a class of un-citizens instantly in the mid 1930s. Legal historian James Whitman showed how a committee of Nazi German lawyers studied US states' laws as inspiration for the anti-miscegenation, anti-immigration, and second-class citizenship laws that would come to be known as the Nuremberg Laws.[37] They even toured the USA to see Jim Crow in action.

The Nazis argued that they were more civilized in their white race terror and enforcement of race-separation, though. When non-Jewish Germans rampaged down the main shopping street in Berlin wrecking Jewish-owned stores, when a mob paraded so-called Aryan "race-traitors" (people with Jewish romantic partners) through Nuremberg, a newspaper editor pointed out that no one was killed. He wrote that the world press shouldn't criticize Germany: "instead report about lynch justice in America. We pay no attention to Negro executions, so people should not bother us when we lead racial offenders through the streets."[38] Like the Americans, like the British in India, Germans performed ritual displays of public humiliation of imagined lesser races.[39]

(In 1919 Amritsar, Punjab, India, British officials forced Indians to crawl in order to cross a major thoroughfare as collective ritual punishment for a crime just days before the infamous Amritsar Massacre. Led by a British officer, the Indian Army opened fire on peaceful protestors gathered in a large courtyard, murdering at the very least several hundreds. A couple of decades later, Adolf Hitler spoke with admiration about how the British held down India with a microscopic force of white men. Should he have to take over the administration of India, though, he intended to make even harsher examples of Indian offenders.[40])

Besides parading "race-traitors," Austrian Nazis forced Viennese Jews to scrub the streets on their hands and knees, to name just one example.[41] And this raises the old paradox of white supremacy's own lack of confidence: it feels it must publicly debase those who, according to white supremacy's own theories, must already be *obviously* lesser.

Adolf Hitler (1889–1945) and the Nazi party were great believers in eugenics and its ability to purify and strengthen the white race. And American eugenicists seemed downright envious of how the single-party German state could enact it. Hitler was making eugenic measures compulsory, lamented the head of the American Eugenics Society, "while we are pussyfooting around."[42] The popular American race-theorist Lothrop Stoddard, whom you encountered in the previous chapter, traveled to Germany in 1940 and celebrated how effectively the Nazis were "weeding out the worst strains in Germanic stock in a scientific and truly humanitarian way."[43] The Nazis, in turn, admired American eugenics policies and later, through their propaganda machine, assured the German people that eugenicists around the globe supported their policies.[44] German doctors and nurses performed 400,000 forced sterilizations on gay people, trans women, deaf people, and mixed-race people (and they considered the Roma all mixed-race) during the Nazi period.[45] In their first mass murder, they killed 300,000 psychiatric patients and children with disabilities.[46] Some they murdered using gas chambers.[47]

For the Nazi leaders, the purpose of the state was to nourish the race, defend it, and – in the spirit of Social Darwinism – to test it against its race rivals.[48] For the Nazis, the Jews, though a super-minuscule minority in Germany, were the internal threat to race hygiene. In the works of British race theorist Houston Stewart Chamberlain, Hitler read that Jews harbored a "peculiarly and absolutely un-Aryan spirit."[49] Their blood could infect the pure Aryan blood until a mixed people replaced "real" Germans. Slavs, meanwhile, were supposed to be a parasitical subspecies like Jews. The external threat from the Slavs to the east, as Madison Grant's *Passing of the Great Race* taught Hitler, was the peril of the Red "Slavic horde" and central Asian "Orientals." (Hitler never declared the Japanese "honorary Aryans," as is often reported, but at least since 1900 American and European race scientists granted them semi-whiteness.[50]) Hitler saw Stalin's Soviet Union as an ideological threat, and that was also part of its being a racial threat. For Hitler, as he wrote in *Mein Kampf*, "struggle is always a means for improving a species' health and power of resistance and, therefore, a cause of its higher evolution."[51] (He reads almost exactly like Karl Pearson or any number of Victorian Social Darwinists.) Socialism, which Hitler called "Bolshevism," stunted Darwinian struggle through sharing and cooperation and was therefore to be eliminated. The vast war Hitler started, historians tend to agree, was a racial war, a racial test, in his mind.[52]

Over in the USA, members of the "America First" movement, including Henry Ford (1863–1947) and aviation hero Charles Lindbergh (1902–1974), watched the beginning of Hitler's war with gloom – but not because of Germany's victories or who the Nazis were. The problem was that white men were fighting white men. Recall some things you read about in the previous chapter: the issues of the Yellow Peril and white global unity. Lindbergh, famous for making the first nonstop flight from New York to Paris, wrote that the power of flight was a God-given gift permitting "the White race to live at all in a pressing sea of Yellow, Black, and Brown."[53] He spoke on all the major US radio networks in 1939 two weeks after the start of the war, arguing that, far from fighting Germany, the USA and all white countries must unite to "defend the white race against foreign invasion." The true threat, he argued even after the attack on Pearl Harbor and the USA's own entry into the war, came from the Asians, with whom he lumped the Soviets.[54] He was aided in this cause by people like the most powerful press owner of his day, William Randolph Hearst (1863–1951).[55] One of his newspapers ran an editorial in 1943 suggesting that the worst thing about Nazi Germany was the way, in allying with Japan, it fought "against its own race with the yellow peril."[56]

It's impossible to separate Yellow Perilism from Australia, Canada, and the USA's forced relocation and internment of people of Japanese descent during the Second World War. That is, Franklin Roosevelt's sinister Executive Order 9066 has to be viewed as part of a deeper history, not just as an overwrought security measure. In part, it was based on the theory that Asians, "Orientals," were secretive, unintegrated, clannish, a subterranean threat.[57] This call for white unity will remind you of earlier calls for a unified Anglo-Saxondom to withstand nonwhite nations, combined with arguments in the style of *The Passing of the Great Race*.

British Racism Comes Home from the Empire

After the revelations of the nature and extent of the Holocaust, there was pressure on white elites to change the terms of their scientific racism and eugenics.[58] Meanwhile, civil rights activists drew the connection between Nazi race hierarchies and those in the USA.[59] And the Holocaust was a key reference point for Black anti-colonial leaders around the world.[60]

But the discrediting of Nazi race terror hardly ended it in the white home fronts of the English-speaking world. For example, in 1958, white mobs attacked Black residents of West London. The Notting Hill race riots of that year saw young white men chasing Black Londoners shouting "lynch him!" and attacking the homes of West Indian immigrants.[61] *The Times* attributed the trouble to "the [poor] housing situation plus white women associating with coloured men in the area."[62] But recent research showed that the whites who attacked Black Britons tended *not* to be from the same West London neighborhoods, suggesting they weren't competitors for housing or women. White attackers *traveled to* immigrant neighborhoods to terrorize them. Historian Christopher Hillard found that the attacks were more about the white Londoners reasserting "the proper order of things."[63] And another scholar found that fascist and white supremacist parties like Oswald Mosley's[64] (1896–1980) Union Movement and the White Defence League were "on the ground in Notting Hill shortly before, during and after the racist riots in 1958." A local newspaper reported this at the time:

> In the middle of a mob of screaming, jeering youths and adults, a speaker from the Union Movement was urging his excited audience to "get rid of them (the coloured people)." . . . Suddenly hundreds of leaflets were thrown over the crowd, a fierce cry rent the air and the mob rushed off in the direction of Latimer Road shouting, "Kill the n–s!"[65]

Another paper quoted a white rioter as saying "just tell your readers that Little Rock learned us a lesson."[66] (The prior year, the Governor of Arkansas had ordered the state's National Guard to bar the integration of Little Rock schools. More on that below.) A year later, a gang of five whites stabbed Antiguan Kelso Cochrane in West London, having shouted to him, "hey, Jim Crow!" just before.[67]

While it was a very old story in the USA and elsewhere in the English-colonized world, a noxious root of white supremacy emerged in Britain between the end of the Second World War and 1970: politicians used race-baiting to win votes. In particular, they started arguing that nonwhite immigrants were violent and overrunning the country, displacing "real" Britons. This was clearly tied up with the end of the British Empire – the world's largest, longest-lived engine for race superiority – and how colonial attitudes came "home" to a diminished island.[68]

The immigrants who came to Britain with full rights and permanent residency after 1948 were called the "Windrush Generation" after the huge ship that brought many people from the Caribbean, HMT *Empire Windrush*. But, invited to a UK in great need of labor, migrants came from many British Empire and Commonwealth[69] countries in this period to work in the transport industry, work as nurses in the new National Health Service, and more. While hateful expressions like the Notting Hill attacks started with this invitation to Commonwealth peoples to come "home" to the UK to rebuild it, the tactic of fearmongering peaked with MP Enoch Powell's (1912–1998) infamous "Rivers of Blood" speech in 1968.[70] Referring to an oracle's vision in the *Aeneid*, Powell said, "I seem to see 'the River Tiber foaming with much blood.'" He made clear that he meant he foresaw the streets of British cities flowing with blood from a race war should immigration of nonwhites continue. First, he told the story of how a constituent, an elderly white woman, had written to tell him of her fear as house after house on her street was "taken over" by "Negroes," who harassed her after she refused to let them use her phone.[71] He went on to say that not only were immigrants refusing to integrate, but also they, with Labour party co-conspirators, would eventually come to "dominat[e] . . . the rest of the population." Should it come to that, he implied, the streets would run with blood.[72] In part, he was referring to protests against police violence Powell saw in some US cities in those years. (And the American conservative press applauded Powell as a maverick truth-teller.)[73]

To their credit, his party, the Tories, immediately demoted Powell for the racist speech; to their shame, they soon reversed course, embracing nativism and anti-immigration in reaction to the popular embrace of Powell's message, with marchers parading through Birmingham with signs reading "we support Powell and Britain."[74] The Conservatives wanted a shot of this new electoral adrenaline.

Let's return to recent decades' politics of race-baiting, as well as nonwhite race perils, further below.

Midcentury Civil Rights Movements

Race-baiting, Jim Crow laws and segregation, white terror: there were extraordinary, vast, global movements against these evils in the twentieth century. Their victims, as well as other justice-minded people, were never silent about them, never accepted them as their era's sole possibility. They spoke truth to power in the form of the US Supreme Court, the governors of the British Empire, the cowardly KKK, or the puffed-up fascist Blackshirts parading through East London. And the forces of white power fought back, whether through the stroke of court clerks' pens, the colonial police-man's lathi stick, or the burning cross. In the face of this, the advances of the global civil rights and anti-colonial movements were victories clawed from deeply entrenched white supremacy that gripped power violently. They came at the cost of blood and time in prison or on the chain gang. The victories of the midcentury years were taken, not given. They were distinctly *not* the natural result of white leaders learning – for the first time and to their horrified astonishment – that systematic racism was wrong.

In the USA, there was the famous Civil Rights Movement that, among other things, made huge inroads against Jim Crow segregation and voter suppression. The path to securing the Civil and Voting Rights Acts in the 1960s and an amendment to the US Constitution stretched over years. It involved boycotts, legal chal-lenges, sit-ins, marches, and canvasing for voter registration. (And, in reaction, whites erected Confederate monuments, or named institu-tions after Confederates, during the civil rights struggle at a rate only surpassed during the beginnings of Jim Crow.[75])

In the USA, Black people led the movement, and allies of all kinds backed them, just like during the abolition movement. Jewish Americans, aware that they'd been largely admitted to whiteness after the Second World War, marched and were beaten and arrested, and had their synagogues dynamited and otherwise targeted by the KKK.[76] (An anti-Jewish terrorist murdered eleven people at Pittsburgh's Tree of Life synagogue in 2018 for reasons similar to why the KKK attacked synagogues in midcentury years. He was reacting to liberal Jews' advocacy for the well-being of Latin American immigrants.)

I'll finish a story I alluded to earlier. After a 1954 Supreme Court ruling determined that "separate but equal" school segrega-tion was unconstitutional, the National Association for the Advancement of Colored People (NAACP) sought to integrate Little Rock's best high school. In response, the Arkansas governor ordered the state's National Guard to essentially barricade the school; the US President, in turn, federalized the National Guard and ordered them to *help* integrate, along with US Army airborne troops. Thus, in 1957, nine courageous young African American students attended the school under armed guard. When Little Rock's whites threatened and shouted down the students, some white students at the school were outraged at their neighbors' behavior. Speaking of the mob's intimidation, one white student said at the time, "I thought it was downright un-American. ... I always thought that all men were created equal."[77] And, unlike Thomas Jefferson, she spoke the words without hypocrisy.

Activists in Australia and Canada struggled for the rights for Indigenous people there in the same 1960s years. In Australia, First Peoples achieved guaranteed voting rights in a 1967 referendum and, after political agitation and a mass sit-in – the "Aboriginal Tent Embassy" on the lawn of the Australian Parliament – in 1972, won significant rights to lands historically occupied by First Nations peoples.[78] The 1960s and 1970s saw Canadian First Nations organize, too, to defeat a 1969 Bill for enforcing assimilation and eliminating any notion of First Nation sovereignty. That movement then won victories in gaining recognition of Indigenous rights to certain lands.[79]

Around the same time, Native Americans fought for greater civil rights, as well. This looked a little different because what various Indigenous societies chiefly sought was greater self-determination for *their* nations. Besides that, the American Indian Movement was launched in the late 1960s to advocate for the safety and well-being of native peoples in American cities. And a movement called Indians of All Tribes famously occupied Alcatraz Island in San Francisco Bay in 1969, setting the tone for occupations and attempts to reclaim stolen land to the present day.[80]

Other campaigns against white supremacy across the globe were as linked as whiteness itself was global. The civil disobedience campaigns of Martin Luther King, Jr. (1929–1968) and others were explicitly inspired, in part, by those of Mohandas Gandhi (1869–1948).[81] Gandhi, who first experienced systematic white supremacy as a young lawyer in South Africa, called whiteness a "fetish of predestined superiority."[82] After making a start as a campaigner in Africa, Gandhi returned to India to organize vast anti-colonial boycotts, marches, and strikes. He organized massive movements to opt out of the British imperial economy: the non-cooperation movement.

Churchill reviled him.[83] Campaigners against white supremacy – besides King, the African National Congress in South Africa – honored him.[84]

Still other anti-colonial, anti-white supremacy activists made common cause. From 1919, American W. E. B. Du Bois helped lead Pan-African Congresses that united West Indian and African anti-colonial and anti-white supremacy movements. US officials, meanwhile, watched proceedings aghast and British colonial authorities tried denying passports to activists in their colonies.[85] The 1945 Congress was perhaps the most important, with a massive meeting in Manchester, England uniting Black Britons with those who worked against white imperialism in Kenya, Malawi, Nigeria, and elsewhere, along with South African proto-Apartheid. Champions like West Indian campaigners Amy Ashwood Garvey (1897–1969), George Padmore (1903–1959), and C. L. R. James (1901–1989) joined Du Bois at his Congress. It was timely. From 1945, this period marked the beginning of the end for the British Empire, which died within a few decades.

In sum, like these anti-colonialists, decent people of all kinds identified and spoke out against every evil of white supremacy in this chapter. You already know about the fights against segregation. And you know about the irrepressible Ida B. Wells. But Black women arguably spearheaded the anti-lynching movement of the early 1900s, with marches and conventions and political agitation.[86] Black activists, meanwhile, called out medical racism, citing unequal levels of tuberculosis.[87] Some scientists in late-1920s Germany published articles against the heartlessness of eugenics.[88] And Black writers railed against anti-Jewishness in Germany and beyond before the USA entered the war.[89] Anti-white supremacists were as much "people of their time" as white supremacists.

Capital's Segregation

In the last half century, capitalism has continued to reinforce white supremacy. For example, decades after civil rights campaigners brought an end to legal segregation in housing, over half of the major US cities are more segregated today than they were in 1990.[90] That's because nonwhites earn less, possess less capital, are closer to the brink of ruin by an exceptional expense like a medical bill (in the USA, at least), and sometimes have to leave the workforce to care for the young and the elderly in their family. Therefore, there's less left over for rent. The legacy of government redlining contributes to that, since poorer, low-rent housing is still concentrated in formerly red-lined areas.[91] In Australia, there were similar lasting effects: when First Nations people started leaving isolated reserves in large numbers in the 1960s, they arrived in Australian cities with limited wealth because their movement and earning had been so constrained historically.[92] Meanwhile, mortgage lenders in the USA and, it appears, in Canada continue to reject nonwhites at a higher rate than whites, even when factors other than race are controlled for.[93]

Recall the story of President Woodrow Wilson segregating the US federal government bureaucracy in 1913. In 2020, two Berkeley economists conducted an extensive study of those employees and found that Wilson's segregation quickly doubled the income gap between Black and white workers. But the effects didn't stop there. Tracing the fate of these employees' families, researchers found that segregation not only led to a decline in home ownership, but also reduced education, earnings, and social mobility for employees' descendants.[94]

It's easy to see a vicious cycle: job discrimination kept non-whites from good jobs; good jobs led to mortgages; segregated social spaces discouraged solidarity among workers; competition for what jobs there were drove a wedge between Black and Mexican or Irish; nonwhite businesses had a limited and less wealthy clientele; capital didn't accrue in nonwhite hands. Since the days of the Emancipation Proclamation, the share of US wealth in Black hands has barely budged, standing at 1 percent, while Black people constitute about 14 percent of the population.[95] Indigenous people are even worse off.[96] And money buys access: with less money, there's less political sway and access to opportunity. White observers see less inter-generational capital in nonwhite families and believe it's evidence of white superiority and nonwhites' "refusal" to act on opportunity. They see other nonwhite communities of immigrants who've accrued capital faster, and fail to see that *recent* immigrants might be backed with capital from their homelands and haven't experienced cross-generational barriers in America, Canada, or elsewhere.

Denied loans to live in neighborhoods with good schools, denied the opportunity to work in better-paying jobs, nonwhite Americans often had to accept federal low-income housing that concentrated poverty and received inordinate police scrutiny. (When, in fact, federal loans for white people in white neighborhoods were also in a sense federal housing – federal "handouts" to a specific race, if you will.) The situation appears natural, rather than the outcome of very specific and deep history, with "racial preferences" systematically accruing to one race.

Consider job prospects. In the USA, Australia, and elsewhere in the English-speaking world, many job applications ask about the applicant's criminal record, or there's a "police check" as part of the application process. This perpetuates the damage of mass incarceration or different rates of policing for nonwhite and white.[97] Meanwhile, experiments by social scientists in the USA show that someone with a "white-sounding" name is 50 percent more likely to get an interview than others, despite the quality of their resume.[98] In the UK, a similar experiment around 2021 found that applicants with names suggesting they were of African, Pakistani, or Middle Eastern descent also received far fewer interview invitations than those with white-sounding names, including those with names suggesting they were white Eastern Europeans.[99]

White observers then look at areas of concentrated poverty inhabited by nonwhites and attribute it, in the words of economic historian Mehrsa Baradaran, "to some cultural failing such as family breakdown or lack of education."[100] These "cultural failing" arguments are only the slightest bit removed from arguments about the *nature* of races that people have made continuously for centuries.[101] Individual members of, say, the UK Independence Party, Trump's Republican party, or other nativist parties in the English-speaking world will sometimes repudiate biologically racist arguments; but their arguments for British or "Anglo-Saxon" culture as superior, or arguments about how immigrants "refuse to assimilate," are the same in essence, resulting in all-too-familiar repression, denial of opportunity, dehumanization, anti-democracy, and so on.[102]

Unequal Policing

The roots of unequal policing today also lay in the factors with which you're now familiar. There's the appeal to racist white voters; there's the capitalist dynamics that concentrate poverty in certain quarters and deny better jobs; and there's the centuries-old view of nonwhites being essentially violent or criminal, among others.[103] Besides these, politicians seeking votes calculated that

they needed to appeal to white identity and promise white dominance – cast as security – in new ways. As part of this, they used
phrases like "war on crime" and "war on drugs" as coded language
for keeping nonwhites in line. Richard Nixon (president 1969–1974)
made such declarations of war, clearly seeing an opportunity to
attract southern US Democrats to his Republican party.[104] Reagan,
Bush, and Democrat Bill Clinton (president 1993–2001) also campaigned on long prison sentences for drug offenses, also presented in
popular media and the news as a problem of Blackness.[105] The result
was mass incarceration in the USA, with more prisoners in American
jails than ever before, and Black people jailed at five times the rate of
white.[106]

Meanwhile, neighborhoods with more Black, Indigenous,
and other nonwhite residents got – get – more police scrutiny. This
wasn't isolated to the USA. Studies of British policing, for example,
show that nonwhites get stopped and searched at an inordinately
high rate: Black people eight times as often as whites; South Asians
around twice as often.[107] And nonwhites are stopped at an exceptional rate on wealthier streets, as if the police see their job as
protecting wealth from nonwhite interlopers.[108] In Canada, individual city studies have shown that Indigenous people are roughly one
and a half times more likely than whites to be stopped by police.[109]
Researchers have found that, while Black and Latin American drivers
in the USA were far more likely to be pulled over by police during
daylight hours, they're pulled over at the same rate as whites during
nighttime hours. By night, it's harder for police to distinguish drivers'
skin color.[110] Meanwhile, three out of five white Americans don't
think there's an over-policing problem.[111]

Over-policing and mass incarceration stem from the "war
on crime" and the concentration of poverty, but other factors appear
to be at play. For example, today's nonwhite students in the USA are
punished or expelled from school at far higher rates than white
students, with research suggesting that teachers-in-training perceive
anger in the facial expressions of nonwhite students where they don't
in exactly the same expression on a white face.[112]

At the same time as there was over-policing of nonwhites,
they couldn't expect the protection of the police or courts to the same
degree as whites. For example, North American and Australian
Indigenous and First Nations peoples were murdered and went
missing – mostly from urban areas – at a vastly higher rate than

they were represented in the population. Their identities and those of the perpetrators also went undiscovered at an inordinate rate.[113] In the UK, to name just one example, there was the infamous case of Stephen Lawrence, murdered by a group of teenagers for being Black in the wrong place at the wrong time in London in 1993. His killers, though their identities were strongly suspected by locals and known to police, went free. Subsequent government investigations revealed that inspectors were incompetent and racist, with one officer ordered to "smear" Lawrence's family to divert pressure. It took until 2012 to convict just two of the perpetrators, whose identities had been well known for years.[114] In the USA, Black males are over twice as likely to die in a police encounter as white males, with Indigenous people and those of Latin American descent about half again as likely.[115] Meanwhile, whites receive lesser sentences than the nonwhite minority. For example, in the USA, Black and Latin American men arrested for firearms offenses were 40 and 30 percent less likely, respectively, to receive probation rather than jail.[116]

Playing the (White) Race Card a Bit More Subtly

Nation-states remain race-states, and that's one of the most powerful reinforcements of white supremacy in the post-civil rights era. As much as vast blocs of voters in Australia, Britain, or the USA want their countries to be comprised of *citizens*, powerful people and forces insist that their countries are comprised of the white race. In other words, some want "we, the people" of the country to mean "we, the citizens (of whatever color)," while others – still enough to elect presidents and prime ministers – insist "we, the people" are white. Those who believe the sovereign power of the state flows from its citizens of any color are "civic nationalists"; those who cling to the idea that power flows from the "true" race of the homeland are "race nationalists." And they are legion.

Running boldly through the fabric of the USA, UK, or Canada are messages that they are, in their essence, white. For example, US schoolchildren learn the fable of the "first Thanksgiving," which tells them that the nation was founded by – and is thus the property of – benign whites who feasted peacefully with Indian neighbors.[117] British students learn that the UK is a bequest shared with them by white Christian kings and queens and Royal Navy captains carved in stone and mounted on plinths. Not to be outdone, the US capital is studded with monuments to slaveholders, which declare that the country is white and that venerating slavers is not just acceptable but encouraged. Canada Day and Australia Day celebrate when white people "founded" those countries instead of describing how whiteness came into being in the process of dispossessing the people who already lived there. These and countless other influences have strange outcomes: they "racialize" their states – that is, make them "white" – but also hide race. That is, they make whiteness "normal," the status quo. It's as if white people don't have *any* race; only nonwhites have race.[118]

In the post-Civil Rights Acts era, when politicians wanted to cash in on white identity concerns, or stoke the idea that the "white man's country" was being lost to nonwhites, politicians spoke of defending white supremacy in coded language.[119] You've already read about this in the context of the "war on crime." A campaign advisor for Ronald Reagan (president 1981–1989) and George H. W. Bush (president 1989–1993), Lee Atwater (1951–1991) put it this way:

> You start out in 1954 by saying, "n–, n–, n–." By 1968, you can't say "n–" – that hurts you. Backfires. So, you say stuff like "forced busing," "states' rights," and all that stuff. You're getting so abstract now … these things you're talking about are totally economic things, [but] a byproduct of them is [that] blacks get hurt worse than whites. [I]f it is getting that abstract, and that coded, [we're still] doing away with the racial problem one way or the other. … [S]aying, "we want to cut this," is much more abstract than even the busing thing, and a hell of a lot more abstract than "n–, n–."[120]

"Forced busing" was a reference to efforts to desegregate schools by dispersing white students to schools outside their immediate neighborhoods to diversify student bodies. Politicians took advantage of this to frighten white parents with the prospect of their children going to schools in "slums." Former President Joe Biden insisted his steadfast opposition to busing as a Delaware senator was based on the argument that it didn't work or was being done the wrong way, despite the fact that Wilmington parents appeared loudly to oppose it on less principled grounds. Researchers who studied the life paths of minority students bussed to better-funded white-majority schools found lifelong benefits for those students.

They also found that white students experienced no negative consequences.[121]

In short, politicians telegraphed to white voters that their party would keep nonwhites in their place and, reminiscent of the things Eugene Debs wrote, they assured the most "ignorant, lazy, unclean, totally void of ambition" white person that they could "esteem themselves immeasurably above the cleanest, most intelligent and self-respecting" nonwhite. Atwater's tactic became central to the US Republican Party bringing racist Democratic Party voters in southern states into their fold from the later 1960s: the "Southern Strategy."

This trend of talking about the preservation of white national dominance in coded language – sometimes called "dog-whistling" because the carefully chosen language sends a figurative ultrasonic signal about race – was hardly restricted to the USA.[122] In the 1980s, Australian Member of Parliament John Howard paid a political price for the targeted opposition of Asian immigrants to the country.[123] He learned a lesson, because in the 1990s, *Prime Minister* John Howard didn't target Asian immigrants, he merely raised questions about the wisdom of welcoming *undefined* people who lack "Australian values" and the effects on "national identity."[124] In Canada in 2015, Prime Minister Stephen Harper appeared to borrow the tactic, saying that immigrants shouldn't receive better healthcare than "old stock Canadians" suggesting, without offering evidence, that they were getting special privileges. His government's immigration minister also proposed a new act titled "Zero Tolerance for Barbaric Practices." Without naming Muslims, they said it was needed to fight child marriage, polygamy, and honor killings (all Orientalist tropes and all already illegal under Canadian law). The apparent aim was to show that the Harper government was being tough on Muslims and defending some kind of white culture.[125]

So we arrive at the new race peril of the 1990s to the present. This was a new variation of Yellow Perilism: the peril of the Muslim. Adherents of Islam, of course, are of a vast range of origins, ethnicities, and surface physical characteristics. But, amid the panic stirred up about them, they became a race, not a religion. Whites in Scotland, England, or the USA believed they could spot a Muslim on sight: they looked like the terrorists depicted in films, the men bearded, the women covered.[126] But, of course, they couldn't, since

Indonesia has the world's largest Muslim population and distinguishing between a Muslim from Turkey and a Christian from Bulgaria would be a fool's errand on many levels. After a small group of hijackers, mainly Saudi Arabian, conducted the 9/11 attacks, Sikhs were murdered and beaten in the USA and Australia.[127] After a July 2005 attack in London, some Sikhs wore stickers reading, "Don't freak, I'm a Sikh."[128]

The imagined Muslim was supposed to fit Orientalist stereotypes: separate, clannish, inscrutable, cunning – with a curved dagger always behind his back. They were also supposed to "hate freedom" and be violent and rageful, as suggested by magazine covers emblazoned with "The Roots of Muslim Rage."[129]

Overall, they were not welcome members of the white man's country. As if Muslims shared a sole makeup the world over, they were all supposed to share a sole "cultural identity" (really, a sole racial identity) that was diametrically opposed to "the West," the good, "normal" white race. This idea was pushed in a popular book called *The Clash of Civilizations*.[130] Meanwhile, Muslims were supposed to be planting alien beachheads in supposedly white homelands. They were "conquering Europe's cities, street by street."[131] They were creating "no-go" zones in Birmingham, UK; they were threatening the USA with the imposition of Sharia law.[132] None of this, of course, was real; but the politics of describing the loss of white territory to racist voters was real and seemingly effective.

On the other hand, race perilism focused on dark-skinned Muslims wasn't new. Lothrop Stoddard, the 1920s–1930s bestselling white supremacist, warned against the "ferment" he saw rising among "the ignorant, brutal Oriental masses" of Muslims in North Africa and West Asia in 1922.[133] And, in the late 1960s, Enoch Powell didn't stop with demonizing Black West Indians, but warned of the "Oriental colonisation" of Britain by South Asian immigrants.[134] Below, we'll bring this story of Muslim race peril up to the moment, in the hands of Trumpism. These panics span centuries because race nationalism spans centuries.

The Crisis

That brings us to the sharpest crisis of whiteness in the last generation: the election of Barack Obama (in office 2009–2017) to the presidency of the USA. In books and speeches, Obama was explicit in saying that he, a mixed-race individual, literally embodied the end – or at least the beginning of the end – of race nationalism or ethnocracy in the USA.[135] In him, whiteness was no longer a prerequisite qualification for the highest office in the land. If the First Citizen was Black, then it followed that real citizenship extended to all, regardless of race.[136] That's not at all to say that Obama directly aimed to – or could possibly – dismantle the deep-stretching underpinnings of white supremacy or even the notion that the USA is a white race-nation.

The extraordinary reaction to Obama's election echoed the fevered refrains repeated in this book. Motivated by a "deep-seated hatred of white people," in the words of a rightwing activist, Obama would usher in a race war. Or his Black appointees would seek revenge. He'd deprive *real* Americans of power.[137] Campaigning in 2008, Republican vice-presidential candidate Sarah Palin suggested Obama was a Jihadist "palling around with terrorists," apparently tasked with the role in that campaign of suggesting Obama wasn't a real American.[138] In a democracy, it's expected that a rival party will resist the one in charge; but the campaign against Obama, and Republicans' promise to reject everything he proposed, seemed based on the idea that Obama and his voters were illegitimate – or that treating them as such appealed to Republican voters.[139]

Enter Donald Trump (1946–) in the run-up to Obama's 2012 reelection campaign. Trump's foray into national politics began with casting doubt on Obama's legitimacy. He didn't invent it, but he certainly harnessed, "birtherism," the theory that there was a conspiracy to hide the fact Obama wasn't born in the USA.[140] This would not only mean that Obama wasn't qualified to run for President, but also included the suggestion that he was a secret Muslim (which was supposed to be obviously disqualifying, too). Practically, it was a way for those who feared for white ethnocracy's longevity to oppose Obama without direct reference to his being Black.[141] They were still taking lessons from Lee Atwater, it seems.

Trump rode his leadership of birtherism into the national political spotlight and straight through the walls of the Republican Party establishment. Indeed, using rhetoric that left MP Enoch Powell in the rearview mirror, he made dust of the Republican establishment. Trump effectively made clear, in his promise to "make American great again," that he was really promising a kind of racial restoration. The old order was back. Candidate Trump questioned the legitimacy of a judge of Mexican descent who crossed him; and candidate Trump said he'd close mosques, while President Trump banned immigration from majority-Muslim countries. In an extraordinary feat of synthesis, during his second campaign, he warned that Mexican immigrants – overwhelmingly Catholic – were carrying Muslim prayer rugs across the US border.[142] In his inauguration speech, he declared that he'd bring order to the "inner city," bringing an end to "American carnage" there.[143] He's made his white race-nationalist – or white identitarian – views even more clear since then – all old wine in new bottles.[144]

Anti-democracy in the name of preserving white power, that very old story, appeared in radical new forms in the hands of the Trumpists. Most visible was the insurrectionist riot of January 6, 2021, when pro-Trump assailants stormed the US Capitol with the express intent of arresting Democratic legislators, zip-tie cuffs in hand, while chanting "hang Mike Pence," the "traitorous" Republican vice president who refused to interfere with the election.[145] Besides this spectacular instance of anti-democracy, the USA's Republican Party has carried on a more muted, but more powerful and persistent, campaign of voter suppression aimed at limiting the nonwhite vote. The two main tactics for this are passing voter ID laws, falsely arguing that there's significant voting fraud; and limiting opportunities to cast ballots, especially in predominantly nonwhite areas.[146] ID laws disproportionately discourage nonwhite people from voting, and polling stations in key nonwhite voting districts are inordinately fewer than in white-majority areas.[147] Trump, though, didn't resuscitate white supremacist anti-democracy; it was already there. Studying data from the two decades before Trump's candidacy, researchers identified a connection between voters' racial prejudice and their distaste for democracy.[148]

In 2024, Trump promised not to accept an electoral loss; but that was moot because, in the end, roughly half of all US voters put him back in the White House.[149] If anything, Trump ran his second presidential campaign more explicitly on white identity and racial fear-mongering. Careful to consistently mispronounce her name on the 2024 campaign trail, Trump repeatedly called Kamala Harris (1964–), of Jamaican and South Asian descent, "dumb," and the "DEI candidate."[150] The former California Attorney General and US senator was supposed to be unqualified, in her position solely due to affirmative action quotas. Meanwhile, Trump said, Harris "played the race card on a level you rarely see."[151] Besides traditional race-baiting for his white followers, the implicit message was that Harris *had* race and he didn't, thus only she could "play the race card." At the very same time, he said there was anti-white racism in the country that he'd fix in a second term.[152]

Anti-immigration remained the bread and butter he fed his audiences. Debating Kamala Harris, he depicted the USA as being under siege by savages in terms that not only skipped dog-whistling, but might embarrass Enoch Powell. Of Haitian immigrants in an Ohio town, Trump said, "they are eating the pets of the people that live there."[153] Migrants were "poisoning the blood of our country," there were many murderers among them, with "murder ... in their genes. And we got a lot of bad genes in our country right now."[154]

Speaking of anti-immigration, it's time to address Brexit in the UK. Backing up to around 2010, a major campaign was well under way long before Donald Trump's first victory. In those years, an anti-immigrant party, the UK Independence Party (UKIP), and its press allies attacked the establishment Conservative party from the right. UKIP targeted Eastern European immigrants living and working in the UK under the EU's liberal residency rules, and they campaigned to leave the EU for that reason. But they traded on opposing nonwhite immigration as a central tactic, even though EU membership didn't have much bearing on the rate of nonwhite immigration to the UK. Nigel Farage, UKIP's leader, argued in 2013 that Muslim immigrants to the UK were "coming here to take us over," and called Enoch Powell a political hero.[155] "Our once well-ordered civilisation is sliding towards chaos in the face of the unprecedented, colossal influx of foreign arrivals," wrote a *Daily Express* columnist in late 2015, his rhetoric nearly identical to that warning of immigration's existential threat to white civilization from a century before.[156]

The Brexiteers led the UK from the EU in a June 2016 referendum. Areas in the UK with fewer immigrants voted for Brexit at a higher rate than those with more.[157] As in the USA, research suggests Brexit voters were motivated by the belief that Britain was a white nation and nonwhites (or suspect whites, like the "Polish plumber" caricature) had encroached for too long.[158]

The success of Brexit and Trump's election emboldened those who support white ethnocracy. The first weeks and months after the Brexit vote saw an increase in attacks on nonwhite, Jewish, and Eastern European residents and British citizens.[159] That violence was far exceeded in the summer of 2024, with white mobs burning mosques and nonwhite businesses and attacking foreign-seeming nonwhites in the streets, shouting "we want our country back," a slogan familiar from Brexiteers' rallies.[160] In the USA, the infamous fascist march in Charlottesville, Virginia in 2017 was a similarly diabolical instance of white nationalists emboldened by a race-nationalist regime. The same went for white terror murderers who attacked mosques in Quebec City and Christchurch, New Zealand (Muslims, again, having been transformed into a race). The Quebec City killer appeared inspired by President Trump's "Muslim ban" and the Canadian prime minister's repudiation of it. He believed that murdering Muslims would ultimately save white Canadians' lives.[161] The white supremacist who committed the Christchurch mosque murders praised Donald Trump as a "a symbol of renewed white identity" and titled his manifesto "The Great Replacement," keeping Madison Grant and Lothrop Stoddard's replacement theory bloodily relevant.[162]

But, horrible as these flashpoints are, white supremacy persists because of centuries-old, subterranean, clinging tentacles. Donald Trump, the Brexiteers, and white nationalist parties in Australia or New Zealand are in part manifestations of the enduring dynamics of white supremacy; they don't create or sustain it by themselves.[163]

Final Thoughts

The past century showed the persistence of centuries-old dynamics, but also white supremacy's evolution to fit the times. It also showed the insecurity and even brittleness that's been there since the beginning.

These developments include:

- Public **displays of violence** meant to show the danger of challenging whiteness. They also showed how the public, police, and courts would hold the line together against nonwhites. These weren't limited to the torture and murder of individual nonwhite men, nor even nonwhite businesses, but, in places like Tulsa, went as far as warlike assaults on entire quarters of cities.
- When whites didn't dispossess nonwhites with brute force, they did it with redlining or job discrimination. Across generations, whites have **kept capital out of nonwhite hands**, reinforcing their sense of superiority.

- Race science and Social Darwinism – global race logic – reached **its logical conclusion in the hands of Nazis** and their allies in the middle of the twentieth century. The Nazis drew inspiration from the USA's segregation system, and American eugenicists admired Nazi eugenic policy, in turn. America First, which feared the Yellow Peril, advocated staying out of war with Germany.
- After the Second World War, with Britain becoming more diverse, the race superiority long practiced in the empire was reborn at home, with leaders making political capital by stoking fear.
- At the turn of the twenty-first century, **new race perils** like an imagined "Muslim" threat played into the hands of leaders pushing anti-immigration throughout the English-speaking world.
- In the middle and later twentieth century, movements for justice in every corner of the British Empire and in the USA **supported and reinforced each other**, drawing the conclusion that they all opposed a globe-spanning whiteness.
- Leaders have continued to operate as if they don't have race and don't appeal to **white identity politics**. This stems from the persistent fact that the nation-states of the English-speaking world are ethnostates. Protestant whites are the *real* citizens of these states, with all others, in the words of Franklin Roosevelt, there "on sufferance."[164]
- Leaders' attacks on "critical race theory" or DEI or "uncontrolled" immigration" were subtle and not-so-subtle promises to their white electorate: we'll protect you, the true Briton, American, or Australian, from nonwhite usurpation. **Unequal policing** went hand-in-hand with that.

***

There's no one better to whom to grant the last word of this chapter than James Baldwin. Reflecting on the struggle of the US Civil Rights Movement, he wrote with a kind of wonder at the intransigence of whiteness. White supremacy was at once "shameful ... [and] also something of an achievement." It was a feat. It wasn't at all that whiteness was unassailable, smashing its rivals easily like a giant swatting gnats. Far from it. He wrote that white supremacy faced a "perpetual challenge" from its nonwhite victims and fair-minded whites; yet this challenge, this "problem was always, somehow, perpetually met."[165]

On the other hand, the achievements of Brexit, Trumpism, and other white identity movements aren't really successes by many measures. Brexit appears to have cost British households significantly.[166] Economists argue that Trump's anti-immigration policies hurt white, unskilled, non-urban Americans, too – white people on public assistance – because second-generation immigrant workers pay the bill for those programs.[167] Meeting the challenge against whiteness seems to degrade the white ethnostate. As Pankaj Mishra wrote, "as Brexit and Trump show, the capacity for self-harm has grown ominously."[168]

FINAL REFLECTIONS AND PROSPECTS FOR THE FUTURE

"Intractable," or supremely stubborn and unmoving, seems a good word to describe white supremacy. That is, the problem of white supremacy seems intractable, stuck and unyielding like a massive granite monument for over three centuries.

Yet I want to raise a red flag about words like "intractable." What I mean is, when you hear or read someone describing white supremacy or race-hate as "intractable," "deep-seated," "timeless," or "complicated," listen closely. Is the speaker describing it that way, as difficult and unyielding, so that listeners understand how ending it will require shifting vast, fundamental realities? Or, instead, is the speaker offering a picture meant to excuse their – and your – inaction or lack of hard thinking? It's like they're saying, "what good is it to shake one's fist at something as timeless as the ocean or to try to move something as immovable as a mountain?" The other thing this framing encourages is an incrementalist, gradual approach. They're saying, "you can't change an ageless force of nature like a tide, but maybe we can pass a law to clean up a little after it floods." Notice that such messages usually come from people whose houses stand well above the flood zone.

But things will change. That's all an historian can guarantee. Things have never not changed – and they regularly change drastically on a large scale. The creation of whiteness in the context of colonialism, slavery, and early capitalism was one such fast, vast change. Crises occur. Systems fail and new ones arise. As the great author Ursula K. Le Guin said, "we live in capitalism, its power seems inescapable – but then, so did the divine right of kings. Any human power can be resisted and changed by human beings."[1]

While it's endured over three centuries, people of all kinds have resisted white supremacy the entire time. It's periodically been in grave danger and, for at least fifty years, in a near-constant fight for its life, propped up by adherents ranging from devoted to unwitting.

Watching US state legislatures issue educational gag orders banning the teaching of white supremacy's history in 2023, Ta-Nehisi Coates saw reason for hope. "Backlashes ... generally come, and are generally more ferocious, when the forces that would like to maintain the status quo are most afraid."[2]

And those forces should be. The work against the status quo of whiteness and white ethnocracy has probably never before been so widely shared. More than ever, movements for justice in a variety of fields work together in solidarity, knowing that success in one area for one group means success for others. White supremacy draws power from capitalism, sexism and gender conformity, state authority, and much more. And today, its opponents of many backgrounds acknowledge and act on this, aiming broadly at this network of power, allying with those working on divergent, intersecting fronts across the globe.

The simultaneous success of Brexit and Trump pushed me finally to write this book; but the spring 2020 street execution of George Floyd shoved me down the path. That's not because there was something particularly rare about the killing of a Black or Indigenous person in police custody in any corner of the English-speaking world. It's because people of all kinds took to the streets of cities large and small in every corner of the English-speaking world (and beyond), in solidarity and outrage at a murder in distant Minneapolis. And their words and actions showed they were also standing against white supremacy broadly in Australia, Britain, Canada, and elsewhere. In Bristol, UK, people pulled down the statue of Edward Colston (1636–1721), who made his fortune on Royal African Company slaving, and pushed it into Bristol harbor. In New Zealand, Māori people said they marched "to defend Black Lives overseas and to fight for our own lives against our own racist police."[3] In Adelaide, Australia, marchers called their rally "Solidarity with Minneapolis," while nonwhite Australians spoke about deaths of indigenous Australians at the hands of police.[4]

In George Floyd Square today, besides the area – constantly renewed with flowers – showing the place of his murder, there's a monumental steel fist raised in defiance of Minnesota's weather extremes. But there's more. There's a sign that reads "Land Back," which calls for restoration or restitution for the Indigenous people of the land they never left, only lost. And there's a spot with free clothes for people in need. And recently there was a sign calling for the end of apartheid in Israel–Palestine. Another sign reads, "END FASCISM." Perhaps intersecting movements for justice and freedom embody the power of *and*. And perhaps its power has yet to be fully unleashed.

In the meantime, whiteness is self-destructive. If you measure the success of a country by the well-being and prosperity of its people, there's no sound argument that white supremacy is good for the whites of English-speaking lands. The people elected, and the policies adopted, to preserve white power have been abject failures at improving the well-being and prospects of whites themselves.

I hope this deep history has helped you reflect on what will need to change to end whiteness and white supremacy. I suggest thinking of a time after it without stopping yourself for being "unrealistic," or feeling that you must plot the specific steps that'd be required to overcome it. Don't police yourself, don't stop *yourself* from thinking about a world after whiteness when there are 1,000 messages trying to stop you, inundating you at all times, telling you that whiteness is natural or the default. It might also take one of the great accidents or crises of history to push it over the edge. But there was a time before whiteness; there'll be a time after it.

ACKNOWLEDGMENTS

For discussions about this project, thank you to Tommy Curry, John Flores, Ted McCormick, Manisha Sinha, and Noel Voltz. Thanks very much to Cambridge University Press's peer reviewers. Thanks to Thomas Haynes, Steven Holt, Rosa Martin, and Michael Watson at Cambridge University Press. Many thanks, also, to undergraduate and graduate students of my Comparative White Supremacy seminar for discussions that opened my eyes and suggested the way. Those students read drafts of some of this book. This book is also dedicated to future students. For Ken Ledford's and Jonathan Sadowsky's support, thank you. This book was made possible by a sabbatical granted by the Department of History and College of Arts and Sciences, Case Western Reserve University. Thank you to the history departments of Stanford University and the University of Maine.

FIGURES

NOTES

Introduction

1. Robin DiAngelo, *Nice Racism: How Progressive White People Perpetuate Racial Harm* (Boston: Beacon Press, 2021), xix.
2. Some scholars prefer to think of racism in much broader terms as something like "race thinking" and structural racism. Pioneering historian George Fredrickson defined racism *not* as a hateful attitude arising from white supremacy, but more along the lines of how I defined white supremacy: systemic. He wrote "racism . . . is not merely an attitude or set of beliefs; it also expresses itself in the practices, institutions, and structures that a sense of deep difference justifies or validates." Far be it from me to correct him. But I suggest that it helps us to distinguish between "white supremacy," a specific power pattern, and "racism," something common across the world since the invention of race as we know it. A member of a national minority, then, can be a crude racist – hate the majority race *for* their race. But without the power to, say, infuse their society's institutions with discrimination, that racism ends as an odious, but impotent, attitude. George Fredrickson, *Racism: A Short History* (Princeton: Princeton University Press, 2002), 6.
3. Martin Luther King, Jr., *Letter from a Birmingham Jail*, April 16, 1963.
4. Just for a handful of examples, Ta-Nehisi Coates, *Between the World and Me* (New York: One World, 2015); Reni Eddo-Lodge, *Why I'm No Longer Talking to White People about Race* (London: Bloomsbury Circus, 2017); Ibram X. Kendi, *Stamped from the Beginning: The Definitive History of Racist Ideas in America* (New York: Bold Type Books, 2017).
5. James Baldwin interview with the editors of *Esquire* (July 1968).

Chapter 1: Before Whiteness, 400s BCE–1600

1. Karen E. Fields and Barbara J. Fields, *Racecraft: The Soul of Inequality in American Life* (New York: Verso, 2012), 121.

2. For a columnist having some fun with the news that one of the oldest skeletons ever found in England suggested its owner had brown skin, see Brian Reade, "Dark-Skinned Cheddar Man Is Hard Cheese for the Racist Morons of the Far Right," *The Mirror*, February 10, 2018. For someone with a different reaction, see Sinclair Lewis, "A Tale of Two Discoveries," *American Renaissance*, February 13, 2018. For the heated reactions to scholar Mary Beard's observations that some Roman Britons would have come from places like Africa, see Mary Beard, "Roman Britain in Black and White," *Times Literary Supplement*, August 3, 2017.

3. Cheddar Man is the name given to a human who lived 10,000 years ago near today's Cheddar Gorge in Somerset. DNA analysis of his skull suggested he was dark-skinned.

4. Hella Eckardt, Gundula Müldner, and Mary Lewis, "People on the Move in Roman Britain," *World Archaeology* 46 (2014): 534–550.

5. Laurens E. Tacoma, Tatiana Ivleva, and David J. Breeze, "Lost Along the Way: A Centurion Domo Britannia in Bostra," *Britannia* 47 (2016): 31–42.

6. David Dabydeen, John Gilmore, and Cecily Jones, eds., *Oxford Companion to Black British History* (Oxford: Oxford University Press, 2008), 422.

7. Pallab Ghosh, "DNA Study Finds London Was Ethnically Diverse from Start," *BBC News*, November 23, 2015, www.bbc.com/news/science-environment-34809804.

8. Hakim Adi, ed., *Black British History: New Perspectives* (London: Zed, 2019), 4–6.

9. Kostas Vlassopoulos, *Historicising Ancient Slavery* (Edinburgh: Edinburgh University Press, 2021), chapters 5 and 6.

10. Kathryn Lomas, Andrew Gardner, and Edward Herring, "Creating Ethnicities and Identities in the Roman World," *Bulletin of the Institute of Classical Studies. Supplement* 120 (2013): 1–10.

11. Talawa Adodo, "Herodotus and the Black Body: A Critical Race Theory Analysis," *Journal of Black Studies* 46 (2015): 723–741.

12. Ibid., 733.

13. For an overview of this, see A. Bashford and S. W. Tracy, "Introduction: Modern Airs, Waters, and Places," *Bulletin of the History of Medicine* 86 (2012): 495–514.

14. John P. Jackson, Jr. and Nadine M. Weidman, *Race, Racism, and Science* (New Brunswick, NJ: Rutgers University Press, 2004), 1–4.

15. Clare Downham, "The Viking Slave Trade: Entrepreneurs or Heathen Slavers?" *History Ireland* 17, no. 3 (2009): 15–17.

16. For a good overview from a classicist who's expert on the subject, see Rebecca Futo Kennedy, "Airs, Waters, Metals, Earth: People and

Environment in Archaic and Classical Greek Thought," in Rebecca Futo Kennedy and Molly Jones-Lewis, eds., *The Routledge Handbook to Identity and the Environment in the Classical and Medieval Worlds* (London: Routledge, 2016), 9–28. To name just a few more select resources of many, see I. Hannaford, *Race: The History of an Idea in the West* (Washington, D.C.: Woodrow Wilson Center Press, 1996); Benjamin Isaac, "Proto-racism in Graeco-Roman Antiquity," *World Archaeology* 38 (2006): 32–47; Benjamin Isaac, *Invention of Racism in Classical Antiquity* (Princeton, NJ: Princeton University Press, 2004); Rachana Kamtekar, "Distinction without a Difference? Race and Genos in Plato," in J. Ward and T. Lott, eds., *Philosophers on Race: Critical Essays* (Malden, MA: Wiley-Blackwell 2002), 1–13.

17. Rebecca Futo Kennedy, "Otis T. Mason and Hippocratic Environmental Theory at the Smithsonian Institution in the Nineteenth and Early Twentieth Centuries," in Emily Varto, ed., *Brill's Companion to Classics and Early Anthropology* (Leiden: Brill, 2018), 154–182, 160.

18. Septimius Severus (ruled 193–211). For the image, see the so-called "Severan Tondo," Altes Museum, Berlin.

19. Futo Kennedy, "Airs, Waters, Metals, Earth," 22–23.

20. For just one example of this persistence out of many, see Linda Nash, *Inescapable Ecologies: A History of Environment, Disease, and Knowledge* (Berkeley, CA: University of California Press, 2006).

21. Caitlin Greene, "A Note on the Evidence for African Migrants in Britain from the Bronze Age to the Medieval Period," May 23, 2016, www.caitlingreen.org/2016/05/a-note-on-evidence-for-african-migrants.html.

22. Florence H. R. Scott, "The North Elmham and Fairford Women: Two Black Women in Tenth-Century England," *Ælfgif-who? Newsletter* no. 4, April 19, 2021, https://florencehrs.substack.com/p/northelmham fairfordwomen; Adi, *Black British History*, 6–7.

23. Bede, *Ecclesiastical History of England*, book IV, chapter 1.

24. Adi, *Black British History*, 9, citing the *Patent Rolls of Henry III* (https://catalog.hathitrust.org/Record/000270470). Medievalists don't think someone called an "Ethiopian" had to be from today's Ethiopia. They tend to think it indicates a dark-skinned African. See Dorothy Hoogland Verkek, "Black Servant; Black Demon: Color Ideology in the Ashburnham Pentateuch," *Journal of Medieval and Early Modern Studies* 31 (2001): 57–78, 64.

25. Hakim Adi cautions us to be very careful about drawing the over-easy conclusion that Africans in medieval England must have been slaves. He's right. And Florence H. R. Scott does a good job of revealing a particularly disgusting instance of this, too. See Scott, "The North

Elmham and Fairford Women." But, in the case of the Ipswich Man of Greyfriars, we can be pretty suspicious that he'd been enslaved because, around the time Ipswich Man arrived in England, two Greyfriars patrons are recorded as bringing "four captive Saracens" to England from Tunis on their return from a crusade. Adi points this out; see Adi, *Black British History*, 8. Ipswich Man's burial in the monastery churchyard means that the institution considered him, whatever his rank at death – and we don't know it – a genuine community member.

26. Jessica A. Coope, *The Most Noble of People: Religious, Ethnic, and Gender Identity in Muslim Spain* (Ann Arbor, MI: University of Michigan Press, 2017), 32.

27. Hannah Barker, *That Most Precious Merchandise: The Mediterranean Trade in Black Sea Slaves, 1260–1500*, 1st ed. (Philadelphia, PA: University of Pennsylvania Press, 2019).

28. There were also crusades against non-Christian pagans in eastern or northeastern lands of what we today call Europe, sometimes called the Baltic Crusades, at the same time. Earlier, around the reign of Charlemagne in 800, the so-called "Holy Roman Empire" launched wars of conquest against non-Christians to the east. This, despite some debate, appears to be the root of the English word "slave." The people who called themselves "Slavs" were the source of enslaved prisoners of war – *sclavi* in the late Latin of Charlemagne's age.

29. Indeed, the new enemy was powerful enough that sometimes the Christians had to pay ransoms to Muslim, "Saracen," captors of Christian sailors and soldiers to free them from slavery. See Robert C. Davis, "Counting European Slaves on the Barbary Coast," *Past and Present* 172 (August 1, 2001): 87–124.

30. John Victor Tolan, *Saracens: Islam in the Medieval European Imagination* (New York: Columbia University Press, 2002). Sometimes medieval observers lumped their imagined Muslim opposites under the terms "Turk," "Infidel," or "Arab."

31. "Because of its geographical indeterminacy, the idea and boundaries of Europe have been conceived as much in opposition to other cultural and political zones as in relation to what 'Europeans' have had in common," wrote Bruce Baum of this period. See Bruce Baum, *The Rise and Fall of the Caucasian Race: A Political History of Racial Identity* (New York: New York University Press, 2006), 27.

32. Gerard Delanty offers a review of the debates about the origins of a coherent sense of Europe. Naturally, as a good scholar, he shows that the evolution was complicated and subtle. But I think my broad-stroke picture is supported by the date. See Gerard Delanty, "The Origins of the Idea of Europe," in Gerard Delanty, ed., *Inventing Europe: Idea, Identity, Reality* (London: Palgrave Macmillan, 1995), 16–29.

33. Sethina Watson, "Introduction: The Moment and Memory of the York Massacre of 1190," in Sethina Watson and Sarah Rees Jones, eds., *Christians and Jews in Angevin England: The York Massacre of 1190, Narratives and Contexts* (London: Boydell & Brewer, 2013), 1–14.

34. Edgar Samuel, "The Readmission of the Jews to England in 1656, in the Context of English Economic Policy," *Jewish Historical Studies* 31 (1988): 153–169.

35. Scholar Geraldine Heng is among those who've led the way in sophisticated scholarship on the question of race in medieval Europe. See Geraldine Heng, *The Invention of Race in the European Middle Ages* (Cambridge: Cambridge University Press, 2018). On page 3, she offers an important definition of race: it's "one of the primary names ... for the strategic, epistemological, and political commitments ... to demarcate human beings through differences ... that are selectively essentialized as absolute and fundamental, in order to distribute positions and powers differentially. [It's] a structural relationship for the articulation and management of human difference." While that's a smart, critical definition, for our purposes in this book, we're looking for something more essential in race. That's not at all to deny that demarcation and hard difference-making could certainly lead to terrors, as it did for the Jews of York. Here I am following a certain route through the scholarship of race which holds that medieval and early modern negative views of Jews and the resulting discrimination were quite different from theories of blood-inherited negative qualities of the more modern era. Extremely capable scholars like Heng argue otherwise. You should read what they have to say. But I conclude from my reading of these scholars that at some point the definition of race thinking as we know it becomes too diluted when we go back beyond the pre-colonial era. That's not at all to say there aren't critical pre-modern influences – which I was at pains to distil for readers. Beside Heng, see the essays in Amos Morris-Reich and Dirk Rupnow, eds., *Ideas of "Race" in the History of the Humanities* (Cham: Palgrave Macmillan, 2017). Joan-Pau Rubiés's essay nicely lays out how the debate on the origins of modern race depends on how you define it, see Joan-Pau Rubiés, "Were Early Modern Europeans Racist?" in Amos Morris-Reich and Dirk Rupnow, eds., *Ideas of "Race" in the History of the Humanities* (Cham: Palgrave Macmillan, 2017), 33–88, 33–36.

36. Thomas Wykes, quoted in Simon Jenkins, *A Short History of London* (London: Penguin, 2020), 31.

37. Anidjar, Gil. *Blood: A Critique of Christianity* (New York: Columbia University Press, 2014). Still, in Victorian Britain, probably a much more observant Christian time and place than medieval England, a converted Jew, Benjamin Disraeli, served as prime minister for many years.

38. Marc J. Rosenstein, "The End of Iberian Jewry: Conversion, Expulsion, Diaspora, 1300–1600 CE," in *Turning Points in Jewish History* (Lincoln, NE: University of Nebraska Press, 2018), 195–209. Forced conversion with no chance of expulsion was more the order in the Kingdom of Portugal.

39. Jeffrey Gorsky, "Purity of Blood," in *Exiles in Sepharad: The Jewish Millennium in Spain* (Lincoln, NE: University of Nebraska Press, 2015), 311–328.

40. For a review of debates about this long process of race-making, "racialization," see Max S. Hering Torres, "Purity of Blood: Problems of Interpretation," in María Elena Martínez, David Nirenberg, and Max-Sebastián Hering Torres, eds., *Race and Blood in the Iberian World* (Münster: LIT Verlag, 2012), 11–38; Francisco Bethencourt, "Conclusions," in *Racisms: From the Crusades to the Twentieth Century* (Princeton, NJ: Princeton University Press, 2013), 365–374, 366.

41. Gomes Eanes de Zurara, "How Antam Gonçalvez Brought Back the First Captives," in Charles Raymond Beazley and Edgar Prestage, trans. and eds., *The Chronicle of the Discovery and Conquest of Guinea*, vol. 1: *Chapters I–XI* (Cambridge: Cambridge University Press, 2010), 39–43. Dr. Marcelo E. Fuentes reads de Zurara closely to see hints of religion-based slavery turning into race-based in Marcelo E. Fuentes, "'Crespo e Nuu e Negro': Gomes Eanes de Zurara and the Racialization of Non-Christians by Portuguese Authors," *Essays in Medieval Studies* 34 (January 2018): 17–38.

42. It almost goes without saying that what the Portuguese really wanted to discover in West Africa was gold, more valuable than human trafficking. They often carried out an inter-port trade in enslaved people (and trade goods), trading for gold. See Herbert Klein, "The Atlantic Slave Trade to 1650," in Stuart B. Schwartz, ed., *Tropical Babylons: Sugar and the Making of the Atlantic World, 1450–1680* (Chapel Hill, NC: University of North Carolina Press, 2004), 201–236, 203.

43. For an introduction, see Alice Rio, *Slavery after Rome, 500–1100* (Oxford: Oxford University Press, 2017). Anna Kłosowska offers a tremendous bibliographic review of the literature on medieval slaveries in Anna Kłosowska, "The Etymology of Slave," in Anna Kłosowska and Vincent W. J. van Gerven Oei, eds., *Disturbing Times: Medieval Pasts, Reimagined Futures* (Santa Barbara, CA: Punctum Books, 2020), 151–214.

44. Mary Nyquist, *Arbitrary Rule: Slavery, Tyranny, and the Power of Life and Death* (Chicago, IL: University of Chicago Press, 2013), especially chapter 6, 193–226.

45. Barker, *That Most Precious Merchandise*, 22.

46. Ibid., 18.

47. Rio, *Slavery after Rome*, 32, 58–60.
48. Jeffrey Fynn-Paul describes this sense of being outside Christendom in Jeffrey Fynn-Paul, "Empire, Monotheism and Slavery in the Greater Mediterranean Region from Antiquity to the Early Modern Era," *Past and Present* 205 (2009): 3–40.
49. Eloy Martín Corrales, "The Spain That Enslaves and Expels: Moriscos and Muslim Captives (1492 to 1767–1791)," in *Muslims in Spain, 1492–1814: Living and Negotiating in the Land of the Infidel* (Leiden: Brill, 2020), 67–94. Richard Raiswell writes that the bull was "consciously borrowing from the crusading tradition." See Richard Raiswell, "Nicholas V, Papal Bulls of," in Junius P. Rodriguez, ed., *The Historical Encyclopedia of World Slavery* (Santa Barbara, CA: ABC-CLIO, 1997), 469.
50. Jeffrey Gorsky, "Jewish Blood, Black Blood," in *Exiles in Sepharad: The Jewish Millennium in Spain* (Lincoln, NE: University of Nebraska Press, 2015), 329–339.
51. Onyeka Nubia, "Africans in England and Scotland, 1485–1625," *Oxford Dictionary of National Biography* online (October 2019).
52. David Bates, *William the Conqueror* (New Haven, CT: Yale University Press, 2016), 432–433.
53. Jackson and Weidman, *Race, Racism, and Science*, 4–5.
54. Miranda Kaufmann, *Black Tudors: The Untold Story* (London: Oneworld, 2017), chapter 2 and elsewhere.
55. Onyeka Nubia, "'Blackamoores' Have Their Own Names in Early Modern England," in Hakim Adi, ed., *Black British History: New Perspectives* (London: Zed, 2019), 15–36, 15; Kaufmann, *Black Tudors*, chapter 5.
56. Kaufmann, *Black Tudors*, chapters 3 and 8 and elsewhere.
57. In 1548, Lady Hume of Scotland related a story about a "Moor" who was either Jacques Granado or Pedro Negro, both of whom were knighted for their service against the Scots. See Miranda Kaufmann, "Sir Pedro Negro: What Colour Was His Skin?" *Notes and Queries* 253, no. 2 (June 2008): 142–146, www.mirandakaufmann.com/pedro-negro.html.
58. And, after all, the queen of over twenty years herself was Spanish: Katherine. See Onyeka Nubia, *England's Other Countrymen: Black Tudor Society* (London: Zed, 2019), 26.
59. Gustav Ungerer, "The Presence of Africans in Elizabethan England and the Performance of 'Titus Andronicus' at Burley-on-the-Hill, 1595/96," *Medieval & Renaissance Drama in England* 21 (2008): 19–55. See generally, too, David Olusoga, *Black and British: A Forgotten History*, revised and updated (New York: Picador, 2021).
60. Some readers might notice that I've not dealt with the infamous 1601 Proclamation of Elizabeth I ordering the expulsion of "Negroes and

blackamoors" from England. That's because it's a bit of an historical red herring. It might never have been published and most certainly wasn't enforced. Miranda Kaufmann, 'Caspar van Senden, Sir Thomas Sherley and the 'Blackamoor' Project," *Historical Research* 81, no. 212 (May 2008): 366–371. Nubia wrote of the episode, as well. See Nubia, "Africans in England and Scotland." For scholars seeing an influence of Iberian color-based race-thinking on the English and Scottish, see Nubia, *England's Other Countrymen*, 26–28.

61. See the introduction to Robert C. Schwaller, ed., *African Maroons in Sixteenth-Century Panama: A History in Documents* (Norman, OK: University of Oklahoma Press, 2021).

62. Peter H. Wood, *Strange New Land: Africans in Colonial America* (New York: Oxford University Press, 1996), 15–16.

63. Mark Bailey, *The Decline of Serfdom in Late Medieval England: From Bondage to Freedom* (Woodbridge: Boydell & Brewer, 2014), especially chapter 1.

64. Ali Rattansi, *Racism: A Very Short Introduction*, 1st ed. (Oxford and New York: Oxford University Press, 2007), 105.

65. Kathy Lavezzo, *The Accommodated Jew: English Antisemitism from Bede to Milton* (Ithaca, NY: Cornell University Press, 2016), 72.

66. Onyeka Nubia neatly makes a convincing argument distinguishing between race hate and xenophobia in his study of the apparently racist proclamations against Black Tudors at the end of Elizabeth's reign in Nubia, "'Blackamoores' Have Their Own Names in Early Modern England," 16–17 and elsewhere.

67. Kaufmann, *Black Tudors*, 159–161.

68. Winthrop D. Jordan, *White over Black: American Attitudes toward the Negro, 1550–1812* (Chapel Hill, NC: University of North Carolina Press, 1968) was wonderfully pathbreaking, but is no longer quite the state-of-the-art. I seek to cite the latest scholarly work throughout the book, but there can be no doubt that these scholars are building on the efforts of people like Jordan. See also George M. Fredrickson, *White Supremacy: A Comparative Study in American and South African History* (Oxford: Oxford University Press, 1982); George M. Fredrickson, *Racism: A Short History* (Princeton, NJ: Princeton University Press, 2002); George M. Fredrickson, *The Comparative Imagination: On the History of Racism, Nationalism, and Social Movements* (Berkeley, CA: University of California Press, 2000). You can read an argument for Jordan's great prescience from James Campbell and James Oakes, "The Invention of Race: Rereading *White over Black*," in Richard Delgado and Jean Stefancic, eds., *Critical White Studies: Looking behind the Mirror* (Philadelphia, PA: Temple University Press, 1997), 145–151. Jordan gave some thought to this

question and found a mixed answer. He offered the example of poet John Weever, whose narrator of the poem "In Byrrham" sees a woman's dark skin as an outward sign of impurity. Kim F. Hall considers this and similar contemporary examples in Kim F. Hall, *Things of Darkness: Economies of Race and Gender in Early Modern England* (Ithaca, NY: Cornell University Press, 1995), 130–132 and elsewhere; she transcribes Weever's poem on 272. See also, generally, David Brion Davis, *The Problem of Slavery in Western Culture* (Oxford: Oxford University Press, 1988), 447–448.

69. Jordan pointed to Shakespeare's Sonnet 130 as proof of the pale ideal just after the death of the ideally pale Queen Elizabeth. But the Sonnet itself argues that the narrator is in love with a woman despite her being *not* pale. See Jordan, *White over Black*, 9.

70. Hall, *Things of Darkness*, 67–69 and elsewhere.

71. Jane H. Ohlmeyer, "A Laboratory for Empire?: Early Modern Ireland and English Imperialism," in Kevin Kenny, ed., *Ireland and the British Empire* (Oxford: Oxford University Press, 2005), 26–60.

72. Brendan Smith, *Colonisation and Conquest in Medieval Ireland: The English in Louth, 1170–1330* (Cambridge: Cambridge University Press, 1999), chapter 2, especially.

73. Jane Ohlmeyer, "Conquest, Civilization, Colonization: Ireland, 1540–1660," in Richard Bourke and Ian McBride, eds., *The Princeton History of Modern Ireland* (Princeton, NJ: Princeton University Press, 2016), 21–47.

74. James E. Doan, "'An Island in the Virginian Sea': Native Americans and the Irish in English Discourse, 1585–1640," *New Hibernia Review/Iris Éireannach Nua* 1, no. 1 (1997): 79–99.

75. William Thomas, *The Pilgrim: A Dialogue on the Life and Actions of King Henry the Eighth* (1547), ed. J. A. Froude (London: Parker, 1861), 68.

76. Charles Ivar McGrath, "Politics, 1692–1730," in Jane Ohlmeyer, ed., *The Cambridge History of Ireland*, vol. 2 (Cambridge: Cambridge University Press, 2018), 126, 130–135 and elsewhere.

77. Aziz Rahman, Mary Anne Clarke, and Sean Byrne, "The Art of Breaking People Down: The British Colonial Model in Ireland and Canada," *Peace Research* 49, no. 2 (2017): 15–38.

78. "Slaving is fundamentally a historical process, as slaving strategies achieved prominence primarily in times and places where rapid military or economic expansion facilitated access to outsiders." Joseph C. Miller, "Slaving as Historical Process: Examples from the Ancient Mediterranean and the Modern Atlantic," in Enrico Dal Lago and Constantina Katsari, eds., *Slave Systems: Ancient and Modern* (Cambridge: Cambridge University Press, 2008), 70–102, 70.

79. For the great depth of slaving's persistence, see Christopher Paolella, *Human Trafficking in Medieval Europe: Slavery, Sexual Exploitation, and Prostitution* (Amsterdam: Amsterdam University Press, 2020), 14–18; for the shift to the fringes, see chapter 4 in that book.

80. This isn't a universal claim. The case of the helots, for example, shows that there was a perpetual serf class in the case of ancient Sparta. These serfs were terrorized and harshly subjugated, though they don't seem to have been chattel, exactly. Stephen Hodkinson, "Spartiates, Helots and the Direction of the Agrarian Economy: Toward an Understanding of Helotage in Comparative Perspective," in Enrico Dal Lago and Constantina Katsari, eds., *Slave Systems: Ancient and Modern* (Cambridge: Cambridge University Press, 2008), 285–320.

81. Fynn-Paul, "Empire, Monotheism and Slavery in the Greater Mediterranean Region," 18–20 and elsewhere.

Chapter 2: The Emergence of Whiteness – Gradually and Suddenly, 1400–1730s

1. James Baldwin, "On Being White . . . and Other Lies," (1984) reprinted in David R. Roediger, ed., *Black on White: Black Writers on What It Means to Be White* (New York: Schocken, 1998), 177–180, 178.

2. See a good, fast summary of these developments in William McKee Evans, *Open Wound: The Long View of Race in America* (Urbana, IL: University of Illinois Press, 2009), 13–47.

3. No: the Irish weren't enslaved. See John Donoghue, "The Curse of Cromwell: Revisiting the Irish Slavery Debate," *History Ireland* 25, no. 4 (2017): 24–28. For his helpful correction of an honest error by Donoghue and more elucidation, see also Ted McCormick, "Letters," *History Ireland* 25, no. 6 (2017): 12–15. There was a sadly predictable chapter when people tried to argue that their Irish ancestors were enslaved by the likes of Oliver Cromwell, who *did* transport Irish POWs to Caribbean islands, but as indentured servants. The lives of indentured people were often horrible. But there's a fundamental difference between perpetual and hereditary slaves and indentured people, who overwhelmingly survived their indenture and received their freedom. Indenture wasn't race-based the way slavery became for Africa-descended people. The "Irish slaves" tale is more about the contemporary history of white supremacy than about the history of the Cromwell-era Irish. On the weaponization of the Irish slaves myth, see Liam Stack, "Debunking a Myth: The Irish Were Not Slaves, Too," *New York Times*, March 17, 2017.

4. April 1493 letter of Columbus to Rafael Sanchez, treasurer to the Spanish Crown; facsimile of published version and translation, Letter of Christopher Columbus to Rafael Sanchez (Chicago: Lowdermilk, 1893), 13; also quoted in Hans Koning, *Columbus: His Enterprise. Exploding the Myth* (New York: New York University Press, 1992), 64. See also Tink Tinker and Mark Freeland, "Thief, Slave Trader, Murderer: Christopher Columbus and Caribbean Population Decline," *Wičazo Ša Review* 23 (April 2008): 25–50.

5. October 14, 1492 entry from Columbus's journal, "Christopher Columbus: Extracts from Journal," *Internet Medieval Sourcebook*, https://origin.web.fordham.edu/halsall/source/columbus1.asp.

6. Canarian land grants were based on a model established during the Iberian conquest. See Alberto Vieira, "Sugar Islands: The Sugar Economy of Madeira and the Canaries, 1450–1650," in Stuart B. Schwartz, ed., *Tropical Babylons: Sugar and the Making of the Atlantic World, 1450–1680* (Chapel Hill, NC: University of North Carolina Press, 2004), 42–84, 43, 50.

7. In fact, around the time Columbus was exploring, Canarian/Guanches warriors utterly routed a Spanish force of around 1,000 in the "First Battle of Acentejo," in 1494. The Spaniards were on horseback in heavy armor and found it difficult to move; the Canarian defenders could simply throw spears and rocks at them. Readers should bear this in mind when they consider the claims that superior European technology determined the outcomes of European colonial invasions. It took far more than "guns" and "steel" to aid European intrusion.

8. Philip D. Curtin, *The Rise and Fall of the Plantation Complex: Essays in Atlantic History*, 2nd ed. (Cambridge: Cambridge University Press, 1998), 4–5. There had already been some sugar cultivation in small corners of Arab-settled lands like Sicily and southern Iberia. See J. H. Galloway, "The Mediterranean Sugar Industry," *Geographical Review* 67, no. 2 (1977): 177–194, 180.

9. Vieira, "Sugar Islands," 56.

10. Kwame Nimako and Glenn Willemsen, *The Dutch Atlantic: Slavery, Abolition and Emancipation* (London and New York: Pluto Press, 2011), 61.

11. William D. Phillips Jr., *Slavery in Medieval and Early Modern Iberia* (Philadelphia, PA: University of Pennsylvania Press, 2013), 62–63; Vieira, "Sugar Islands," 57–61.

12. Ibid., 63.

13. John F. Richards, *The Unending Frontier: An Environmental History of the Early Modern World* (Berkeley, CA: University of California Press, 2003), 327.

14. Ibid., 327–328.

15. Karen F. Anderson-Córdova, *Surviving Spanish Conquest: Indian Fight, Flight, and Cultural Transformation in Hispaniola and Puerto Rico* (Tuscaloosa, AL: University of Alabama Press, 2017), 207.

16. William F. Keegan, "Destruction of the Taino," *Archaeology* (January/February 1992): 51–56; Yale Genocide Studies Program, https://web.archive.org/web/20240328214834/https://gsp.yale.edu/case-studies/colonial-genocides-project/hispaniola.

17. Anderson-Córdova, *Surviving Spanish Conquest*, 133–135.

18. Jane Landers, "Africans in the Spanish Colonies," *Historical Archaeology* 31, no. 1 (1997): 84–103, 85.

19. Guy Cameron and Stephen Vermette, "The Role of Extreme Cold in the Failure of the San Miguel de Gualdape Colony," *The Georgia Historical Quarterly* 96, no. 3 (2012): 291–307, 293.

20. Gillian Brockell, "Before 1619, There Was 1526: The Mystery of the First Enslaved Africans in What Became the United States," *Washington Post*, September 7, 2019, https://web.archive.org/web/20220215184432/https://www.washingtonpost.com/history/2019/09/07/before-there-was-mystery-first-enslaved-africans-what-became-us.

21. Juan Francisco Maura, "Caballeros y rufianes andantes en la costa atlántica de los Estados Unidos de América: Lucas Vázquez de Ayllón y Alvar Núñez Cabeza de Vaca," *Revista Canadiense de Estudios Hispánicos* 35, no. 2 (2011): 305–328, 305.

22. Cameron and Vermette, "The Role of Extreme Cold in the Failure of the San Miguel de Gualdape Colony," 294.

23. Brockell, "Before 1619, There Was 1526." Speaking of the colony's failure, the story of the Spanish in the Americas has a long succession of miserable episodes full of hunger, self-sabotage, disaster, and death. The reason they maintained a presence in the Americas was persistence: because of the lures of sugar, silver, and land, the Spanish kept coming, quite simply.

24. For the many opportunities the English saw in the new Spanish venture and the way that ended when the Spanish decided Elizabeth was lost to Protestantism, see Jorge Canizares-Esguerra, *Entangled Empires: The Anglo-Iberian Atlantic, 1500–1830* (Philadelphia, PA: University of Pennsylvania Press, 2018), 20.

25. James Horn, *A Land as God Made It: Jamestown and the Birth of America* (New York: Basic Books, 2008), 6, 9, 30–31.

26. William D. Phillips Jr., "Slavery in the Atlantic Islands and the Early Modern Spanish Atlantic World," in David Eltis and Stanley L. Engerman, eds., *The Cambridge World History of Slavery*, vol. 3 (Cambridge: Cambridge University Press, 2011), 325–329, 329.

27. Margaret Ellen Newell, *Brethren by Nature: New England Indians, Colonists, and the Origins of American Slavery* (Ithaca, NY: Cornell University Press, 2015), 18–19.

28. Ibid., 31–42. For more on the English comfort with enslaving and transporting POWs in this period, see Samantha Seeley, *Race, Removal, and the Right to Remain: Migration and the Making of the United States* (Chapel Hill, NC: University of North Carolina Press, 2021), 32; Michael L. Fickes, "'They Could Not Endure That Yoke': The Captivity of Pequot Women and Children after the War of 1637," *The New England Quarterly* 73, no. 1 (2000): 58–81, 61–62.

29. Englishmen's perceptions of the physical characteristics of various Indian peoples were mixed. Some colonizers believed native peoples had darker skin chiefly because of exposure to the sun and elements. See James E. Doan, "'An Island in the Virginian Sea': Native Americans and the Irish in English Discourse, 1585–1640," *New Hibernia Review/Iris Éireannach Nua* 1, no. 1 (1997): 79–99, 81. As Doan described, colonizers thought signs like native peoples' dress or weapons were more revealing about their nature. Not surprisingly, Englishmen drew on comparisons to the Irish – or at least the Irish of their imaginations.

30. As Newell wrote: "The Pequot War became a war of captivity because the English – in New England, the Atlantic, and the Caribbean – wanted workers at a time when several empires were engaged in a frenzy of competitive colonial establishment and expansion that pushed labor demands beyond what the supply of European servants could satisfy." Newell, *Brethren by Nature*, 42.

31. Michael Guasco, "To 'Doe Some Good upon Their Countrymen': The Paradox of Indian Slavery in Early Anglo-America," *Journal of Social History* 41, no. 2 (2007): 389–411.

32. Newell, *Brethren by Nature*, 37.

33. Alden T. Vaughan, *Roots of American Racism: Essays on the Colonial Experience* (Oxford: Oxford University Press, 1995), 41.

34. Jean M. O'Brien is excellent on colonizers' contemporary attempts to expunge Indigenous peoples, including the Pequot, from history. See Jean M. O'Brien, *Firsting and Lasting: Writing Indians Out of Existence in New England* (Minneapolis, MN: University of Minnesota Press, 2010), 156 and elsewhere. See also Newell, *Brethren by Nature*, 38.

35. O'Brien, *Firsting and Lasting*, 65.

36. At almost the same time, in 1621, the Dutch East India Company launched a campaign of total elimination of the nutmeg-cultivating Banda people (in today's Indonesia) who resisted their conquest. Directly or indirectly, the Dutch killed 2,800 and kidnapped 1,700 and trafficked them as slaves.

37. See the UN's definition: www.un.org/en/genocide-prevention/definition.
38. On the question of ethnic cleansing versus genocide – which is a matter of technical definition and *not* degree of inhumanity, see Michael Freeman, "Puritans and Pequots: The Question of Genocide," *The New England Quarterly* 68 (1995): 278–293.
39. Did James really say this? My trail through the sources ends in 1875, so I can't be certain. D.M., "Cromwell in Ireland," *The Irish Monthly* 3 (1875): 158–167, 159.
40. Michael Guasco, *Slaves and Englishmen: Human Bondage in the Early Modern Atlantic World* (Philadelphia, PA: University of Pennsylvania Press, 2017), 180–182; Guasco, "To 'Doe Some Good upon Their Countrymen,'" 389; Ann Marie Plane, *Colonial Intimacies: Indian Marriage in Early New England* (Ithaca, NY: Cornell University Press, 2000), 101 and elsewhere, where Plane shows similar motivations after King Philip's War.
41. Linda Colley wonderfully demonstrated this with a series of examples from North America, northwest Africa, and elsewhere in Linda Colley, *Captives: Britain, Empire, and the World, 1600–1850* (New York: Pantheon Books, 2002).
42. Alan Gallay, *Indian Slave Trade: The Rise of the English Empire in the American South, 1670–1717* (New Haven, CT: Yale University Press, 2002), 8. As Dr. Robbie Ethridge, an anthropologist and scholar of Mississippian native peoples, wrote, "Indians oftentimes used war captives in gift exchanges to broker peace and to secure alliances, among other things. And although in indigenous slavery most war captives became slaves, not all necessarily shared that fate: some were used in further exchanges, some were used as marriage partners, and some were adopted." See Robbie Ethridge, review of Brett Rushforth, *Bonds of Alliance: Indigenous and Atlantic Slaveries in New France*, *American Historical Review* 118 (October 2013), 1140.
43. Gallay, *Indian Slave Trade*.
44. Ibid., 6–7.
45. Brett Rushforth interview with historian Dr. Rebecca Onion quoted in Onion, "America's Other Original Sin," *Slate*, January 18, 2016.
46. Erin Woodruff Stone, "America's First Slave Revolt: Indians and African Slaves in Española, 1500–1534," *Ethnohistory* 60 (April 2013): 195–217. There may have been successful revolts in the same or even earlier years in what today is Panama. See Robert C. Schwaller, ed., *African Maroons in Sixteenth-Century Panama: A History in Documents* (Norman, OK: University of Oklahoma Press, 2021).
47. And it seems that that resistance, the frequency of Amerindians slipping away, hardened the English colonists' desire to make their captivity harsher and closer. Gallay, *Indian Slave Trade*, 90. For escapes in the

Caribbean, too, see Erin Woodruff Stone, *Captives of Conquest: Slavery in the Early Modern Spanish Caribbean* (Philadelphia, PA: University of Pennsylvania Press, 2021), chapter 6. For another example of successful escape to the hinterlands in the English Caribbean, see Alison Games, "'The Sanctuarye of our Rebell Negroes': The Atlantic Context of Local Resistance on Providence Island, 1630–1641," *Slavery and Abolition* 19 (December 1998): 1–21; Junius P. Rodriguez, ed., *Encyclopedia of Slave Resistance and Rebellion*, vol. 2 (Westport, CT: Greenwood, 2007), 579–580. It's a grim fact, too, that some Amerindians who made wealth from slave-raiding *for* the English could, in turn, be kidnapped *by* the English at a later date. See Denise I. Bossy, *The Yamasee Indians: From Florida to South Carolina* (Lincoln, NE: University of Nebraska Press, 2018), 3–4.

48. Lawrence A. Clayton, *Bartolomé de Las Casas and the Conquest of the Americas* (Chichester: Wiley-Blackwell, 2011); Henry Kamen, *Philip of Spain* (New Haven, CT: Yale University Press, 1997), 33, 61.

49. José Lingna Nafafé, *Lourenço Da Silva Mendonça and the Black Atlantic Abolitionist Movement in the Seventeenth Century* (Cambridge: Cambridge University Press, 2022).

50. Guasco, "To 'Doe Some Good upon Their Countrymen.'" For the "Golden Rule," see Jack P. Greene, "'A Plain and Natural Right to Life and Liberty': An Early Natural Rights Attack on the Excesses of the Slave System in Colonial British America," *The William and Mary Quarterly* 57, no. 4 (2000): 793–808, 793.

51. Karen Ordahl Kupperman, *Providence Island, 1630–1641: The Other Puritan Colony* (Cambridge: Cambridge University Press, 1993), 168; Alison Games, *Web of Empire: English Cosmopolitans in an Age of Expansion, 1560–1660* (Oxford: Oxford University Press, 2008), 176.

52. Kupperman, *Providence Island*, 166.

53. Christopher Leslie Brown, *Moral Capital: Foundations of British Abolitionism* (Chapel Hill, NC: University of North Carolina Press, 2006), 42. And yet Rhode Island rolled this back in later decades to facilitate participation in the trade itself. Things shifted. Christy Clark-Pujara, *Dark Work: The Business of Slavery in Rhode Island* (New York: New York University Press, 2018), 11.

54. Katharine Gerbner, "Writing against Slavery: Germantown, Quakers, and the Ethnic Origins of Early Antislavery Thought," in Bethany Wiggin, ed., *Babel of the Atlantic* (Philadelphia, PA: Penn State University Press, 2019), 176 and elsewhere. I've offered just an illustrative handful of anti-slavery statements. I direct readers to an account of a 1710 tract in Greene, "'A Plain and Natural Right to Life and Liberty.'"

55. Guasco, "To 'Doe Some Good upon Their Countrymen,'" 391–392.

56. Guasco, *Slaves and Englishmen*, 14.

57. Michael L. Fickes reminded readers that Englishmen were still being enslaved for crimes in the first half of the seventeenth century in New England, but that such sentences were clearly temporary. He wrote that after the Body of Liberties legal code was published in 1641, references to English slaves essentially ended, replaced by West African and Indian slaves. See Fickes "'They Could Not Endure That Yoke,'" 78.

58. Newell, *Brethren by Nature*, 47.

59. Virginia Bernhard, *Slaves and Slaveholders in Bermuda, 1616–1782* (Columbia, MO: University of Missouri Press, 1999), 49–93, and 65 in particular.

60. Heather Miyano Kopelson, *Faithful Bodies: Performing Religion and Race in the Puritan Atlantic* (New York: New York University Press, 2016), 154; Guasco, *Slaves and Englishmen*, 168.

61. Newell, *Brethren by Nature*, 48.

62. Gerbier's 1660 *A summary description manifesting that greater profits are to bee done in the hott then in the could [sic] parts off the coast off America*, quoted in Eric Otremba, "Enlightened Institutions: Science, Plantations, and Slavery in the English Atlantic, 1626–1700" (Dissertation, Minneapolis, University of Minnesota, 2012), 226.

63. Otremba, "Enlightened Institutions," 226–227.

64. Robin Blackburn, *The Making of New World Slavery: From the Baroque to the Modern, 1492–1800* (London: Verso, 1997), 239.

65. Guasco, "To 'Doe Some Good upon Their Countrymen,'" 395.

66. Virginia Assembly, quoted in Vaughan, *Roots of American Racism*, 59.

67. Nancy Shoemaker, *A Strange Likeness: Becoming Red and White in Eighteenth-Century North America* (Oxford: Oxford University Press, 2004), 129.

68. Ibid., 130.

69. Guasco, *Slaves and Englishmen*, 182.

70. Georgia's founders didn't appear to ban slaveholding on the principle of equality. See Thomas Hart Wilkins, "James Edward Oglethorpe: South Carolina Slaveholder?" *The Georgia Historical Quarterly* 88 (2004): 85–94.

71. Guasco, *Slaves and Englishmen*, 173.

72. Anthony Shoplik and Jeffrey Glover, "James Indian, 'Answers': An Indigenous Freedom Suit in Massachusetts Bay," *The New England Quarterly* 95, no. 1 (2022): 66–84.

73. Ibid., "James Indian," 71.

74. Ibid., "James Indian," 72.
75. Miranda Kaufmann, "English Common Law, Slavery and," in Eric Martone, ed., *Encyclopedia of Blacks in European History and Culture*, vol. I (Westport, CT: Greenwood Press, 2008): 200–203.
76. George van Cleve, "'Somerset's Case' and Its Antecedents in Imperial Perspective," *Law and History Review* 24, no. 3 (2006): 601–646, 604 and elsewhere.
77. This was the 1720 Yorke–Talbot slavery opinion of the Attorney General and Solicitor General.
78. Historian Lee Wilson showed that, although new laws in American colonies were innovations, making what had formerly been a group of unfortunate people "property," slaveholders defended this time and again using ancient English laws re-affirmed by English/British judges. In other words, while there was essentially no chattel slavery in Britain, British judges repeatedly confirmed British subjects' "rights" to treat humans as property abroad. Don't let the English off the hook as being somehow guiltless of American slaveholding. See Lee B. Wilson, *Bonds of Empire: The English Origins of Slave Law in South Carolina and British Plantation America, 1660–1783* (Cambridge: Cambridge University Press, 2021), 15, 23, and elsewhere.
79. Who commented on England's "free air" and when is a bit complicated, but it entered the legal conversation from the 1640s. For commentary by an early modern legal historian, see Krista J. Kesselring, "Slavery and Cartwright's Case before Somerset," https://legalhistorymiscellany.com/2018/10/10/slavery-and-cart wrights-case-before-somerset.
80. Taunya Lovell Banks, "Dangerous Woman: Elizabeth Key's Freedom Suit – Subjecthood and Racialized Identity in Seventeenth Century Colonial Virginia," *Akron Law Review* 41, no. 3 (2008): 799–837, 811–812 and elsewhere. Historian Jennifer Morgan tells and contextualizes this story, as well. See Jennifer L. Morgan, *Reckoning with Slavery: Gender, Kinship, and Capitalism in the Early Black Atlantic* (Durham, NC: Duke University Press, 2021), Introduction.
81. It's getting ahead of ourselves here, but ultimately, we'll see later how the Supreme Court of the eventual USA put a total and unmistakable stop to any possibility of freedom suits by people deemed "Black." In 1857, it said the US Constitution never intended to include slave-descended people in its rights and citizenship. For the Dred Scott v. Sandford decision, March 1857, see www.law.cornell.edu/supre mecourt/text/60/393.
82. Ira Berlin, *Many Thousands Gone: The First Two Centuries of Slavery in North America* (Cambridge, MA: Belknap Press of Harvard University Press, 1998), 26. Russell R. Menard reminded historians

that slavery and indenture on Barbados preceded the sugar revolution, which helped them to see that slavery in its deeper historical context rather than as a part of the explosive expansion of sugar cultivation. That's important. But he also showed the massive pace of growth of enslaved labor later. See Russell R. Menard, *Sweet Negotiations: Sugar, Slavery, and Plantation Agriculture in Early Barbados* (Charlottesville, VA: University of Virginia Press, 2006). To a limited scope, there was slavery for criminals, POWs, and others in West Africa prior to large-scale European trafficking, too. But these slaves had certain right and privileges and were not a perpetual class. See Paul E. Lovejoy, *Transformations in Slavery: A History of Slavery in Africa*, 3rd ed. (Cambridge: Cambridge University Press, 2012), 8–18.

83. Holly Brewer, "Slavery, Sovereignty, and 'Inheritable Blood': Reconsidering John Locke and the Origins of American Slavery," *American Historical Review* 122, no. 4 (October 2017): 1038–1078, 1038.

84. The story is told by many, but Berlin's is a good example. See Berlin, *Many Thousands Gone*, chapter 1. Meanwhile, consider this article describing how apologists for European slavery have abused this story: Tyler Parry, "The Curious History of Anthony Johnson: From Captive African to Right-Wing Talking Point," *Black Perspective* (July 2019), www.aaihs.org/the-curious-history-of-anthony-johnson-from-captive-african-to-right-wing-talking-point.

85. Berlin, *Many Thousands Gone*, 34. Casor once claimed he'd been indentured for only seven years and Johnson was holding him captive past his term. See Alejandro de la Fuente, *Becoming Free, Becoming Black: Race, Freedom, and Law in Cuba, Virginia, and Louisiana* (Cambridge: Cambridge University Press, 2021), 14.

86. Ibid., *Becoming Free, Becoming Black*, 15.

87. Richard S. Dunn, *Sugar and Slaves: The Rise of the Planter Class in the English West Indies, 1624–1713* (New York: Norton, 1972), 123; Stuart M. Nisbet, "Early Scottish Sugar Planters in the Leeward Islands, c. 1660–1740," in T. M. Devine, ed., *Recovering Scotland's Slavery Past: The Caribbean Connection* (Edinburgh: Edinburgh University Press, 2015), 62–81, 62.

88. Lorena Walsh, "Slave Life, Slave Society, and Tobacco Production in the Tidewater Chesapeake, 1620–1820," in Ira Berlin and Philip D. Morgan, eds., *Cultivation and Culture: Labor and the Shaping of Slave Life in the Americas* (Charlottesville, VA: University of Virginia Press, 1993), 170–199, 177–178.

89. Howard W. French, *Born in Blackness: Africa, Africans, and the Making of the Modern World, 1471 to the Second World War* (New York: Liveright, 2021), 209.

90. Nisbet, "Early Scottish Sugar Planters in the Leeward Islands," 63–64; Hilary Beckles, *A History of Barbados: From Amerindian Settlement to Nation-State* (Cambridge: Cambridge University Press, 1990), 30–31; Hilary McD. Beckles and Andrew Downes, "The Economics of Transition to the Black Labor System in Barbados, 1630–1680," *The Journal of Interdisciplinary History* 18 (1987): 225–247.

91. John F Richards, *The Unending Frontier: An Environmental History of the Early Modern World* (Berkeley, CA: University of California Press, 2003), 328.

92. Georgia Lynne Fox, *An Archaeology and History of a Caribbean Sugar Plantation on Antigua* (Gainesville, FL: University of Florida Press, 2020), 162.

93. Edward E. Baptist, "Toward a Political Economy of Slave Labor: Hands, Whipping-Machines, and Modern Power," in Sven Beckert and Seth Rockman, eds., *Slavery's Capitalism: A New History of American Economic Development* (Philadelphia, PA: University of Pennsylvania Press, 2016), 31–61, 56.

94. Historian Michael Tadman painstakingly analyzed the demographics of the enslaved in New World sugar-growing areas. It's a complicated mix of factors, but he summarized it like this: "sugar planters, as we have seen, combined extreme labor demands with a long-term insistence on a predominantly male work force, and the combination of burdens they imposed was lethal. The Louisiana case shows that sugar produced natural decrease even when the labor force was American-born. Where (in Brazil or Jamaica, for example) sugar planters bought their slaves from Africa, natural decrease would have been even worse than in Louisiana. Sugar and the Atlantic slave trade represented the worst of all worlds – the extreme demands of the sugar plantation, the urge to import (so as to maintain a male-dominated labor force), and the intensive sucking of Africans into an unfamiliar, and therefore hostile, disease environment." See Michael Tadman, "The Demographic Cost of Sugar: Debates on Slave Societies and Natural Increase in the Americas," *The American Historical Review* 105 (2000): 1534–1575, 1561.

95. Anna Suranyi, *Indentured Servitude: Unfree Labour and Citizenship in the British Colonies* (Montreal: McGill-Queen's Press, 2021), 142–144.

96. Rachel A. Feinstein, *When Rape Was Legal: The Untold History of Sexual Violence during Slavery* (Oxford: Routledge, 2018), 5–6.

97. Bernhard, *Slaves and Slaveholders in Bermuda*, 66.

98. Excellent historians carry on a good debate about the relative degree of daily acts of resistance versus simmering rebellions. I advise readers not to see either as greater or lesser proof of the individualism,

humanity, courage, measure of daily hardship, etc. of the enslaved. See Jason T. Sharples, "Discovering Slave Conspiracies: New Fears of Rebellion and Old Paradigms of Plotting in Seventeenth-Century Barbados," *American Historical Review* 120, no. 3 (June 2015): 811–843; on the relatively few incidents of armed uprising, see 842–843; for the historians' debate, 816.

99. For a helpful list, see Joseph E. Holloway, "Slave Insurrections in the United States: An Overview," http://slaverebellion.info/index.php?page=united-states-insurrections. For a map, see http://slaverebellion.info/index.php?page=maps.

100. Edmund S. Morgan, *American Slavery, American Freedom*, reissue ed. (New York: W. W. Norton & Company, 2003), 591; Ethan A. Schmidt, "Cockacoeske, Weroansqua of the Pamunkeys, and Indian Resistance in Seventeenth-Century Virginia," *The American Indian Quarterly* 36, no. 3 (2012): 288–317, 288 and throughout.

101. Morgan, *American Slavery, American Freedom*, 270, 327, and elsewhere.

102. Wendy Warren, *New England Bound: Slavery and Colonization in Early America* (New York: Liveright, 2016), 190.

103. James Baldwin, "The White Problem," in Robert A. Goodwin, ed., *100 Years of Emancipation* (Skokie, IL: Rand McNally, 1964).

104. Kay Wright Lewis, *A Curse upon the Nation: Race, Freedom, and Extermination in America and the Atlantic World* (Athens, GA: University of Georgia Press, 2019), 34 and elsewhere.

105. Thomas Jefferson, *Notes on the State of Virginia* (1784), chapter 15, https://press-pubs.uchicago.edu/founders/documents/v1ch15s28.html.

106. Bernhard, *Slaves and Slaveholders in Bermuda*, 91.

107. Menard, *Sweet Negotiations*, 112.

108. Oscar Williams, *African Americans and Colonial Legislation in the Middle Colonies* (Oxford: Routledge, 2014), chapter 4.

109. Governor William Gooch to Alured Popple, May 18, 1736, reprinted in Emory G. Evans, "A Question of Complexion: Documents Concerning the Negro and the Franchise in Eighteenth-Century Virginia," *Virginia Magazine of History and Biography* 71, no. 4 (October 1963): 411–415, 414.

110. For a good overview of slave codes and other tactical developments based on fear and "the security of property," see Juan F. Perea, "Policing the Boundaries of the White Republic: From Slave Codes to Mass Deportation," in Kathleen Belew and Ramón A. Gutiérrez, eds., *A Field Guide to White Supremacy* (Berkeley, CA: University of California Press, 2021), 61–84.

111. There are many examples of fear-based torture and killing, but, for some examples, see Andy Doolen, "Reading and Writing Terror: The

New York Conspiracy Trials of 1741," *American Literary History* 16, no. 3 (2004): 377–406; Deborah Gray White, *Ar'n't I a Woman?: Female Slaves in the Plantation South*, revised ed. (New York: W. W. Norton & Company, 1999), 64; Wilma A. Dunaway, *Slavery in the American Mountain South, Studies in Modern Capitalism* (Cambridge: Cambridge University Press, 2003), 168–172.

112. Edward B. Rugemer, "The Development of Mastery and Race in the Comprehensive Slave Codes of the Greater Caribbean during the Seventeenth Century," *William and Mary Quarterly* 70, no. 3 (July 2013): 429–458.

113. Very talented scholars look at the evidence and date color- or race-based slavery (and, practically, color- or race-based "mastery") to the turn of the nineteenth century, not the eighteenth. I believe that's an outlying date, but the point is that good scholars can disagree. In any case, it's worth taking very seriously that the transition may have happened quite slowly or at different paces in different areas or contexts. See Allyson Hobbs, *A Chosen Exile: A History of Racial Passing in American Life* (Cambridge, MA: Harvard University Press, 2014), 36.

114. Morgan Godwyn, *The Negroes Advocate, Suing for Their Admission into the Church* (London: J.D., 1680), 36.

115. De la Fuente, *Becoming Free, Becoming Black*, 15–16.

116. Richard Maguire, *Africans in East Anglia, 1467–1833* (Woodbridge: Boydell & Brewer, 2021), 99–100.

117. William A. Pettigrew, *Freedom's Debt: The Royal African Company and the Politics of the Atlantic Slave Trade, 1672–1752* (Chapel Hill, NC: University of North Carolina Press, 2013), 11–12.

118. For a good introduction to the historiography of racial capitalism, see the introduction to Destin Jenkins and Justin Leroy, eds., *Histories of Racial Capitalism* (New York: Columbia University Press, 2021).

119. Richard Baxter, *Baxter's directions to slave-holders, revived; first printed in London, in the year 1673: To which is subjoined, a letter from the worthy Anthony Benezet . . .* (Philadelphia, PA: Francis Bailey, 1785), 6–7.

120. George Keith and Christian Quakers, *An exhortation & caution to Friends concerning buying or keeping of Negroes* (Philadelphia, PA: William Bradford, 1693), https://quod.lib.umich.edu/e/evans/N00510.0001.001/1:1?rgn=div1;view=fulltext. On this subject and a 1688 statement against slavery by German and Dutch colonists in Pennsylvania, see Katharine Gerbner, "Writing against Slavery: Germantown, Quakers, and the Ethnic Origins of Early Antislavery Thought," in Bethany Wiggin, ed., *Babel of the Atlantic* (Philadelphia, PA: Penn State University Press, 2019), 175–198.

121. William Snelgrave, *A new account of some parts of Guinea, and the slave-trade* (London: P. Knapton, 1734), 160.
122. Samuel Sewall, *The Selling of Joseph: A Memorial* (Boston, MA: Bartholomew Green and John Allen, 1700), https://digitalcommons .unl.edu/cgi/viewcontent.cgi?article=1026&context=etas. Sewall was hardly humane: he was implicated in the Salem Witch Trials and had prejudiced things to say about Africans. But he was categorical in saying that slavery was wrong, against nature and Christianity, and Africans equally human.

Chapter 3: Defining Whiteness through the "Enlightenment," 1600–1800

1. German-speakers used their term for the Enlightenment, *die Aufklärung*, more contemporaneously than English speakers, with Kant publishing the essay *Was ist Aufklärung?* in 1784.
2. For historical writings about how race was still skin-deep, changeable, or conditional around 1600, see Ivan Hannaford, *Race: The History of an Idea in the West* (Baltimore, MD: Johns Hopkins University Press, 1996), 168–173.
3. Efram Sera-Shriar, *Founding the Sciences of Man: The Observational Practices of James Cowles Prichard and William Lawrence* (Pittsburgh, PA: University of Pittsburgh Press, 2016), 29.
4. Dominique Tombal, "Le polygénisme aux XVIIᵉ et XVIIIᵉ siècles: De la critique biblique à l'idéologie raciste," *Revue Belge de Philologie et d'Histoire* 71, no. 4 (1993): 850–874, 850–857.
5. Terence D. Keel, "Religion, Polygenism and the Early Science of Human Origins," *History of the Human Sciences* 26 (2013): 3–32.
6. Siep Stuurman, "François Bernier and the Invention of Racial Classification," *History Workshop Journal* 50 (October 1, 2000): 1–21, 1, see especially note 5. Other near contemporaries doing similar things were Henri de Boulainvilliers (1658–1722) and Georges-Louis Leclerc, the Comte de Buffon (1707–1788).
7. Stuurman, "François Bernier and the Invention of Racial Classification," 4.
8. Ibid., 2. See also Pierre H. Boulle, "François Bernier and the Origins of the Modern Concept of Race," in Sue Peabody, ed., *The Color of Liberty: Histories of Race in France* (Durham, NC: Duke University Press, 2006), 11–27, 12 and elsewhere.
9. Hannaford, *Race*, 205.
10. Bruce Baum, *The Rise and Fall of the Caucasian Race: A Political History of Racial Identity* (New York: New York University Press, 2006), 59.

11. William Petty, "The Scale of Animals," in *The Petty Papers: Some Unpublished Writings of Sir William Petty*, vol. 2 (New York: A. M. Kelley, 1967), 21–34, 31.

12. Emmanuel Chukwudi Eze, "Hume, Race, and Human Nature," *Journal of the History of Ideas* 61, no. 4 (2000): 691–698, 691–692.

13. Deborah K. Heikes, "Race and the Copernican Turn," *The Journal of Mind and Behavior* 36, no. 3/4 (Fall 2015): 139–163, 152. Kant believed there was one human animal, but that lesser races of that animal had appeared through what he called "degeneration." For Kant's race-thinking, there are many sources, but an excellent start is Emmanuel Chukwudi Eze's "The Color of Reason: The Idea of 'Race' in Kant's Anthropology," *The Bucknell Review* (Special Issue on Anthropology and the German Enlightenment, ed. Katherine M. Faull), 38 (1995): 201–241.

14. Christopher L. Miller, *The French Atlantic Triangle: Literature and Culture of the Slave Trade* (Durham, NC: Duke University Press, 2008), 63 and elsewhere.

15. Miles Ogborn and Victoria Pickering examined how Sloane approached and organized his colonial collecting. See Miles Ogborn and Victoria Pickering, "The World in a Nicknackatory: Encounters and Exchanges in Hans Sloane's Collection," in Adriana Craciun and Mary Terrall, eds., *Curious Encounters: Voyaging, Collecting, and Making Knowledge in the Long Eighteenth Century* (Toronto: University of Toronto Press, 2019): 113–138.

16. James Delbourgo, *Collecting the World: The Life and Curiosity of Hans Sloane* (London: Allen Lane, 2017), 43. Thanks very much to Professor Ted McCormick for this and other references in this section.

17. Ibid., 51.

18. Ibid., 58–59.

19. Mark Govier, "The Royal Society, Slavery and the Island of Jamaica: 1660–1700," *Notes and Records of the Royal Society of London* 53, no. 2 (1999): 203–217, 209 and elsewhere. For Sloane's investment, see https://reconstructingsloane.org/wp-content/uploads/2021/01/Case-14-Labels.pdf.

20. Thomas McCarthy, *Race, Empire, and the Idea of Human Development* (Cambridge: Cambridge University Press, 2009), 25. McCarthy points out that, while Locke was a founding shareholder in the company, Locke also wrote that "slavery is so vile and miserable an estate of man, and so directly opposite to the generous temper and courage of our nation, that 'tis hardly to be conceived that an Englishman, much less a gentleman, should plead for it." Cited from Peter Laslett, ed., *Locke: Two Treatises of Government* (Cambridge: Cambridge University Press, 1988), 141. Some nations (races) were naturally the opposite of slaves, it seems, while others were not.

21. For more on Locke's role in Shaftesbury's colonial project and slavery, see Robert Bernasconi and Anika Maaza Mann, "The Contradictions of Racism: Locke, Slavery, and the Two Treatises," in Andrew Valls, ed., *Race and Racism in Modern Philosophy* (Ithaca, NY: Cornell University Press, 2005): 89–107.

22. Ibid., 92.

23. Brad Hinshelwood, "The Carolinian Context of John Locke's Theory of Slavery," *Political Theory* 41, no. 4 (August 2013): 562–590, 577.

24. Anthony Pagden, "The Struggle for Legitimacy and the Image of Empire in the Atlantic to c. 1700," in Alaine Low, Nicholas Canny, and Wm Roger Louis, eds., *The Oxford History of the British Empire*, vol. I: *The Origins of Empire: British Overseas Enterprise to the Close of the Seventeenth Century* (Oxford: Oxford University Press, 1998), 34–54, 43.

25. Speaking of the Royal African Company, other investors transmuted its slave-trade profits into Enlightenment art and science. A major investor and practically one of the company's heads, the Duke of Chandos, provided a church position and regular income to British Enlightenment figure John Theophilus Desaguliers. In the early eighteenth century, Desaguliers studied engineering, hydraulics, and physics as an assistant to Isaac Newton. (He might have interacted with another Chandos benefactor and investor in the Royal African Company, George Frederic Handel, when Handel premiered a water-themed piece before one of Desaguliers's fountains/waterworks.) See Audrey T. Carpenter, *John Theophilus Desaguliers: A Natural Philosopher, Engineer and Freemason in Newtonian England* (London: Bloomsbury, 2011), 158–159; David Hunter, "Handel and the Royal African Company," *Musicology Now* (June 2015), https://musicologynow.org/handel-and-the-royal-african-company. More broadly, historian Stephanie Barczewski did a tremendous job of showing how slavery-connected wealth both led to land investments in England and Scotland with "country houses" built thereon and contributed to the symbolic decorating of those houses with colonial motifs. This country-house building peaked roughly at the same time as British-borne human trafficking toward the end to the eighteenth century. See Stephanie Barczewski, *Country Houses and the British Empire, 1700–1930* (Manchester: Manchester University Press, 2014). Chandos's patronage of Desaguliers wasn't entirely academic. Desaguliers consulted on schemes for importing West African resources and questions related to gold mining. See Larry R. Stewart, *The Rise of Public Science: Rhetoric, Technology, and Natural Philosophy in Newtonian Britain* (Cambridge: Cambridge University Press, 1992), 216, 320, 324; Patricia Fara, *Life after Gravity: Isaac Newton's*

London Career (Oxford: Oxford University Press, 2021), 97. And, while Hans Sloane wasn't on the duke's payroll, Sloane was a fellow stockholder in the company, and Chandos recruited him to investigate West African plant specimens in search of preventatives for smallpox and other illness that struck European slavers and miners on the African coast. See Stewart, *The Rise of Public Science*, 321–322.

26. Patricia Springborg, "Hobbes, Donne and the Virginia Company: 'Terra Nullius' and 'the Bulimia of Dominium,'" *History of Political Thought* 36, no. 1 (2015): 113–164.

27. Eric Otremba, "Enlightened Institutions: Science, Plantations, and Slavery in the English Atlantic, 1626–1700" (Dissertation, Minneapolis, University of Minnesota, 2012), 51, 65, 68–69, 89, 230–231. Otremba notes on page 88 that Boyle may have invested in a Barbadian colonial enterprise, but it's not certain. See John D. Burton, "Crimson Missionaries: The Robert Boyle Legacy and Harvard College," *New England Quarterly* 67, no. 1 (1994): 132–140.

28. James Robertson, "Eighteenth-Century Jamaica's Ambivalent Cosmopolitanism," *History* 99, no. 4 (2014): 607–631.

29. D. J. Bryden, "The Jamaican Observatories of Colin Campbell, F.R.S. and Alexander Macfarlane, F.R.S.," *Notes and Records of the Royal Society of London* 24 (1970): 261–272.

30. Will of Colin Campbell, within UK National Archives file PROB 11/793, transcribed at https://web.archive.org/web/20250306151205/http:/www.jamaicanfamilysearch.com/Members/wills-18.htm.

31. Center for the Study of the Legacies of British Slavery Database, University College London, https://www.ucl.ac.uk/lbs/person/view/2146644157; Bryden, "The Jamaican Observatories," 265.

32. As Bernardin de Saint Pierre, a friend of Rousseau, wrote in 1818, "I am sorry that philosophers who combat abuses with so much courage, have hardly spoken of Negro slavery except to joke about it." For Rousseau, see John Christman, "Rousseau's Silence on Trans-Atlantic Slavery: Philosophical Implications," *European Journal of Philosophy* 30, no. 4 (2022): 1458–1472.

33. Devin J. Vartija, *The Color of Equality: Race and Common Humanity in Enlightenment Thought* (Philadelphia, PA: University of Pennsylvania Press, 2021), 100 and many other places.

34. For this, too, readers should refer to Tyler Stovall, *White Freedom: The Racial History of an Idea* (Princeton, NJ: Princeton University Press, 2021).

35. For contemporary concepts of serf, slave, bondsman, etc., see Betty Wood, *The Origins of American Slavery: Freedom and Bondage in the English Colonies* (New York: Hill and Wang, 1998), 9–19.

36. Gerrard Winstanley, Iohn Baker, and Thomas Star, "An Appeal to the House of Commons," https://quod.lib.umich.edu/e/eebo/ A96689.0001.001?view=toc.

37. Iain McLean, "Before and after Publius: The Sources and Influences of Madison's Political Thought," in Samuel Kernell, ed., *James Madison: The Theory and Practice of Republican Government* (Stanford, CA: Stanford University Press, 2005), 14–40, 18.

38. Historian Holly Brewer put it well in a terrific essay: "slavery was anchored in hierarchical and feudal principles that connected property in land to property in people, principles that were bent to new forms in England and its empire by Stuart kings. By the late 1670s, it was distinguished in the West Indies by a separate legal system that stripped people of their rights, and that had many components (such as slaves' inability to testify against masters). Slavery was created in bits and pieces. Liberalism emerged in reaction to such principles – and not simply in the writings of Locke, though his writings provide a convenient window into that conflict. Liberalism emerged in opposition to slavery and absolutism." Holly Brewer, "Slavery, Sovereignty, and 'Inheritable Blood': Reconsidering John Locke and the Origins of American Slavery," *American Historical Review* 122, no. 4 (October 2017): 1038–1078, 1043.

39. David Eltis, *The Rise of African Slavery in the Americas* (Cambridge: Cambridge University Press, 2000), 5–12, 42–46, and elsewhere.

40. Michael Guasco, *Slaves and Englishmen: Human Bondage in the Early Modern Atlantic World* (Philadelphia, PA: University of Pennsylvania Press, 2017), 170.

41. Christopher L. Miller, *The French Atlantic Triangle: Literature and Culture of the Slave Trade* (Durham, NC: Duke University Press, 2008), 69–70 and elsewhere.

42. Russell R. Menard, *Sweet Negotiations: Sugar, Slavery, and Plantation Agriculture in Early Barbados* (Charlottesville, VA: University of Virginia Press, 2014), 58 and elsewhere.

43. Anthony W. Marx, *Making Race and Nation: A Comparison of South Africa, the United States, and Brazil* (Cambridge: Cambridge University Press, 1998), 2.

44. Joep Leerssen, *National Thought in Europe: A Cultural History*, 3rd revised ed. (Amsterdam: Amsterdam University Press, 2018), 222.

45. For one example, Michael Dietler described how eighteenth-century French elites invented a politically expedient ancient Frank. See Michael Dietler, "'Our Ancestors the Gauls': Archaeology, Ethnic Nationalism, and the Manipulation of Celtic Identity in Modern Europe," *American Anthropologist* 96, no. 3 (1994): 584–605, 587 and elsewhere. See also Baum, *The Rise and Fall of the Caucasian Race*, 123, 132–133; Hannaford, *Race*, 235–236, 251 and many other places.

46. Bronwen Douglas, *Foreign Bodies: Oceania and the Science of Race 1750–1940* (Canberra: Australian National University Press, 2008), 38 and elsewhere. Blumenbach claimed that a colonial governor of Virginia had already made skull comparisons before 1622, per Hannaford, *Race*, 205.

47. David Hume, *Of National Characters*, Essay XXI (1748).

48. Immanuel Kant, "Observations on the Feeling of the Beautiful and Sublime" (1764), in Emmanuel Chukwudi Eze, ed., *Race and the Enlightenment: A Reader* (Oxford: Blackwell, 1997), 49–55.

49. María José Mora and María José Gómez-Calderón, "The Study of Old English in America (1776–1850): National Uses of the Saxon Past," *The Journal of English and Germanic Philology* 97, no. 3 (1998): 322–336, 323.

50. Andrew Galloway, "William Cullen Bryant's American Antiquities: Medievalism, Miscegenation, and Race in 'The Prairies,'" *American Literary History* 22, no. 4 (2010): 724–751, 726 and elsewhere. See also "Letter of John Adams to Abigail Adams, 14 August 1776," https://masshist.org/digitaladams/archive/doc?id=L17760814ja.

51. Benjamin Franklin, *Observations Concerning the Increase of Mankind, Peopling of Countries, etc.* (1751). For an excellent analysis of this and the broader role of Anglo-Saxon race-thinking in America in this period and its brutal consequences, see Kelly Brown Douglas, *Stand Your Ground: Black Bodies and the Justice of God* (Maryknoll, NY: Orbis, 2015), chapter 1.

52. Baum, *The Rise and Fall of the Caucasian Race*, 98.

53. Neil Davidson, *Nation-States: Consciousness and Competition* (Chicago, IL: Haymarket, 2016), chapter 3.

54. For a good statement of the nature of race nationalism, see Ann Laura Stoler, *Race and the Education of Desire: Foucault's History of Sexuality and the Colonial Order of Things* (Durham, NC: Duke University Press, 1995), 92–94.

55. "The modern state, in short, is nothing less than a racial state," wrote David Theo Goldberg, *The Racial State* (Oxford: Blackwell, 2002), 2.

56. Richard McMahon, *The Races of Europe: Construction of National Identities in the Social Sciences, 1839–1939* (London: Palgrave Macmillan, 2016), chapter 4. While I respectfully disagree, and instead see its beginnings around the time of the Glorious Revolution, when Englishmen forcefully asserted the idea that the monarch serves at the pleasure of Parliament (the "people") followed by the Americans' (more English than English) revolt, Ivan Hannaford argues that it was later in the nineteenth century that "state and nation [became] co-terminous and co-extensive with the single, exclusive idea of race." See Hannaford, *Race*, 255.

57. *Federalist Papers* no. 2 text, https://avalon.law.yale.edu/18th_century/fed02.asp.

58. Paine was making the case, stronger than most, for a hard break from Britain, after all; so, the argument that Americans were simply far-flung Britons didn't make sense. Thomas Paine, "Thoughts on the Present State of American Affairs," *Common Sense* 3rd ed. (Philadelphia, PA: Bell, 1776).

59. Kathleen Wilson, *The Island Race: Englishness, Empire and Gender in the Eighteenth Century* (London: Routledge, 2003), 12.

60. Gregory D. Smithers, *Science, Sexuality, and Race in the United States and Australia, 1780–1940* (Lincoln, NE: University of Nebraska Press, 2017), 29.

61. J. V. Lynch, "The Limits of Revolutionary Radicalism: Tom Paine and Slavery," *Pennsylvania Magazine of History and Biography* 123, no. 3 (July 1999): 177–199, 180, 189.

62. Jacob Rader Marcus, *United States Jewry 1776–1985*, vol. 3 (Detroit, MI: Wayne State University Press, 1993), 1121–1122, 1126.

63. Edward Long, *The History of Jamaica: Or, General Survey of the Antient and Modern State of That Island* (London: T. Lowndes, 1774), 27; Catherine Hall, *Lucky Valley: Edward Long and the History of Racial Capitalism* (Cambridge: Cambridge University Press, 2024).

64. Frederic Cople Jaher, *A Scapegoat in the New Wilderness* (Cambridge, MA: Harvard University Press, 1994), chapters 3–4.

65. Ibid., 123 and many other places.

66. See Eli Faber, *Jews, Slaves, and the Slave Trade: Setting the Record Straight* (New York: New York University Press, 1998), including the population figures in his appendices.

67. It's true that this divide wasn't always perfectly clear in the details, given Cherokee slaveholding and Black freemen slaveholding. White slaveholding utterly dwarfed these others. And, to a significant degree, Black slaveholding came down to Black freemen "freeing" their families by purchasing them; emancipating them was often sharply restricted by colonial or state governments, and in some places freemen were barred from remaining in place after emancipation. See David L. Lightner and Alexander M. Ragan, "Were African American Slaveholders Benevolent or Exploitative? A Quantitative Approach," *The Journal of Southern History* 71, no. 3 (2005): 535–558.

68. Cristina Malcolmson, *Studies of Skin Color in the Early Royal Society: Boyle, Cavendish, Swift* (Oxford: Routledge, 2016), 5.

69. Ibid., chapter 4.

70. Ibid., chapter 6.

71. Craig Koslofsky, "Superficial Blackness?: Johann Nicolas Pechlin's *De Habitu et Colore Aethiopum Qui Vulgo Nigritae* (1677)," *Journal for Early Modern Cultural Studies* 18, no. 1 (2018): 140–158.

72. Nathaniel Appleton, *Considerations on slavery. In a letter to a friend* (Boston: Edes and Gill, 1767), 19.

73. Charles W. Mills, *The Racial Contract*, 2nd ed. (Ithaca, NY: Cornell University Press, 2022), 94.

PART II: Redefining the "Master" and Inventing the White Man's Burden

1. Rudyard Kipling, "The White Man's Burden," *McClure's Magazine* 12 (February 1899), n.p.

Chapter 4: The Empire of Whiteness, 1600–1830s

1. It's rather clear that China's Ming dynasty of the early 1400s had more than enough power and technology to colonize overseas – far more ability, frankly, than the Spaniards who sailed west a century later. The Ming emperor sent vast fleets across the Indian Ocean and across what today is Indonesia to collect tribute and perform diplomacy. But particular circumstances of imperial court politics ended such voyages. Meanwhile, around 1480, the Incan emperor Tupac Inca Yupanqui ordered the creation of a vast flotilla of sailing ships and explored westward for a year with a retinue of some thousands. He explored the Galápagos chain, most likely, and perhaps Easter Island and others. He brought back treasures, oddities, and some captives, but lacked practical motivations to colonize in the European fashion.

2. "East Indies: January 1601," in W. Noel Sainsbury, ed., *Calendar of State Papers Colonial, East Indies, China and Japan*, vol. 2: *1513–1616* (London: Her Majesty's Stationery Office, 1864), 118–121, www.british-history.ac.uk/cal-state-papers/colonial/east-indies-china-japan/vol2/pp118-121.

3. For a high-quality, broad background see Atul Kohli, *Imperialism and the Developing World: How Britain and the United States Shaped the Global Periphery* (Oxford: Oxford University Press, 2020), chapter 1.

4. Ron Harris, *Going the Distance: Eurasian Trade and the Rise of the Business Corporation, 1400–1700* (Princeton, NJ: Princeton University Press, 2020), chapter 11.

5. P. Bruce Buchan, "The East India Company 1749–1800: The Evolution of a Territorial Strategy and the Changing Role of the Directors," *Business and Economic History* 23, no. 1 (1994): 52–61, 57.

6. Richard B. Allen, *European Slave Trading in the Indian Ocean, 1500–1850* (Athens, OH: Ohio University Press, 2015), 17.

7. For this general story, see Sugata Bose and Ayesha Jalal, *Modern South Asia: History, Culture, Political Economy*, 3rd ed. (London: Routledge, 2018).

8. Charles Anthony Coke, *Census of the British Empire: Compiled from Official Returns for 1861*, vol. 2 (London: Harrison, 1864), 177.

9. Bernard S. Cohn, *Colonialism and Its Forms of Knowledge: The British in India* (Princeton, NJ: Princeton University Press, 1996), 41.

10. Anonymous columnist in the *Calcutta Gazette*, cited in Tim Keirn and Norbert Schürer, *British Encounters with India, 1750–1830: A Sourcebook* (New York: Palgrave Macmillan, 2011), 157.

11. Cohn, *Colonialism and Its Forms of Knowledge*, 42, 109, and elsewhere.

12. Bose and Jalal, *Modern South Asia*, 64.

13. There are many good choices, but the reader may survey the history and theory of Orientalism from a collected variety of perspectives in A. L. Macfie, ed., *Orientalism: A Reader* (Edinburgh: Edinburgh University Press, 2000).

14. For an example drawn from the years of the first major EIC territorial gains, see John MacDonald, *Memoirs of an Eighteenth-Century Footman: Travels (1745–1779)* (London: George Routledge & Sons, 1927), 145.

15. For countless examples, we might as well start with Georg Hegel and his Lectures on the Philosophy of History from 1822, see Arvind Mandair, "Hegel's Excess: Indology, Historical Difference and the Post-secular Turn of Theory," *Postcolonial Studies* 9, no. 1 (2006): 15–34, 15–16, and elsewhere. Even someone who professed sympathy for Hindus, like Charles Stuart writing in 1808, admitted that they were capable of "progress" and "reason," even if they appeared slow to adopt it. See Charles Stuart, *A Vindication of the Hindoos from the Aspersions of the Reverend Claudius Buchanon, M.A.* (London: Rodwell, 1808), 10.

16. James Mill, *The History of British India*, vol. II (London: Baldwin, Cradock and Joy, 1817), 460; Alexander Dow, *The History of Hindostan, from the Death of Akbar, to the Complete Settlement of the Empire under Aurungzebe* (London: Becket and DeHondt, 1772), cxlii.

17. Tony Ballantyne, *Orientalism and Race: Aryanism in the British Empire* (Houndmills: Palgrave, 2002), 21.

18. Eugene F. Irschick, "Order and Disorder in Colonial South India," *Modern Asian Studies* 23, no. 3 (1989): 459–492, 461 and elsewhere. For one example, Emma Roberts complained about Benares (Varanais), "seat of Hindu superstition," and how it lacked signs of lost, ancient grandeur like other Indian cities. See Emma Roberts, *Scenes and Characteristics of Hindostan, with Sketches of Anglo-Indian Society*, vol. 1 (London: Allen, 1835), 123. The fallen, dilapidated state of things was a constant refrain for her; see ibid., vol. 2, 306, for example. At the turn of the 1800s,

Scottish Enlightenment scholars who'd served in the EIC also argued that Indian kingdoms had proceeded along a course of greater and greater "refinement" like their European contemporaries, only to fall in recent times. See Tony Ballantyne, *Orientalism and Race*, 34.

19. Partha Chatterjee, *The Nation and Its Fragments: Colonial and Postcolonial Histories*, vol. 4 (Princeton, NJ: Princeton University Press, 1993), 10.

20. Aravind Ganachari, "'White Man's Embarrassment': European Vagrancy in 19th Century Bombay," *Economic and Political Weekly* 37, no. 25 (2002): 2477–2486. On this sense of maintaining a prestige somewhat synonymous with whiteness, see Thomas R. Metcalf, *Ideologies of the Raj* (Cambridge: Cambridge University Press, 1998), 121 and elsewhere.

21. *Temperance Gazette* 1846, no. 1 (January), 18. German observer Georg Hegel claimed that "the English, or rather the East India Company, are the lords of the land; for it is the necessary fate of Asiatic Empires to be subjected to Europeans; and China will, some day or other, be obliged to submit to this fate." See Alison Stone, "Hegel and Colonialism," *Hegel Bulletin* 41 (2020): 247–270. Traveler Reginald Heber wrote that, left to their own devices, the Indians would not improve their own land. See Reginald Heber, *Narrative of a Journey through the Upper Provinces of India, from Calcutta to Bombay 1824–1825*, vol 1 (London: John Murray, 1828), 16.

22. Much has been written on this, but readers can make a start with Joshua Ehrlich, "The Crisis of Liberal Reform in India: Public Opinion, Pyrotechnics, and the Charter Act of 1833," *Modern Asian Studies* 52 (2018): 2013–2055. The excellent notes provide a guide to following onward through the literature.

23. John Stuart Mill, *On Liberty* (London: Parker and Son, 1859), 23. Read this along with John Stuart Mill, "A Few Words about Non-intervention," *Fraser's Magazine* (1859), reprinted in *New England Review* 27 (2006): 252–264. In that essay, he wrote that higher civilizations could morally conquer and hold what he considered lesser ones.

24. "Macauley's Minute on Education, February 2, 1835," https://home.iitk.ac.in/~hcverma/Article/Macaulay-Minutes.pdf.

25. Anonymous columnist in the *Calcutta Gazette*, February 9, 1786, 1–2, cited in Keirn and Schürer, *British Encounters with India*, 157.

26. Thomas Skinner, *Excursions in India: Including a Walk over the Himalaya Mountains, to the Sources of the Jumna and the Ganges* (London: R. Bentley, 1833), 131.

27. Robert C.-H. Shell, *Children of Bondage: A Social History of the Slave Society at the Cape of Good Hope, 1652–1838* (Johannesburg: Witwatersrand University Press, 2001), 155.

28. Cecilia Morgan, *Building Better Britains?: Settler Societies in the British World, 1783–1920* (Toronto: University of Toronto Press, 2016), 105.

29. Matt K. Matsuda, *Pacific Worlds: A History of Seas, Peoples, and Cultures* (Cambridge: Cambridge University Press, 2012), 220–221.

30. Julie Evans, Patricia Grimshaw, David Philips, and Shurlee Swain, *Equal Subjects, Unequal Rights: Indigenous People in British Settler Colonies, 1830–1910* (Manchester: Manchester University Press, 2003), 3.

31. Stuart Banner, "Why Terra Nullius? Anthropology and Property Law in Early Australia," *Law and History Review* 23, no. 1 (2005): 95–131. See also Stuart Banner, *Possessing the Pacific: Land, Settlers, and Indigenous People from Australia to Alaska* (Cambridge, MA: Harvard University Press, 2007).

32. Banner, "Why Terra Nullius?" 117 and many other places.

33. Michael-Shawn Fletcher, Tegan Hall, and Andreas Nicholas Alexandra, "The Loss of an Indigenous Constructed Landscape Following British Invasion of Australia: An Insight into the Deep Human Imprint on the Australian Landscape," *Ambio* 50, no. 1 (January 2021): 138–149.

34. Kay Merry, "The Cross-Cultural Relationships between the Sealers and the Tasmanian Aboriginal Women at Bass Strait and Kangaroo Island in the Early Nineteenth Century," *Counterpoints* 3, no. 1 (2003): 80–88.

35. Lyndall Ryan, *Tasmanian Aborigines: A History since 1803* (Sydney: Allen & Unwin, 2012), 14, 43.

36. See the University of Newcastle, Australia's "Colonial Frontier Massacres in Australia, 1788–1930" project at https://c21ch.newcastle.edu.au/colonialmassacres/map.php and its tremendous bibliography, https://c21ch.newcastle.edu.au/colonialmassacres/ColonialMassacres_4_0_Bibliography.pdf.

37. Benjamin Madley, "From Terror to Genocide: Britain's Tasmanian Penal Colony and Australia's History Wars," *Journal of British Studies* 47, no. 1 (2008): 77–106, 78–79.

38. For talk of "extirpation" and "extermination," see ibid., 93–94, 98; Henry Reynolds, *An Indelible Stain?* (Sydney: Penguin, 2001), 52–54.

39. Wilson shows that tales of Captain Cook and his contemporaries set English readers more at ease about colonization. Remember, historians find that colonization and the growing national sense of being responsible for lesser races, even as "jailkeepers" for enslaved people deemed quite capable of violent revolt, did not set people at ease, did not inspire confidence. See Kathleen Wilson, *The Island Race: Englishness, Empire and Gender in the Eighteenth Century* (London: Routledge, 2003), chapter 2 and elsewhere.

40. Indigenous massacre victim data from the "Colonial Frontier Massacres in Australia, 1788–1930" project, https://c21ch.newcastle .edu.au/colonialmassacres/statistics.php.

41. For the prehistory of ethnography and its transition to a discipline in Britain, see Efram Sera-Shriar, *Founding the Sciences of Man: The Observational Practices of James Cowles Prichard and William Lawrence* (Pittsburgh, PA: University of Pittsburgh Press, 2016). The Ethnographical Society of London was founded in 1843.

42. Peter Pels and Oscar Salemink, "Introduction: Locating the Colonial Subjects of Anthropology," in Peter Pels and Oscar Salemink, eds., *Colonial Subjects: Essays on the Practical History of Anthropology* (Ann Arbor, MI: University of Michigan Press, 1999), 1–52, 16–18.

43. Shruti Kapila, "Race Matters: Orientalism and Religion, India and Beyond c. 1770–1880," *Modern Asian Studies* 41, no. 3 (2007): 471–513, 488.

44. George Steinmetz, "'The Devil's Handwriting': Precolonial Discourse, Ethnographic Acuity, and Cross-Identification in German Colonialism," *Comparative Studies in Society and History* 45, no. 1 (2003): 41–95, 42.

45. For a good primer on the roots of ethnology and anthropology in colonialism and exploration, see Pels and Salemink, "Introduction: Locating the Colonial Subjects of Anthropology," 18 and elsewhere.

46. Richard Hakluyt, "First voyage made to the coastes of Americas," *Principall Navigations, Voiages, and Discoveries of the English Nation* (1589), quoted in Peter Mancall, *Hakluyt's Promise: An Elizabethan's Obsession for an English America* (New Haven, CT: Yale University Press, 2007), 160. Hakluyt did report that different American peoples made fierce war on each other.

47. Sarah Rivett, "Empirical Desire: Conversion, Ethnography, and the New Science of the Praying Indian," *Early American Studies* 4, no. 1 (2006): 16–45. For just one classic example, see Samuel Hopkins, *Historical memoirs, relating to the Housatunnuk Indians: or, An account of the methods used, and pains taken, for the propagation of the Gospel among that heathenish-tribe, and the success thereof, under the ministry of the late reverend Mr. John Sergeant* (Boston, MA: S. Kneeland, 1753).

48. Speaking of cruelty, the classic shocking tale, followed by many other periodical captivity narratives, was Mary Rowlandson's *A Narrative of the Captivity, Sufferings, and Removes of Mrs. Mary Rowlandson* (1682). Scholar Yael Ben-zvi argued that such captivity narratives invented a kind of "foreign" Indigenous peoples, which only served to make the newcomers, whose mothers had been born over the ocean, entitled to the land by their imported birthright. See Yael Ben-Zvi, "Ethnography and the Production of Foreignness in Indian Captivity Narratives," *American Indian Quarterly* 32, no. 1 (2008): ix–xxxii, x and elsewhere.

49. For example, Henry Timberlake and Duane H. King, eds., *The Memoirs of Lt. Henry Timberlake: The Story of a Soldier, Adventurer, and Emissary to the Cherokees, 1756–1765* (Cherokee, NC: Museum of the Cherokee Indian, 2007), 93 and elsewhere. Or John Heckewelder, *History, Manners, and Customs of Indian Nations* (1819), described in Gary B. Nash, *Red, White, and Black: The Peoples of Early America* (Englewood Cliffs, NJ: Prentice-Hall, 1974), 15.

50. Peter Pels, "The Rise and Fall of the Indian Aborigines: Orientalism, Anglicanism, and the Emergence of an Ethnology of India, 1833–1869," in Peter Pels and Oscar Salemink, eds., *Colonial Subjects: Essays on the Practical History of Anthropology* (Ann Arbor, MI: University of Michigan Press, 1999), 82–116, 83.

51. Benjamin Smith Barton, *New Views of the Origin of the Tribes and Nations of America* (Philadelphia, PA: John Bioren, 1797), https://arch ive.org/details/newviewsoforiginoobart/page/n1/mode/2up?ref=ol& view=theater; David R. Wilcox and Don D. Fowler, "The Beginnings of Anthropological Archaeology in the North American Southwest: From Thomas Jefferson to the Pecos Conference," *Journal of the Southwest* 44, no. 2 (2002): 121–234, 125 and elsewhere; Elias Boudinot, *A Star in the West, or, A Humble Attempt to Discover the Long Lost Ten Tribes of Israel, Preparatory to Their Return to Their Beloved City, Jerusalem* (Trenton, NJ: D. Fenton, S. Hutchinson and J. Dunham, 1816), https:// archive.org/details/starinwestorhumbooboudarch. There are countless examples of Anglo-American looting in the name of Enlightenment-style discovery, including by Thomas Jefferson, which he describes in *Notes on the State of Virginia* (1785), part XI. See, for example, Bernard C. Peters, "Indian-Grave Robbing at Sault Ste. Marie, 1826," *Michigan Historical Review* 23 (Fall 1997): 49–80.

52. Ballantyne, *Orientalism and Race*, 60.

53. Kapila, "Race Matters," 478–479.

54. Ibid., 471–472.

55. Bruce Baum, *The Rise and Fall of the Caucasian Race: A Political History of Racial Identity* (New York: New York University Press, 2006), 100.

56. Ibid., 102; John P. Jackson, Jr. and Nadine M. Weidman, *Race, Racism, and Science* (New Brunswick, NJ: Rutgers University Press, 2004), 42.

57. Baum, *The Rise and Fall of the Caucasian Race*, 131; Jackson and Weidman, *Race, Racism, and Science*, 74.

58. Paul Turnbull, "British Anatomists, Phrenologists and the Construction of the Aboriginal Race, c. 1790–1830," *History Compass* 5, no. 1 (January 2007): 26–50, 28.

59. Thomas McCarthy, *Race, Empire, and the Idea of Human Development* (Cambridge: Cambridge University Press, 2009), 73–74.

60. Jackson and Weidman, *Race, Racism, and Science*, 47. See the story of Morton and his contemporary skull-collectors in Ann Fabian, *The Skull Collectors: Race, Science, and America's Unburied Dead* (Chicago, IL: University of Chicago Press, 2010).

61. Jackson and Weidman, *Race, Racism, and Science*, 47; Baum, *The Rise and Fall of the Caucasian Race*, 106.

62. Baum, *The Rise and Fall of the Caucasian Race*, 108.

63. Manisha Sinha, *The Slave's Cause: A History of Abolition* (New Haven, CT: Yale University Press, 2016), 1–2 and elsewhere.

64. Tom Zoellner, *Island on Fire: The Revolt That Ended Slavery in the British Empire* (Cambridge, MA: Harvard University Press, 2020); Michael Craton, *Testing the Chains: Resistance to Slavery in the British West Indies* (Ithaca, NY: Cornell University Press, 1983), 319–323.

65. Catherine Hall, *Civilising Subjects: Metropole and Colony in the English Imagination, 1830–1867* (Chicago, IL: University of Chicago Press, 2002).

66. Kremena Todorova, "'I Will Say the Truth to the English People': The History of Mary Prince and the Meaning of English History," *Texas Studies in Literature and Language* 43 (2001): 285–302.

67. Malcolm Chase, "Wedderburn, Robert (1762–1834/5)," *Oxford Dictionary of National Biography*, www.oxforddnb.com/view/10.1093/ref:odnb/9780198614128.001.0001/odnb-9780198614128-e-47120; Iain McCalman, "Anti-slavery and Ultra-radicalism in Early Nineteenth-Century England: The Case of Robert Wedderburn," *Slavery & Abolition* 7, no. 2 (1986): 99–117.

68. Robert Wedderburn, *The Horrors of Slavery* (London: Wedderburn, 1824); Iain McCalman, ed., *The Horrors of Slavery and Other Writings by Robert Wedderburn* (Princeton, NJ: Wiener, 1991), 87–90. Scholar Ryan Hanley reviews a curious document from Wedderburn written – if truly written by him – late in life in which he radically softened his abolitionist stance. See Ryan Hanley, "A Radical Change of Heart: Robert Wedderburn's Last Word on Slavery," *Slavery & Abolition* 37 (2016): 423–445.

69. Human trafficking numbers come from the tremendous, multi-university Slave Voyages Project, www.slavevoyages.org. Profit rates can be measured in many ways – as profit on trafficking and returns on investment, profits from sugar or textiles, and many more. See Alan Rice, "The Economic Basis of the Slave Trade," *Revealing Histories: Remembering Slavery*, http://revealinghistories.org.uk/how-did-money-from-slavery-help-develop-greater-manchester/articles/the-economic-basis-of-the-slave-trade.html; David Eltis and Stanley L. Engerman, "The Importance of Slavery and the Slave Trade to Industrializing Britain," *The Journal of Economic History* 60, no. 1 (2000): 123–144, 135 and elsewhere.

70. James Beattie, *The Works of James Beattie*, vol. 8: *Elements of Moral Science* (Philadelphia, PA: Hopkins and Earle, 1809), 225–232. Beattie originally published this material in 1792.

71. Christopher D. E. Willoughby, *Masters of Health: Racial Science and Slavery in U.S. Medical Schools* (Chapel Hill, NC: University of North Carolina Press, 2022), 36–37.

72. Eric Eustace Williams, *Capitalism and Slavery* (Chapel Hill, NC: University of North Carolina Press, 1944). Williams's personal biography makes tremendous reading, from trailblazer as a student to first Prime Minister of Trinidad and Tobago. The bibliography of works devoted solely to the ideas and legacy of Williams's works is vast and tremendously productive. I'll say here only that no one in Britain would publish the book for decades, objecting, it seems, that it didn't highlight the "heroic" story of white British abolitionists.

73. Selwyn H. H. Carrington, *The Sugar Industry and the Abolition of the Slave Trade, 1775–1810* (Gainesville, FL: University of Florida Press, 2002).

74. Anthony E. Kaye, "Nationalism and Abolitionist Politics in Great Britain and the United States," *Review (Fernand Braudel Center)* 35, no. 2 (2012): 135–167, 136–137 and elsewhere.

75. Michael E. Woods, "A Theory of Moral Outrage: Indignation and Eighteenth-Century British Abolitionism," *Slavery & Abolition* 36 (2015): 662–683.

76. Christopher Leslie Brown, *Moral Capital: Foundations of British Abolitionism* (Chapel Hill, NC: University of North Carolina Press, 2006), 155 and elsewhere.

77. William Cowper, "The Task," 1785.

78. Samuel North, "Remembering Slavery in Urban Cape Town: Emancipation or Continuity?" *International Review of Social History* 65 (April 2020): 197–223, 199.

79. Henrice Altink, "Slavery by Another Name: Apprenticed Women in Jamaican Workhouses in the Period 1834–8," *Social History* 26, no. 1 (2001): 40–59, 45 and elsewhere.

80. Diana Patton, ed., *A Narrative of Events since the First of August, 1834, by James Williams, an Apprenticed Labourer in Jamaica* (Durham, NC: Duke University Press, 2001); Richard Huzzey, *Freedom Burning: Anti-slavery and Empire in Victorian Britain* (Ithaca, NY: Cornell University Press, 2012), 11.

81. *The Spectator*, March 31, 1838, 13.

82. Frederick Cooper, *Beyond Slavery: Explorations of Race, Labor, and Citizenship in Postemancipation Societies* (Chapel Hill, NC: University of North Carolina Press, 2000), 34.

83. Kris Manjapra, "The Scandal of the British Slavery Abolition Act Loan," *Social and Economic Studies* 68, no. 3/4 (2019): 165–184, 165.
84. Nicholas Draper, "Possessing People: Absentee Slave-Owners within British Society," in Catherine Hall, Nicholas Draper, Keith McClelland, Katie Donington, and Rachel Lang, *Legacies of British Slave-Ownership: Colonial Slavery and the Formation of Victorian Britain* (Cambridge: Cambridge University Press, 2014), 34–77; Catherine Hall, "The Slavery Business and the Making of 'Race' in Britain and the Caribbean," *Current Anthropology* 61, no. S22 (October 2020): S172–S182.
85. Catherine Hall, Nicholas Draper, Keith McClelland, Katie Donington, and Rachel Lang, "Introduction," in Catherine Hall, Nicholas Draper, Keith McClelland, Katie Donington, and Rachel Lang, *Legacies of British Slave-Ownership: Colonial Slavery and the Formation of Victorian Britain*, illustrated ed. (Cambridge: Cambridge University Press, 2014), 1–33.
86. Manjapra, "The Scandal of the British Slavery Abolition Act Loan."

Chapter 5: Between White Father and Elimination, 1800–1865

1. Historians have done good work examining how this distinction was made, because that dividing point reveals so much about the thinking of past actors. Of course, along the way, these historians have shown how arbitrary, obsessive, and sometimes ridiculous these divisions were. Clearly, many Europeans who happened to be somewhat dusky of skin with black hair were often darker than victims of slavers. See Ariela J. Gross, "Litigating Whiteness: Trials of Racial Determination in the Nineteenth-Century South," *The Yale Law Journal* 108 (1998): 109–188; Daniel Sharfstein, "Crossing the Color Line: Racial Migration and the One-Drop Rule, 1600–1860," *Minnesota Law Review* 91 (January 2007): 592–656; Allyson Hobbs, *A Chosen Exile: A History of Racial Passing in American Life* (Cambridge, MA: Harvard University Press, 2016).
2. For just one example of the literature on this contrast with the Spaniards, see Gabriel Glickman, *Making the Imperial Nation: Colonization, Politics, and English Identity, 1660–1700* (New Haven, CT: Yale University Press, 2023), 56–84.
3. Nicholas Guyatt, *Bind Us Apart: How Enlightened Americans Invented Racial Segregation* (New York: Basic Books, 2016).
4. For Washington's tireless pursuit of one who successfully escaped him, see Erica Armstrong Dunbar, *Never Caught: Ona Judge, the Washingtons, and the Relentless Pursuit of Their Runaway Slave*

(New York: Simon and Schuster, 2017), esp. 147–153. Washington was quite willing to have her kidnapped off the streets of Portsmouth, New Hampshire and returned in chains to Virginia. But the people helping Washington in New Hampshire warned that abolition-minded folk, black and white, might very well physically block this, or at least shout to the heavens, if the self-liberated woman were seized. Washington never backed down, but historian Dunbar clearly shows that he wanted to keep his pursuit quiet. He was well aware that some ordinary folk of all kinds – "men of their time" – in New England would think his pursuit shameful.

5. Guyatt, *Bind Us Apart*, 28 and elsewhere.
6. For those who demanded that the new USA support the rebellion for freedom and independence, see Tim Matthewson, "Abraham Bishop, 'The Rights of Black Men,' and the American Reaction to the Haitian Revolution," *The Journal of Negro History* 67 (1982): 148–154; Tim Matthewson, "Jefferson and the Nonrecognition of Haiti," *Proceedings of the American Philosophical Society* 140, no. 1 (1996): 22–48; Timothy M. Matthewson, "George Washington's Policy toward the Haitian Revolution," *Diplomatic History* 3, no. 3 (2007): 321–336.
7. James Sullivan, quoted in Guyatt, *Bind Us Apart*, 21.
8. Joseph Eaton, "Lost in Translation: David Bailie Warden, the Abbé Grégoire's *De la littérature des Nègres*, and the Limits to Franco-Jeffersonian Cultural Exchange," *Transactions of the American Philosophical Society* 110 (2022): 219–240.
9. Grégoire, quoted by Bruce Dain, *A Hideous Monster of the Mind: American Race Theory in the Early Republic* (Cambridge, MA: Harvard University Press, 2002), 114–115.
10. See Graham Russell Hodges, "Introduction," in Henri Grégoire, *An Enquiry Concerning the Intellectual and Moral Faculties, and Literature of Negroes* (1808) (Oxford: Routledge, 1997), ix–xxiv.
11. George Tucker relating arguments he heard in Virginia, quoted in Guyatt, *Bind Us Apart*, 20.
12. Jack N. Rakove, *James Madison and the Creation of the American Republic*, 2nd ed. (New York: Longman, 2002), 231.
13. For Washington on slavery, see Philip D. Morgan, "'To Get Quit of Negroes': George Washington and Slavery," *Journal of American Studies* 39 (2005): 403–429. It's debatable, but he may have understood that slavery was hypocritical among those who pleaded for liberty from Britain. See F. Nwabueze Okoye, "Chattel Slavery as the Nightmare of the American Revolutionaries," *The William and Mary Quarterly* 37, no. 1 (1980): 3–28, 13.
14. "From James Madison to James Madison, Sr., 8 September 1783," https://founders.archives.gov/documents/Madison/01-07-02-0170.

15. John Adams to George Churchman and Jacob Lindley, January 24, 1801. See "John Adams on the Abolition of Slavery, 1801," Gilder Lehrman Collection, Yale, www.gilderlehrman.org/history-resources/spotlight-primary-source/john-adams-abolition-slavery-1801.

16. John Craig Hammond, "Slavery, Settlement, and Empire: The Expansion and Growth of Slavery in the Interior of the North American Continent, 1770–1820," *Journal of the Early Republic* 32, no. 2 (2012): 175–206, 204.

17. Henry Clay, quoted in Paul Frymer, *Building an American Empire* (Princeton, NJ: Princeton University Press, 2017), 228. Frymer's chapter 6, "A Second Removal," in that book is, together with its bibliography, an ideal overview of the colonization question.

18. Guyatt, *Bind us Apart*, 28; James Thome, *Emancipation in the West Indies* (New York: American Anti-Slavery Society, 1837), 159.

19. Anonymous, "The Riot in Philadelphia," *American and Foreign Anti-slavery Reporter* article reprinted in the *British and Foreign Anti-slavery Reporter* 3 (September 1842): 151–152.

20. Readers will find an excellent overview of the questions and debates within this history in the introduction and contents of Beverly C. Tomek and Matthew J. Hetrick, eds., *New Directions in the Study of African American Recolonization* (Gainesville, FL: University Press of Florida, 2017).

21. Peter S. Onuf, "'To Declare Them a Free and Independant People': Race, Slavery, and National Identity in Jefferson's Thought," *Journal of the Early Republic* 18, no. 1 (1998): 1–46, 31.

22. Nicholas Guyatt, "The American Colonization Society: 200 Years of the 'Colonizing Trick,'" *Black Perspectives* (December 22, 2016), www.aaihs.org/the-american-colonization-society-200-years-of-the-colonizing-trick.

23. Toyin Falola and Raphael Chijioke Njoku, *United States and Africa Relations, 1400s to the Present* (New Haven, CT: Yale University Press, 2020), 84.

24. Francis D. Adams and Barry Sanders, *Alienable Rights: The Exclusion of African Americans in a White Man's Land, 1619–2000* (New York: HarperCollins, 2003); G. S. Boritt, "The Voyage to the Colony of Linconia: The Sixteenth President, Black Colonization, and the Defense Mechanism of Avoidance," *The Historian* 37 (1975): 619–632. For an excellent overview of the question of Lincoln's relative commitment to colonization, see Allen C. Guelzo, review of *Colonization After Emancipation: Lincoln and the Movement for Black Resettlement*, by Phillip W. Magness and Sebastian N. Page, *Journal of the Abraham Lincoln Association* 34, no. 1 (2013): 78–87.

25. J. R. Oldfield, *The Ties That Bind: Transatlantic Abolitionism in the Age of Reform, c. 1820–1865* (Liverpool: Liverpool University Press, 2020), 18 and elsewhere.

26. Frymer, *Building an American Empire*, 261.

27. Douglass speech before the American Antislavery Society (May 11, 1869), quoted in ibid., 220.

28. William Lloyd Garrison, *Thoughts on African Colonization* (Boston, MA: Garrison and Knapp, 1832), 11.

29. Lee Jenkins, "Beyond the Pale: Frederick Douglass in Cork," *The Irish Review*, no. 24 (Autumn 1999): 80–95, 80.

30. Pauline Collombier-Lakeman, "Daniel O'Connell and India," *Études Irlandaises* 38 (2013): 41–54.

31. Christine Kinealy, *Daniel O'Connell and the Anti-slavery Movement* (London: Pickering & Chatto, 2014), chapter 2 and elsewhere. For Washington, see O'Connell's speech paraphrased in Howard Temperley, "The O'Connell–Stevenson Contretemps: A Reflection of the Anglo-American Slavery Issue," *The Journal of Negro History* 47 (1962): 217–233.

32. Natalie Joy, "The Indian's Cause: Abolitionists and Native American Rights," *Journal of the Civil War Era* 8 (2018): 215–242.

33. Mary Hershberger, "Mobilizing Women, Anticipating Abolition: The Struggle against Indian Removal in the 1830s," *The Journal of American History* 86, no. 1 (1999): 15–40.

34. Tiya Miles, "'Circular Reasoning': Recentering Cherokee Women in the Antiremoval Campaigns," *American Quarterly* 61, no. 2 (2009): 221–243, 230.

35. Andrew Jackson, "Fifth Annual Message" (December 3, 1833), American Presidency Project, www.presidency.ucsb.edu/documents/fifth-annual-message-2.

36. Michel Hogue, *Metis and the Medicine Line: Creating a Border and Dividing a People* (Chapel Hill, NC: University of North Carolina Press, 2015), 6–8 and elsewhere.

37. NSW Department of Planning, Industry and Environment, "Living on Aboriginal Reserves and Stations" (2012), www.environment.nsw.gov.au/chresearch/ReserveStation.htm.

38. Edward Parmelee Smith, "Circular Letter to Superintendents and Agents of the Indian Department," Commissioner of Indian Affairs (October 21, 1873), 1, https://web.archive.org/web/20240912133311/https:/plateauportal.libraries.wsu.edu/digital-heritage/circular-letter-superintendents-agents-indian-department.

39. For just a pair of examples among very many, see Everard Home, *Observations on Cancer: Connected with Histories of the Disease* (London: W. Bulmer, 1805), 153 and many other places;

Abraham Rees, *The Cyclopaedia; Or, an Universal Dictionary of Arts, Sciences, and Literature: In Thirty-Nine Volumes* (London: Longman, 1819), n.p.

40. To name just a few examples, William Pitt, *A General View of the Agriculture of the County of Leicester* (London: Richard Phillips, 1809), 90; John Sinclair, *The Code of Agriculture, Including Observations on Gardens, Orchards, Woods, and Plantations*, 3rd ed. (London: Constable, 1821), 291; John J. Thomas and M. B. Bateham, eds., *The New Genesee Farmer and Gardener's Journal*, vol. 3 (Rochester, NY: Bateham & Crosman, 1840), 89.

41. Ann Curthoys, "Genocide in Tasmania: The History of an Idea," in A. Dirk Moses, ed., *Empire, Colony, Genocide: Conquest, Occupation, and Subaltern Resistance in World History* (Oxford: Berghahn Books, 2010), 229–252, 231. People used it in reference to Indigenous removal/elimination, in earlier years, too, it's just that the early 1800s seemed its heyday. For example, in his 1791 *Autobiography*, Ben Franklin wrote that, if "it be the design of Providence to extirpate these savages in order to make room for cultivators of the earth, it seems not improbable that rum may be the appointed means." See Franklin quoted in Patrick Brantlinger, *Dark Vanishings: Discourse on the Extinction of Primitive Races, 1800–1930* (Ithaca, NY: Cornell University Press, 2003), 47.

42. On the other hand, scholar Jeffrey Ostler believes that those who used the word "extirpation" in this period meant something more violent, more purposefully attacking or offensive, and he finds grounds. See Jeffrey Ostler, *Surviving Genocide: Native Nations and the United States from the American Revolution to Bleeding Kansas* (New Haven, CT: Yale University Press, 2019), 99. On balance, though, I think the evidence, including that in his own book on page 340, supports the idea that colonizers employed the word as a sort of distancing one; when colonizers wanted to talk about war-making, attacks, they used words other than "extirpation." Of course, minor disagreements of this sort are what keep scholars digging and thinking.

43. Jean M. O'Brien, *Firsting and Lasting: Writing Indians Out of Existence in New England* (Minneapolis, MN: University of Minnesota Press, 2010), xv, 165; Ostler, *Surviving Genocide*, 340.

44. Brantlinger, *Dark Vanishings*, 130–131.

45. Alan Lester, "Humanitarians and White Settlers in the Nineteenth Century," in Norman Etherington, ed., *Missions and Empire* (Oxford: Oxford University Press, 2005), 64–85, 73–75.

46. Homi Bhabha, "The Other Question: Difference, Discrimination and the Discourse of Colonialism," in Russell Ferguson, Martha Gever, Trinh T. Minh-ha, and Cornell West, eds., *Out There: Marginalization*

and Contemporary Culture (Cambridge, MA: MIT Press, 1990), 71–88, 75.

47. Anonymous, "Book Review, Charles Ritter, *The Colonization of New Zealand*," *The Literary Gazette and Journal of Belles Lettres, Arts, Sciences, Etc.* (London: H. Colburn, 1842), 340–341. This was a review of a German book, but the British reviewer provided the quote.

48. Robert van Krieken, "Rethinking Cultural Genocide: Aboriginal Child Removal and Settler-Colonial State Formation," *Oceania* 75, no. 2 (2004): 125–151, 126.

49. Ibid., 127.

50. Sometimes white elites pointed to race-mixing as the cause of white degradation, but that wasn't a necessary component. See Adam J. Pratt, *Toward Cherokee Removal: Land, Violence, and the White Man's Chance* (Athens, GA: University of Georgia Press, 2020), 40.

51. For perceptions of "degraded whites" in Australia, see Anna Johnston, "Writing the Southern Cross: Religious Travel Writing in Nineteenth-Century Australasia," in Tim Youngs, ed., *Travel Writing in the Nineteenth Century: Filling the Blank Spaces* (London: Anthem Press, 2006), 201–218, 205 and elsewhere. For an example from 1830s Florida, including respectable whites' derision of the poor whites who forced them to intervene, see John T. Ellisor, *The Second Creek War: Interethnic Conflict and Collusion on a Collapsing Frontier* (Lincoln, NE: University of Nebraska Press, 2010), 411–412.

52. Ostler, *Surviving Genocide*, 96; Samantha Seeley, *Race, Removal, and the Right to Remain: Migration and the Making of the United States* (Chapel Hill, NC: University of North Carolina Press, 2021), 60; Sidney L. Harring, *White Man's Law: Native People in Nineteenth-Century Canadian Jurisprudence* (Toronto: University of Toronto Press, 1998), 179–180.

53. Joel Palmer, quoted in Ronald Spores, "Too Small a Place: The Removal of the Willamette Valley Indians, 1850–1856," *American Indian Quarterly* 17, no. 2 (1993): 171–191, 180. See also, among many other possible examples, O'Brien, *Firsting and Lasting*, 83, on how colonialism was supposed to have benefited the Mohegans.

54. Guyatt, *Bind Us Apart*, 151.

55. For bibliographic direction on this colonial governmental theory in Africa, see Thomas Spear, "Invention of Tradition," *Oxford Bibliographies*, African Studies, www.oxfordbibliographies.com/view/document/obo-9780199846733/obo-9780199846733-0002.xml.

56. Jeffrey Ostler, "Genocide and American Indian History," *Oxford Research Encyclopedia of American History* (March 2, 2015), https://oxfordre.com/americanhistory/display/10.1093/acrefore/9780199329175.001.0001/acrefore-9780199329175-e-3.

57. This "logic of elimination" was encapsulated in Patrick Wolfe, "Land, Labor, and Difference: Elementary Structures of Race," *American Historical Review* 106, no. 3 (June 2001): 866–905, 868. See also Patrick Wolfe, "Structure and Event: Settler Colonialism, Time, and the Question of Genocide," in A. Dirk Moses, ed., *Empire, Colony, Genocide: Conquest, Occupation, and Subaltern Resistance in World History* (New York: Berghahn Books, 2010), 102–132.

58. Benjamin Madley, *An American Genocide: The United States and the California Indian Catastrophe, 1846–1873* (New Haven, CT: Yale University Press, 2016), 11, 51; Ed Castillo, "Short Overview of California Indian History," California Native American Heritage Commission, https://nahc.ca.gov/native-americans/california-indian-history.

59. Madley, *An America Genocide*, 12.

60. Ibid., 352–353.

61. John Weller, quoted in ibid., 353.

62. Stacey L. Smith, *Freedom's Frontier: California and the Struggle over Unfree Labor, Emancipation, and Reconstruction* (Chapel Hill, NC: University of North Carolina Press, 2013), 109–140.

63. Raymond Evans, "'Pigmentia': Racial Fears and White Australia," in A. Dirk Moses, ed., *Genocide and Settler Society: Frontier Violence and Stolen Indigenous Children in Australian History* (Oxford: Berghahn Books, 2012), 103–124, 104 and elsewhere.

64. John Harris, "Hiding the Bodies: The Myth of the Humane Colonisation of Aboriginal Australia," *Aboriginal History* 27 (2003): 79–104, 81.

65. Jane Lydon, "'No Moral Doubt ...': Aboriginal Evidence and the Kangaroo Creek Poisoning, 1847–1849," *Aboriginal History* 20 (1996): 151–175, 159–160.

66. Timothy Bottoms, *Conspiracy of Silence: Queensland's Frontier Killing Times* (Crows Nest, NSW: Allen & Unwin, 2013), 218 and elsewhere.

67. Harris, "Hiding the Bodies," 81.

68. Edward Wilson, *Melbourne Argus*, March 17, 1856, quoted in Harris, "Hiding the Bodies, 82. The California horror also didn't go unnoticed, and some decent people spoke up. J. Ross Browne published a piece in *Harper's New Monthly Magazine* in 1861 with an engraving showing white gunmen massacring native Californian women and children. It was mordantly titled "Protecting the Settlers," https://digitalcollec tions.nypl.org/items/510d47e1-170a-a3d9-e040-e00a18064a99.

69. James Stephen, Colonial Office minute, quoted in Ann Curthoys and Jessie Mitchell, *Taking Liberty: Indigenous Rights and Settler Self-Government in Colonial Australia, 1830–1890* (Cambridge: Cambridge University Press, 2018), 134–135.

70. Such assimilationist schooling in what would become Canada was far older than the 1870s. See Robert Carney, "Aboriginal Residential Schools before Confederation: The Early Experience," *Historical Studies* 61 (1995): 13–40. See also David B. MacDonald, "Genocide in the Indian Residential Schools: Canadian History through the Lens of the UN Genocide Convention," in Andrew Woolford, Jeff Benvenuto, and Alexander Laban Hinton, eds., *Colonial Genocide in Indigenous North America* (Durham, NC: Duke University Press, 2014), 306–324, 307–308.

71. Commission de vérité et réconciliation du Canada, *Canada's Residential Schools: The History, Part 1: Origins to 1939: The Final Report of the Truth and Reconciliation Commission of Canada*, vol. I (Montreal: McGill-Queen's University Press, 2016), 164.

72. Egerton Ryerson's 1847 report appended to an 1898 report, *Indian Schools in the Dominion* (Ottawa: Government Printing Bureau, 1898).

73. These figures are only for the national system after the mid 1800s; the numbers, therefore, are low. See Truth and Reconciliation Commission of Canada, "Honouring the Truth, Reconciling for the Future: Summary of the Final Report of the Truth and Reconciliation Commission of Canada" (2015), 91–94, https://ehprnh2mwo3 .exactdn.com/wp-content/uploads/2021/01/Executive_Summary_ English_Web.pdf. This focus on schooling doesn't mean that there weren't other kinds of eliminationist practices in Canada. In Canada, too, white settlers and the government combined to eliminate native peoples. Yes, there were massacres. In 1873, for example, American and Canadian trappers killed at least thirteen villagers at Cypress Hills, Saskatchewan, claiming they'd stolen horses. But Canadian settlers and their government supporters contributed to far more death and devastation by the wholesale slaughter of bison in the name of farm and ranch profits. For this horrible 1870s tale, see James W. Daschuk, *Clearing the Plains: Disease, Politics of Starvation, and the Loss of Aboriginal Life* (Regina: University of Regina Press, 2013), especially chapter 7.

74. Margaret Connell Szasz, "'I Knew How to Be Moderate. And I Knew How to Obey': The Commonality of American Indian Boarding School Experiences, 1750s–1920s," *American Indian Culture and Research Journal* 29, no. 4 (2005): 75–94.

75. Sari Horwitz, Dana Hedgpeth, Emmanuel Martinez, Scott Higham, and Salwan Georges, "'In the Name of God': Native American Children Endured Years of Sexual Abuse at Boarding Schools," *Washington Post*, May 29, 2024, www.washingtonpost.com/investigations/inter active/2024/sexual-abuse-native-american-boarding-schools.

76. "Found: Raj-Razed town," *The Telegraph* (of Kolkata), December 8, 2008, www.telegraphindia.com/leisure/found-raj-razed-town/cid/518617.

77. See the text of the "Humble Petition of the Poor People of Jamaica and the Parish of St. Ann" and the so-called "Queen's Advice," actually the words of Edward Cardwell, Secretary of State for the Colonies, in Thomas Harvey and William Brewin, *Jamaica in 1866: A Narrative of a Tour through the Island* (London: Bennet, 1867), 101–104.

78. Alan Lester, Kate Boehme, and Peter Mitchell, *Ruling the World: Freedom, Civilisation and Liberalism in the Nineteenth-Century British Empire* (Cambridge: Cambridge University Press, 2021), 277.

79. Catherine Hall, "The Economy of Intellectual Prestige: Thomas Carlyle, John Stuart Mill, and the Case of Governor Eyre," *Cultural Critique*, no. 12 (1989): 167–196.

Chapter 6: Creating the White Man's Burden, 1865–1930s

1. President Warren Harding recommended his listeners read Lothrop Stoddard in an October 1921 speech in Birmingham, Alabama. See https://voicesofdemocracy.umd.edu/warren-g-harding-address-at-birmingham-speech-text.

2. Stoddard quoted in Carol M. Taylor, "W. E. B. DuBois's Challenge to Scientific Racism," *Journal of Black Studies* 11, no. 4 (1981): 449–460, 449.

3. See the speech of Dr. Effa Muhse, eugenicist, to the American Association of University Women: Effa Muhse, "Heredity and Problems in Eugenics," *AAUW Journal* 8 (March 1915): 49–64.

4. John Waller, "The Rise of the Professional," *Nature* 433 (2005): 688.

5. Christopher D. E. Willoughby, *Masters of Health: Racial Science and Slavery in U.S. Medical Schools* (Chapel Hill, NC: The University of North Carolina Press, 2022), 94. Writing of eugenics, specifically, Saul Dubow wrote that "the development of eugenics can therefore be seen to have been closely bound up with the professionalization and institutionalization of knowledge in the expanding university and state sectors." See Saul Dubow, *Scientific Racism in Modern South Africa* (Cambridge: Cambridge University Press, 1995), 133.

6. Evelynn Maxine Hammonds and Rebecca M. Herzig, *The Nature of Difference: Sciences of Race in the United States from Jefferson to Genomics* (Cambridge, MA: MIT Press, 2008), 63–64.

7. Lundy Braun, *Breathing Race into the Machine: The Surprising Career of the Spirometer from Plantation to Genetics* (Minneapolis, MN: University of Minnesota Press, 2014), 33.

8. "The Impossibility of Acclimatizing Races," *Medical and Surgical Reporter* 5 (March 1861): 624.

9. Thomas Mays, "Does Pulmonary Consumption Tend to Exterminate the American Indian?" *New York Medical Journal* 45 (May 1887): 510.

10. Rutledge M. Dennis, "Social Darwinism, Scientific Racism, and the Metaphysics of Race," *The Journal of Negro Education* 64, no. 3 (1995): 243–252, 244.

11. William Graham Sumner, *Earth Hunger and Other Essays* (New Haven, CT: Yale University Press, 1914), 48.

12. Edward Burnett Tylor, *Primitive Culture: Researches into the Development of Mythology, Philosophy, Religion, Art, and Custom* (J. Murray, 1871), quoted in George W. Stocking, *Race, Culture, and Evolution: Essays in the History of Anthropology: With a New Preface,* Phoenix ed. (Chicago, IL: University of Chicago Press, 1982), 116.

13. The third chapter of *On the Origin of Species* is titled "The Struggle for Existence." See Charles Darwin, *The Origin of Species by Means of Natural Selection* (London: John Murray, 1859).

14. Charles Darwin, *The Descent of Man, and Selection in Relation to Sex* (London: D. Appleton and Company, 1871), 34, 151.

15. Ibid., 160, 174.

16. Mike Hawkins, *Social Darwinism in European and American Thought, 1860–1945: Nature as Model and Nature as Threat* (Cambridge: Cambridge University Press, 1997), 113; Katy Soar, "Edward Tylor, Archaeologist? The Archaeological Foundations of 'Mr. Tylor's Science,'" in Paul-François Tremlett, Graham Harvey, and Liam T. Sutherland, eds., *Edward Burnett Tylor, Religion and Culture* (London: Bloomsbury Publishing, 2017), 141–162, 142, 146, 155.

17. Peter J. Bowler, *Evolution: The History of an Idea,* 25th anniversary ed. (Berkeley, CA: University of California Press, 2009), 286.

18. Lewis Henry Morgan, *Ancient Society, Or Researches in the Lines of Human Progress from Savagery through Barbarism to Civilization* (London: Macmillan, 1877), 60.

19. Tasha Hubbard and Theodore Fontaine, "Buffalo Genocide in Nineteenth-Century North America: 'Kill, Skin, and Sell,'" in Andrew Woolford, Jeff Benvenuto, and Alexander Laban Hinton, eds., *Colonial Genocide in Indigenous North America* (Durham, NC: Duke University Press, 2014), 292–305; H. W. Koch, *The Origins of the First World War* (London: Palgrave, 1984), 319–342.

20. Herbert Spencer, *The Study of Sociology* (London: King and Co., 1873), 193.

21. Cecil Rhodes, "Confession of Faith" (1877), https://pages.uoregon.edu/kimball/Rhodes-Confession.htm. His support of the Jameson Raid in 1895 as an opportunity to expand his own power and wealth fooled few in his day. For just one example, see Miles Taylor, "Patriotism, History and the Left in Twentieth-Century Britain," *The Historical Journal* 33, no. 4 (1990): 971–987, 974.

22. Donald Paul Nurse, "An Amateur Barbarian: The Life and Career of Sir Richard Francis Burton, 1821–1890" (Dissertation, Toronto, 1999), 145, 147.

23. Joseph Le Conte, *The Race Problem in the South* (New York: D. Appleton and Company, 1892), 359–360.

24. Churchill's evidence before the Peel Commission of 1937, quoted in Warren Dockter, *Churchill and the Islamic World: Orientalism, Empire and Diplomacy in the Middle East* (London: Bloomsbury Publishing, 2015), 178.

25. For the quote, thanks to Jeffrey O'Connell and Michael Ruse, *Social Darwinism* (Cambridge: Cambridge University Press, 2021); Theodore Roosevelt, *The Strenuous Life* (New York: Century Company, 1901), 20.

26. Letter from Theodore Roosevelt to Bessie Van Vorst, October 18, 1902. Theodore Roosevelt Papers. Library of Congress Manuscript Division, reproduced by the Theodore Roosevelt Digital Library. Dickinson State University.

27. Diana Preston, *The Boxer Rebellion: The Dramatic Story of China's War on Foreigners That Shook the World in the Summer of 1900* (New York: Walker, 2000), 350–351.

28. Michael Keevak, *Becoming Yellow: A Short History of Racial Thinking* (Princeton, NJ: Princeton University Press, 2001), 41–47 and elsewhere.

29. Charles J. McClain, *In Search of Equality: The Chinese Struggle against Discrimination in Nineteenth-Century America* (Berkeley, CA: University of California Press, 1994), 79 and elsewhere.

30. Gustavus A. Ohlinger, "Winston Spencer Churchill: A Midnight Interview," *Michigan Quarterly Review* 5 (April 1966), 77.

31. Letter of Houston Stewart Chamberlain, quoted in Geoffrey G. Field, *Evangelist of Race: The Germanic Vision of Houston Stewart Chamberlain* (New York: Columbia University Press, 1981), 357.

32. Edward Ross Dickinson, "Sex, Masculinity, and the 'Yellow Peril': Christian von Ehrenfels' Program for a Revision of the European

Sexual Order, 1902–1910," *German Studies Review* 25, no. 2 (2002): 255–284, 263 and elsewhere.

33. Letter of Hearst quoted in Ian Mugridge, *View from Xanadu: William Randolph Hearst and United States Foreign Policy* (Montreal: McGill-Queen's University Press, 1995), 110.

34. For Canadian "Anglo-Saxondom" writings, see Tanja Bueltmann, "Anglo-Saxonism and the Racialization of the English Diaspora," in Tanja Bueltmann, David T. Gleeson, and Donald M. MacRaild, eds., *Locating the English Diaspora, 1500–2010* (Liverpool: Liverpool University Press, 2012), 118–134.

35. See, generally, Duncan Bell, *The Idea of Greater Britain: Empire and the Future of World Order, 1860–1900* (Princeton, NJ: Princeton University Press, 2011), 6–7. And see, for his view, and his quote of J. Arthur Balfour along the same lines, Charles Beresford, "The Future of the Anglo-Saxon Race," *The North American Review* 171, no. 529 (1900): 802–810, 809.

36. Adams was the eventual head of my own professional organization – the American Historical Association. My profession has been far from free of white supremacy.

37. George Burton Adams, "The United States and the Anglo-Saxon Future," *The Atlantic*, July 1896, www.theatlantic.com/magazine/arch ive/1896/07/the-united-states-and-the-anglo-saxon-future/525690.

38. Bell, *The Idea of Greater Britain*, 263 and elsewhere. Cecil Rhodes, in his "confession of Faith," argued for a secret cabal that would work towards a global white race union, as well, in 1877. He wrote that he heard the idea in college.

39. David R. Bellhouse, "Karl Pearson's Influence in the United States," *International Statistical Review/Revue Internationale de Statistique* 77, no. 1 (2009): 51–63, 52–53, 55, 59.

40. Karl Pearson , *National Life from the Standpoint of Science : An Address Delivered at Newcastle, November 19, 1900* (London: Adam and Charles Black, 1901), 34, https://archive.org/details/galton labo17/page/n9/mode/2up.

41. Hawkins, *Social Darwinism in European and American Thought*, 113.

42. Anna Stubblefield, "'Beyond the Pale': Tainted Whiteness, Cognitive Disability, and Eugenic Sterilization," *Hypatia* 22, no. 2 (Spring 2007): 162–181, 163–164.

43. Alexandra Minna Stern, *Eugenic Nation: Faults and Frontiers of Better Breeding in Modern America* (Berkeley, CA: University of California Press, 2016), 25, 123, and elsewhere; Marie Kaniecki, Nicole L. Novak, Sarah Gao et al., "Racialization and Reproduction: Asian Immigrants and California's Twentieth-Century Eugenic Sterilization Program," *Social Forces* 102, no. 2 (December 2023): 706–729.

44. Karen Stote, *An Act of Genocide: Colonialism and the Sterilization of Aboriginal Women* (New York: Columbia University Press, 2015).

45. Miroslava Chávez-García, "Intelligence Testing at Whittier School, 1890–1920," *Pacific Historical Review* 76, no. 2 (2007): 193–228.

46. Thanks to historian Emmanuel Mehr for this reference. See Harry H. Laughlin, "American History in Terms of Human Migration, Extract from Hearings before the Committee on Immigration and Naturalization" (US House of Representatives, March 1928), https://manuscripts.truman.edu/repositories/2/archival_objects/28047.

47. Image from J. E. Wallace Wallin, "A Practical Guide for Administering the Binet–Simon Scale for Measuring Intelligence," *The Psychological Clinic* 5, no. 7 (March 1911): 217–238.

48. John P. Jackson, Jr. and Nadine M. Weidman, "The Origins of Scientific Racism," *The Journal of Blacks in Higher Education*, no. 50 (Winter 2005): 66–79, 66.

49. H. B. Fantham, "Some Factors in Eugenics, Together with Notes on Some South African Cases," *South African Journal of Science* 22, no. 11 (1925): 400–421, 412.

50. Stephen William Daniel Appel, "To Maintain the Living, but Not the Living Deficient – Harold Benjamin Fantham, Eugenics and Educability" (M.Phil. Thesis, Johannesburg, University of the Witwatersrand, 1988), 71.

51. Rebecca Hodes and Rodney H. Reznek, "The Intertwining of Antisemitism and Racism in Modern South Africa, c. 1880–1939," *Jewish Historical Studies* 55, no. 1 (January 2024): 27–50, 41. They also point out that a number of English, German, and Scottish race scientists of the late 1800s and early 1900s started their careers by studying native people in South Africa.

52. Attorney General Alfred Deacon, in Australia, House of Representatives, September 12, 1901, https://historichansard.net/hofreps/1901/19010912_REPS_1_4_c1.

53. William Wilks, in ibid.

54. Churchill letters quoted in Martin Gilbert, "Churchill and Eugenics" (2009), https://winstonchurchill.org/publications/finest-hour-extras/churchill-and-eugenics-1.

55. Bertrand Russell, *Principles of Social Reconstruction* (London: Routledge, 1997), 126.

56. Susanne M. Klausen, "Eugenics and the Maintenance of White Supremacy in Modern South Africa," in Diane B. Paul, John Stenhouse, and Hamish G. Spencer, eds., *Eugenics at the Edges of Empire: New Zealand, Australia, Canada and South Africa* (Cham: Palgrave Macmillan, 2018), 294, 303, and elsewhere.

57. David N. Livingstone, "Science and Society: Nathaniel S. Shaler and Racial Ideology," *Transactions of the Institute of British Geographers* 9, no. 2 (1984): 181–210, 189 and elsewhere; Erika Lee, "The Chinese Exclusion Example: Race, Immigration, and American Gatekeeping, 1882–1924," *Journal of American Ethnic History* 21, no. 3 (2002): 36–62, 47.

58. Ward quoted in Daniel Okrent, *The Guarded Gate: Bigotry, Eugenics, and the Law That Kept Two Generations of Jews, Italians, and Other European Immigrants Out of America* (New York: Scribner, 2019), 227. For Ward, see Colm Lavery, "Situating Eugenics: Robert DeCourcy Ward and the Immigration Restriction League of Boston," *Journal of Historical Geography* 53 (July 2016): 54–62.

59. James Renton, "The End of the Semites," in Ben Gidley and James Renton, eds., *Antisemitism and Islamophobia in Europe: A Shared Story?* (London: Palgrave Macmillan, 2017), 99–140, 103.

60. Bruce Baum, *The Rise and Fall of the Caucasian Race: A Political History of Racial Identity* (New York: New York University Press, 2006), 110, 113, and elsewhere.

61. Leonard Rogoff, "Is the Jew White?: The Racial Place of the Southern Jew," *American Jewish History* 85, no. 3 (1997): 195–230, 199–200.

62. Keevak, *Becoming Yellow*, 16.

63. Joseph Jacobs and Isidore Spielman, "On the Comparative Anthropometry of English Jews," *Journal of the Anthropological Institute of Great Britain and Ireland* 19 (1890): 75–88, 82–88 and elsewhere.

64. John M. Efron, "Commentary: Jewish Genetic Origins in the Context of Past Historical and Anthropological Inquiries," *Human Biology* 85, no. 6 (2013): 901–918, 910.

65. Dylan Weir, "Displacement and Replacement: The Political History of David Duke, Patrick Buchanan, and Racial Resentment," *Journal of Hate Studies* 18, no. 1 (January 2023): 1–16, 2 and elsewhere.

66. Michael Biddiss, "History as Destiny: Gobineau, H. S. Chamberlain and Spengler," *Transactions of the Royal Historical Society* 7 (1997): 73–100, 81.

67. Houston Stewart Chamberlain, *Foundations of the Nineteenth Century*, vol. 1 (New York: J. Lane, 1910), 330.

68. Ibid., 330–331.

69. Ibid., 330.

70. Biddiss, "History as Destiny," 86–87.

71. Nathan Vernon Madison, "Isolationism, Internationalism and the 'Other': The Yellow Peril, Mad Brute and Red Menace in Early to Mid Twentieth Century Pulp Magazines and Comic Books," M.A. thesis (Richmond, VA, Virginia Commonwealth University, 2010), 27–28.

72. Madison Grant, *The Passing of the Great Race: Or the Racial Basis of European History* (New York: Scribner's Sons, 1916), 16, 91.

73. Noel Hartman, "'The Passing of the Great Race' @ 100," *Public Books* (July 2016), www.publicbooks.org/the-passing-of-the-great-race-at-100.

74. Jonathan Peter Spiro, *Defending the Master Race: Conservation, Eugenics, and the Legacy of Madison Grant* (Burlington, VT: University of Vermont Press, 2009), xii–xiii.

75. Charles Franklin Thwing, *Human Australasia: Studies of Society and of Education in Australia and New Zealand* (New York: Macmillan, 1923), 248–250. See also throughout the book Thwing's almost ecstatic elevation of the supreme Anglo-Saxon race, 24–25, 206, 230, and elsewhere.

76. Brian Regal, "Madison Grant, Maxwell Perkins, and Eugenics Publishing at Scribner's," *The Princeton University Library Chronicle* 65, no. 2 (Winter 2004): 317–342, 334.

77. David A. Bateman, *Disenfranchising Democracy: Constructing the Electorate in the United States, the United Kingdom, and France* (Cambridge: Cambridge University Press, 2018), 9.

78. Julie Evans, Patricia Grimshaw, David Phillips, and Shurlee Swain, *Equal Subjects, Unequal Rights: Indigenous People in British Settler Colonies, 1830–1910* (Manchester: Manchester University Press, 2003).

79. Ibid., 53.

80. Donald G. Nieman, *Promises to Keep: African Americans and the Constitutional Order, 1776 to the Present* (Oxford: Oxford University Press, 2020), 102–108.

81. Marilyn Lake, "From Mississippi to Melbourne via Natal: The Invention of the Literacy Test as a Technology of Racial Exclusion," in Ann Curthoys and Marilyn Lake, eds., *Connected Worlds: History in Transnational Perspective* (Canberra: Australian National University Press, 2005), 209–230; Sue Yong and Rob Vosslamber, "Race and Tax Policy: The Case of the Chinese Poll Tax," *Journal of Australian Taxation* 20 (November 2020): 147–164.

82. Richard M. Valelly, *The Two Reconstructions: The Struggle for Black Enfranchisement* (Chicago, IL: University of Chicago Press, 2004), chapter 8.

83. Xi Wang, *The Trial of Democracy: Black Suffrage and Northern Republicans, 1860–1910* (Athens, GA: University of Georgia Press, 1997), 260.

84. Daniel McCool, Susan M. Olson, and Jennifer L. Robinson, *Native Vote: American Indians, the Voting Rights Act, and the Right to Vote* (Cambridge: Cambridge University Press, 2007), chapter 1.

85. Evans, Grimshaw, Phillips, and Swain, *Equal Subjects, Unequal Rights*, 50.

86. Woodrow Wilson, "Character of Democracy in the United States," *The Atlantic*, November 1889, n.p.

87. McCool, Olson, and Robinson, *Native Vote*, 3–5.

88. Violet R. Markham, *The South African Scene* (London: Smith, Elder, and Co., 1913), 341. Markham, a "convinced imperialist," in her own words, was hardly an outlier as a pro-empire, pro-white-supremacy, anti-suffrage female figure. See Julia Bush, *Edwardian Ladies and Imperial Power* (London: A & C Black, 2000), 45, 62, 108, and elsewhere.

89. David R. Roediger, *Working toward Whiteness: How America's Immigrants Became White: The Strange Journey from Ellis Island to the Suburbs* (New York: Basic Books, 2006).

90. David A. Wilson, "Comment: Whiteness and Irish Experience in North America," *Journal of British Studies* 44, no. 1 (2005): 153–160.

91. This figure was extrapolated from the 1871 census that put the number of Indians in the extent of British rule and the client Princely States at 238.8 million. See "The Census of British India of 1871–72," *Journal of the Statistical Society of London* 39, no. 2 (June 1876): 411–416, 411. Historians believe there were about 60,000–100,000 Britons in that land in 1871. Using the high estimate of 100,000, Britons comprised about 0.04 percent. See Tim Dyson, "Company and Crown (c. 1821 to c. 1871)," in Tim Dyson, ed., *A Population History of India: From the First Modern People to the Present Day* (Oxford: Oxford University Press, 2018), 94–112, 102.

92. Carl Husemoller Nightingale, *Segregation: A Global History of Divided Cities* (Chicago, IL: University of Chicago Press, 2012), 113–118.

93. Sumanta Banerjee, "A Tale of Three Towns: Black, White, and South," in Sumanta Banerjee, ed., *Memoirs of Roads: Calcutta from Colonial Urbanization to Global Modernization* (Oxford: Oxford University Press, 2016), 48–54.

94. John Whitson Cell, "Anglo-Indian Medical Theory and the Origins of Segregation in West Africa," *American Historical Review* 91 (April 1986): 307–335, 307.

95. Husemoller Nightingale, *Segregation*, chapter 6.

96. Whitson Cell, "Anglo-Indian Medical Theory and the Origins of Segregation in West Africa," 332.

97. Husemoller Nightingale, *Segregation*, 162.

98. Francis Dube, "Public Health and Racial Segregation in South Africa: Mahatma (M. K.) Gandhi Debates Colonial Authorities on Public Health Measures, 1896–1904," *Journal of the Historical Society of Nigeria* 21 (2012): 21–40.

99. Andrea Patterson, "Germs and Jim Crow: The Impact of Microbiology on Public Health Policies in Progressive Era American South," *Journal of the History of Biology* 42, no. 3 (Fall 2009): 529–559, 532–533 and elsewhere; Samuel Roberts, *Infectious Fear: Politics, Disease, and the Health Effects of Segregation* (Chapel Hill, NC: University of North Carolina Press, 2009), 110, 124, and elsewhere.

100. Margaret Humphreys, *Malaria: Poverty, Race, and Public Health in the United States* (Baltimore, MD: Johns Hopkins University Press, 2003), chapter 3.

101. Husemoller Nightingale, *Segregation*, 307.

102. Josiah Royce, *Race Questions, Provincialism, and Other American Problems* (New York: Macmillan, 1908), 275.

103. Tommy J. Curry, "Royce, Racism, and the Colonial Ideal: White Supremacy and the Illusion of Civilization in Josiah Royce's Account of the White Man's Burden," *The Pluralist* 4, no. 3 (October 2009): 10–38, 21.

104. This story is wonderfully told in Husemoller Nightingale, *Segregation*, 1–2.

105. *Aukland Star*, February 1959, 3, quoted in full in Robert E. Bartholomew, *No Māori Allowed: New Zealand's Forgotten History of Racial Segregation: How a Generation of Māori Children Perished in the Fields of Pukekohe*, updated ed. (Auckland: Bartholomew, 2022), 206. See many other instances of segregation throughout, including, on 101–102, segregation of schools and swimming pools.

106. Constance Backhouse, *Colour-Coded: A Legal History of Racism in Canada, 1900–1950* (Toronto: Osgoode Society for Canadian Legal History by University of Toronto Press, 1999), 226.

107. Kennetta Hammond Perry, "'Little Rock' in Britain: Jim Crow's Transatlantic Topographies," *Journal of British Studies* 51, no. 1 (2012): 155–177, 175.

108. James B. Waldram, Ann Herring, and T. Kue Young, *Aboriginal Health in Canada: Historical, Cultural, and Epidemiological Perspectives*, 2nd ed. (Toronto: University of Toronto Press, 2006), 196.

109. Harriet A. Washington, *Medical Apartheid: The Dark History of Medical Experimentation on Black Americans from Colonial Times to the Present* (New York: Anchor Books, 2008), chapters 6–9.

110. Maureen K. Lux, *Separate Beds: A History of Indian Hospitals in Canada, 1920s–1980s* (Toronto: University of Toronto Press, 2016), 109–111.

111. Take rates of breast cancer in the USA, for example. See Clement G. Yedjou, Jennifer N. Sims, Lucio Miele et al., "Health and Racial

Disparity in Breast Cancer," *Advances in Experimental Medicine and Biology* no. 1152 (2019): 31–49. For disparities in outcomes, including highly treatable ailments, in Canada, see Jungwee Park, "Mortality among First Nations People, 2006 to 2016," Statistics Canada (October 20, 2021), https://www150.statcan.gc.ca/n1/pub/82-003-x/2021010/article/00001-eng.htm. On mistrust of medicine by First Nations people, see Lux, *Separate Beds*, 110–112.

112. The program offered Federal Housing Administration insurance for loans originating from private lenders.

113. Federal Housing Administration, *Underwriting Manual: Underwriting and Valuation Procedure under Title II of the National Housing Act* (Washington, DC: US Government Printing Office, 1936), part II, 333.

114. Richard Rothstein interviewed by Terry Gross, "A 'Forgotten History' of How the U.S. Government Segregated America," *Fresh Air* (3 May 2017), www.npr.org/2017/05/03/526655831/a-forgotten-history-of-how-the-u-s-government-segregated-america.

115. Homer Hoyt, *One Hundred Years of Land Values in Chicago: The Relationship of the Growth of Chicago to the Rise in Its Land Values, 1830–1933* (Chicago, IL: University of Chicago Press, 1933), 315–316. Thanks, for leading me to this source, to Andrew Herscher, "The Urbanism of Racial Capitalism: Toward a History of 'Blight,'" *Comparative Studies of South Asia, Africa, & the Middle East* 40, no. 1 (May 2020): 57–65.

116. Thanks to M. Nolan Gray, *Arbitrary Lines: How Zoning Broke the American City and How to Fix It* (Washington, DC: Island Press, 2022).

117. Richard Rothstein, *The Color of Law: A Forgotten History of How Our Government Segregated America*, reprint ed. (New York and London: Liveright, 2018), 179–180.

118. Adele N. Norris and Gauri Nandedkar, "Ethnicity, Racism and Housing: Discourse Analysis of New Zealand Housing Research," *Housing Studies* 37, no. 8 (September 2022): 1331–1349, 1333.

119. John H. Flores, *The Mexican Revolution in Chicago: Immigration Politics from the Early Twentieth Century to the Cold War* (Urbana, IL: University of Illinois Press, 2018), 85.

120. Backhouse, *Colour-Coded*, 133–135.

121. Desmond King and Stephen Tuck, "De-centring the South: America's Nationwide White Supremacist Order after Reconstruction," *Past & Present* 194, no. 1 (February 2007): 213–253, 225.

122. Jacqueline Leckie, "In Defence of Race and Empire: The White New Zealand League at Pukekohe," *New Zealand Journal of History* 19, no. 2 (1985): 103–129, 114–115, 120–121.

123. Rothstein, *The Color of Law*, 43.
124. Eugene V. Debs, "The Negro in the Class Struggle," *International Socialist Review* 4, no. 5 (November 1903): 257–260.
125. Wolfgang Mieder, "'The Only Good Indian Is a Dead Indian': History and Meaning of a Proverbial Stereotype," *The Journal of American Folklore* 106, no. 419 (1993): 38–60, 45–46.
126. Braun, *Breathing Race into the Machine*, 30–31.
127. Frederick Douglass, *"The Claims of the Negro Ethnologically Considered," a speech at Commencement of Western Reserve College, 12 July 1854* (Rochester, NY: Lee, Mann, and Co., 1854), n.p.
128. Taylor, "W. E. B. DuBois's Challenge to Scientific Racism"; Ian Frazier, "When W. E. B. Du Bois Made a Laughingstock of a White Supremacist," *The New Yorker*, August 19, 2019.
129. See William Graham Sumner papers, https://archives.yale.edu/reposi tories/12/resources/4424/collection_organization.
130. See Stanford University's "Reports of the Advisory Committee on Renaming Jordan Hall and Removing the Statue of Louis Agassiz" (2020), 17, https://campusnames.stanford.edu/wp-content/uploads/ sites/14/2020/10/Jordan-report.pdf.
131. Michael Boulter, *Bloomsbury Scientists: Science and Art in the Wake of Darwin* (London: UCL Press, 2017), 104–107.
132. Timothy J. Stanley, *Contesting White Supremacy: School Segregation, Anti-racism, and the Making of Chinese Canadians* (Vancouver: University of British Columbia Press, 2011), 82–83.
133. David Hawley, *Theodore Roosevelt, Preacher of Righteousness* (New Haven, CT: Yale University Press, 2008), 31 and elsewhere in chapter 3; Nathaniel Southgate Shaler, *Nature and Man in America* (New York: C. Scribner's Sons, 1891), 280. These pages also convey some of Shaler's "Great Replacement" fears: an idea still in vogue among American white supremacists.
134. Richard T. Ely, "Fraternalism vs. Paternalism in Government," *The Century Magazine* (March 1898), 781; Thomas C. Leonard, *Illiberal Reformers: Race, Eugenics and American Economics in the Progressive Era* (Princeton, NJ: Princeton University Press, 2016), xii, 10, 121–122, and elsewhere. On Wilson's cordial comfort with segregation and his nativism, see Mario R. DiNunzio, *Woodrow Wilson: Essential Writings and Speeches of the Scholar-President* (New York: New York University Press, 2006), 21–22 and elsewhere; Lloyd E. Ambrosius, "Woodrow Wilson and The Birth of a Nation: American Democracy and International Relations," *Diplomacy & Statecraft* 18, no. 4 (December 2007): 689–718, 694 and elsewhere.

Chapter 7: White Supremacy's Death-Grip, 1930s-Present

1. Southern Poverty Law Center, "Whose Heritage: Public Symbols of the Confederacy" (2016), 14–15, www.splcenter.org/sites/default/files/com_whose_heritage.pdf.

2. See, for just two examples, the Vancouver 1907 white race terror and, in Australia, the attacks in Kalgoorlie, 1919 and 1934.

3. Toni Morrison interview with Charlie Rose, 1993, quoted in Joshua Barajas, "Lessons We Can Learn from Toni Morrison," *PBS News*, August 6, 2019, www.pbs.org/newshour/arts/lessons-we-can-learn-from-toni-morrison.

4. Daniel Byman, "White Supremacy, Terrorism, and the Failure of Reconstruction in the United States," *International Security* 46, no. 1 (July 19, 2021): 53–103. See also Tim Wilson, "Rightist Violence: An Historical Perspective," Report of the International Centre for Counter-Terrorism (2020), https://icct.nl/publication/rightist-violence-historical-perspective.

5. David F. Krugler, *1919, the Year of Racial Violence: How African Americans Fought Back* (New York: Cambridge University Press, 2015), 9.

6. Ken Gonzales-Day, *Lynching in the West: 1850–1935*, new ed. (Durham, NC: Duke University Press, 2006), chapter 1 and appendices 1–2; Michael J. Pfeifer, "Daniel F. Littlefield Jr.'s Seminole Burning and the Historiography of the Lynching of Native Americans," *Journal of the Gilded Age & Progressive Era* 20, no. 1 (January 2021): 81–86.

7. Laura M. Westhoff, *A Fatal Drifting Apart: Democratic Social Knowledge and Chicago Reform* (Columbus, OH: Ohio State University Press, 2007), 205.

8. Mattias Smångs, "Doing Violence, Making Race: Southern Lynching and White Racial Group Formation," *American Journal of Sociology* 121, no. 5 (2016): 1329–1374, 1337–1338.

9. Thomas Dixon, *The Leopard's Spots: A Romance of the White Man's Burden 1865–1900* (New York: Doubleday, Page & Co., 1902), 372. D. W. Griffiths adapted Dixon's 1905 book *The Clansman: A Historical Romance of the Ku Klux Klan* into his 1915 film *The Birth of a Nation*, infamously screened in the White House by Woodrow Wilson.

10. Westhoff, *A Fatal Drifting Apart*, 202.

11. James W. Clarke, "Without Fear or Shame: Lynching, Capital Punishment and the Subculture of Violence in the American South," *British Journal of Political Science* 28, no. 2 (1998): 269–289.

12. Lester F. Ward, *Pure Sociology: A Treatise on the Origin and Spontaneous Development of Society*, 2nd ed. (New York: Macmillan, 1907), 359. See also Mattias Smångs, "Race, Gender, and the Rape–Lynching Nexus in the U.S. South, 1881–1930," *Social Problems* 67 (November 2020): 616–636; Sandra Gunning, *Race, Rape, and Lynching: The Red Record of American Literature, 1890–1912* (New York: Oxford University Press, 1996), 21–22, 30, 41.

13. Kwame Ture (formerly Stokely Carmichael), interview on Howard University's (WHUT) Evening Exchange (1991), quoted in Ornette D. Clennon, *Black Scholarly Activism between the Academy and Grassroots: A Bridge for Identities and Social Justice* (Cham: Palgrave Macmillan, 2018), 2.

14. Mike Cole, *Racism: A Critical Analysis* (London: Pluto Press, 2016), 140.

15. Thalia Anthony, *Indigenous People, Crime and Punishment* (Abingdon: Routledge, 2013), 46; Thalia Anthony and Stephen Gray, "Was There Slavery in Australia? Yes. It Shouldn't Even Be up for Debate," *The Conversation* (June 11, 2020), https://theconversation.com/was-there-slavery-in-australia-yes-it-shouldnt-even-be-up-for-debate-140544.

16. Penelope Edmonds, *Urbanizing Frontiers: Indigenous Peoples and Settlers in 19th-Century Pacific Rim Cities* (Vancouver: University of British Columbia Press, 2010), 101.

17. Thalia Anthony, "Two Laws: Indigenous Justice Mechanisms in Context," *Journal of Australian Indigenous Issues* 18, no. 1 (2015): 99–115, 102.

18. Elizabeth A. Herbin-Triant, "Southern Segregation South Africa-Style: Maurice Evans, Clarence Poe, and the Ideology of Rural Segregation," *Agricultural History* 87, no. 2 (2013): 170–193, 186–187.

19. Ivan Evans, *Cultures of Violence: Lynching and Racial Killing in South Africa and the American South* (Manchester: Manchester University Press, 2009), 93–94.

20. *The Appeal*, March 26, 1892, 1.

21. This story is told well by Damon Mitchell, "The People's Grocery Lynching, Memphis, Tennessee," *JSTOR Daily*, January 24, 2018, https://daily.jstor.org/peoples-grocery-lynching.

22. She laid this out in her pamphlet, Ida B. Wells, *Southern Horrors: Lynch Law in All Its Phases* (New York: New York Age, 1892).

23. Ida B. Wells's autobiography, quoted in Megan Ming Francis, "Ida B. Wells and the Economics of Racial Violence," *Items. Social Science Research Council*, January 2017, https://items.ssrc.org/reading-racial-conflict/ida-b-wells-and-the-economics-of-racial-violence.

24. M. McLaughlin, *Power, Community, and Racial Killing in East St. Louis* (New York: Springer, 2005), 53 and elsewhere; Allison Keyes, "The East St. Louis Race Riot Left Dozens Dead, Devastating a Community on the Rise," *Smithsonian Magazine Online*, June 30, 2017, www.smithsonianmag.com/smithsonian-institution/easr-st-louis-race-riot-left-dozens-dead-devastating-community-on-the-rise-180963885.

25. Oklahoma Commission to Study the Tulsa Race Riot of 1921, *Report on Tulsa Race Riot of 1921* (2001), 13, 23, www.okhistory.org/research/forms/freport.pdf; Tim Madigan, *The Burning: Massacre, Destruction, and the Tulsa Race Riot of 1921* (New York: Thomas Dunne Books/St. Martin's Press, 2001), 224 and elsewhere.

26. Guy Lancaster, "Nightriding and Racial Cleansing in the Arkansas River Valley," *The Arkansas Historical Quarterly* 72, no. 3 (2013): 242–264.

27. William F. Holmes, "Whitecapping: Agrarian Violence in Mississippi, 1902–1906," *The Journal of Southern History* 35, no. 2 (1969): 165–185, 169.

28. Richard Rothstein, *The Color of Law: A Forgotten History of How Our Government Segregated America*, reprint ed. (New York: Liveright, 2018), 138–142 and elsewhere.

29. Christopher Robert Reed, *The Chicago NAACP and the Rise of Black Professional Leadership, 1910–1966* (Bloomington, IN: Indiana University Press, 1997), 151.

30. James G. Hollandsworth, *An Absolute Massacre: The New Orleans Race Riot of July 30, 1866* (Baton Rouge, LO: Louisiana State University Press, 2001); Lee W. Formwalt, "The Camilla Massacre of 1868: Racial Violence as Political Propaganda," *The Georgia Historical Quarterly* 71, no. 3 (1987): 399–426.

31. Paul Ortiz, *Emancipation Betrayed: The Hidden History of Black Organizing and White Violence in Florida from Reconstruction to the Bloody Election of 1920* (Berkeley, CA: University of California Press, 2005), 214–220 and elsewhere.

32. David Zucchino, *Wilmington's Lie: The Murderous Coup of 1898 and the Rise of White Supremacy* (New York: Grove Press, 2021).

33. For an overview of the Wilmington coup, see H. Leon Prather, Sr., "We Have Taken a City," in David S. Cecelski and Timothy B. Tyson, eds., *Democracy Betrayed: The Wilmington Race Riot of 1898 and Its Legacy* (Chapel Hill, NC: University of North Carolina Press, 2000), 15–42. See also David Zucchino, *Wilmington's Lie: The Murderous Coup of 1898 and the Rise of White Supremacy* (New York: Grove Press, 2021).

34. J. Michael Martinez, *Carpetbaggers, Cavalry, and the Ku Klux Klan: Exposing the Invisible Empire during Reconstruction* (Washington, D.C.: Rowman & Littlefield, 2007), 24–26 and elsewhere.

35. Robert Knox, *Races of Men, a Fragment* (Philadelphia, PA: Lea and Blanchard, 1850), 7, 14.

36. Langston Hughes, "Too Much of Race," *The Crisis* 44 (September 1937), 272. The charge of vagrancy, so vague that it let the state define it largely at will, was a favored tactic for enforcing white supremacy. For the Australian case, see Amanda Nettelbeck, "Creating the Aboriginal Vagrant: Protective Governance and Indigenous Mobility in Colonial Australia," *Pacific Historical Review* 87, no. 1 (2018): 79–100.

37. James Q. Whitman, *Hitler's American Model: The United States and the Making of Nazi Race Law* (Princeton, NJ: Princeton University Press, 2018). This was far from being the sole additional example. Richard E. Frankel emphasizes the similarities between US and German anti-Jewishness before the Nazis. See Richard E. Frankel, *Antisemitism before the Holocaust: Re-evaluating Antisemitic Exceptionalism in Germany and the United States, 1880–1945* (New York: Routledge, 2023).

38. Nazi newspaper editor Julius Streicher, quoted in S. Jonathan Wiesen, "American Lynching in the Nazi Imagination: Race and Extra-legal Violence in 1930s Germany," *German History* 36, no. 1 (2018): 38–59, 38.

39. Jane Caplan, *Nazi Germany: A Very Short Introduction* (Oxford: Oxford University Press, 2019), 67–68.

40. Norman Cameron and R. H. Stevens, *Hitler's Table Talk, 1941–1944* (New York: Enigma, 2000), 16, 657.

41. This is one of many examples, including forcing German Orthodox Jews to cut each other's beards in public. See Ilana Fritz Offenberger, *The Jews of Nazi Vienna, 1938–1945: Rescue and Destruction* (New York: Springer, 2017), 41–43 and elsewhere.

42. Leon F. Whitley, quoted in Robert W. Sussman, *The Myth of Race: The Troubling Persistence of an Unscientific Idea* (Cambridge, MA: Harvard University Press, 2014), 109.

43. Stefan Kühl, *The Nazi Connection: Eugenics, American Racism, and German National Socialism* (New York: Oxford University Press, 1994), 61–62.

44. Kühl, *The Nazi Connection*, 1 and elsewhere.

45. W. Jake Newsome, *Pink Triangle Legacies: Coming out in the Shadow of the Holocaust* (Ithaca, NY: Cornell University Press, 2022), 27, 49, and elsewhere; Robert Proctor, *Racial Hygiene: Medicine under the Nazis* (Cambridge, MA: Harvard University Press, 2002), 123;

Paul Weindling, "The Dangers of White Supremacy: Nazi Sterilization and Its Mixed-Race Adolescent Victims," *American Journal of Public Health* 112, no. 2 (February 2022): 248–254; United States Holocaust Memorial Museum, *Nazi Ideology and the Holocaust* (Washington, D.C.: United States Holocaust Memorial Museum, 2007), 78.

46. Michael Robertson, Astrid Ley, and Edwina Light, *The First into the Dark: The Nazi Persecution of the Disabled* (Sydney: University of Technology Sydney, 2019), 39; Thorsten Noack and Heiner Fangerau, "Eugenics, Euthanasia, and Aftermath," *International Journal of Mental Health* 36, no. 1 (2007): 112–124, 117.

47. Karl Kessler, "Physicians and the Nazi Euthanasia Program," *International Journal of Mental Health* 36, no. 1 (2007): 4–16.

48. This "testing" also circles back on to race hygiene because, as historian Karl Kessler wrote, "starting war was itself related to racial hygiene, because war was the ultimate test of a nation's 'fitness.'" See ibid., 9. For a review of the arguments about Nazis' Social Darwinism, see Richard Weikart, "The Role of Darwinism in Nazi Racial Thought," *German Studies Review* 36, no. 3 (October 2013): 537–556.

49. Houston Stewart Chamberlain, *Foundations of the Nineteenth Century*, trans. John Lees (London: John Lane, 1899), 329.

50. Sarah Panzer, "Honorary Aryans? Japanese German *Mischlinge* and the Negotiation of Identity in Nazi Germany," *Contemporary European History* 33, no. 4 (July 2023): 1300–1314.

51. Adolf Hitler, *Mein Kampf*, vol. 1, chapter 11, quoted in Weikart, "The Role of Darwinism in Nazi Racial Thought," 541.

52. Henry J. Gwiazda, "The Nazi Racial War: The First Stage in Building the New Order in Poland," *The Polish Review* 59, no. 4 (2014): 45–72; Alexander D. Barder, "Nazi Grand Strategy, Genocide, and Dismantlement of the State System, 1941–1945," in Alexander D. Barder, ed., *Global Race War: International Politics and Racial Hierarchy* (Oxford: Oxford University Press, 2021), 113–134; Michael Bess, *Choices under Fire: Moral Dimensions of World War II* (New York: Knopf Doubleday Publishing Group, 2009), chapter 1. In the end, ever clinging to Social Darwinism, Hitler deemed the Aryan race to have been weighed in the balance and found wanting against the Slavs. He was supposed to have said to Albert Speer, "the nation has proved to be weak, and the future belongs entirely to the strong people of the East." See Thomas Childers, *The Third Reich: A History of Nazi Germany* (New York: Simon & Schuster, 2017), 561.

53. Charles Lindbergh, "Aviation, Geography, and Race," *Reader's Digest* 35, no. 211 (November 1939): 64–67, 64.

54. Lindbergh's speech of September 1941, quoted in Lynne Olson, *Those Angry Days: Roosevelt, Lindbergh, and America's Fight over World War II, 1939–1941* (New York: Random House, 2013), 72. Even after the Pearl Harbor attack, Lindbergh warned his colleagues that Asians were "really bound together against the white race," though wisely behind closed doors. See anonymous, "Voices of Defeat," *Life Magazine*, April 13, 1942, 86–100, 99. In a September 1941 speech, Lindbergh said that it was no wonder that American Jews supported aiding Britain, given the persecution of Jews in Germany but that, should the war come to the USA, Jews' toleration in America might very well be rescinded. Simply put, they were tolerated "on sufferance," as Roosevelt himself said. See Rafael Medoff, *The Jews Should Keep Quiet: Franklin D. Roosevelt, Rabbi Stephen S. Wise, and the Holocaust* (Lincoln, NE: University of Nebraska Press and The Jewish Publication Society, 2019), 293. In his speech, Lindbergh concluded that the Jews' "greatest danger to this country lies in their large ownership and influence in our motion pictures, our press, our radio, and our government."

55. Kathryn S. Olmsted, *The Newspaper Axis: Six Press Barons Who Enabled Hitler* (New Haven, CT: Yale University Press, 2022), 212–213 and elsewhere.

56. "Remember Tarawa," *San Francisco Examiner*, December 7, 1943, quoted in Olmsted, *The Newspaper Axis*, 6.

57. Geoffrey S. Smith, "Racial Nativism and Origins of Japanese American Relocation," in Roger Daniels, Sandra C. Taylor, and Harry H. L. Kitano, eds., *Japanese Americans: From Relocation to Redress*, revised ed. (Seattle, WA: University of Washington Press, 1991), 79–87. Hearst's newspapers encouraged forcing Japanese and Japanese Americans into concentration camps. See Olmsted, *The Newspaper Axis*, 213.

58. Stefan Kühl, *The Nazi Connection: Eugenics, American Racism, and German National Socialism* (Oxford: Oxford University Press, 1994), xiv–xvi.

59. Joachim Prinz's speech at the 1963 March on Washington, www .joachimprinz.com/civil-rights.html.

60. Besides Leopold Senghor and Kwame Nkrumah, Frantz Fanon compared Nazism and colonial white supremacy in his chapter "Colonial War and Mental Disorders" in Frantz Fanon, *The Wretched of the Earth*, trans. Constance Farrington (New York: Grove Press, 1963 [1961]), 249–310.

61. Kennetta Hammond Perry, "'Little Rock' in Britain: Jim Crow's Transatlantic Topographies," *Journal of British Studies* 51, no. 1 (2012): 155–177, 156.

62. *The Times*, September 17, 1958, quoted in Christopher Hilliard, "Mapping the Notting Hill Riots: Racism and the Streets of Post-war Britain," *History Workshop Journal* 93, no. 1 (April 2022): 47–68, 48.

63. Ibid., 48.

64. Oswald Mosley was the founder of the British Union of Fascists in 1932, led a fascist paramilitary organization called the "Blackshirts" that conducted anti-Jewish marches, and sympathized with Nazi Germany. He was placed under house arrest during the Second World War.

65. C. Eales, "Witness to Violence," *Kensington News and West London Times*, September 5, 1958, 1, quoted in Liam Liburd, "The Politics of Race and the Future of British Political History," *The Political Quarterly* 94, no. 2 (2023): 244–250, 247.

66. *Manchester Guardian Weekly*, September 4, 1958, quoted in Clive Webb, "Brotherhood, Betrayal, and Rivers of Blood: Southern Segregationists and British Race Relations," in R. Kelley and S. Tuck, eds., *The Other Special Relationship: Race, Rights, and Riots in Britain and the United States* (New York: Springer, 2016), 225–241, 232.

67. Perry, "'Little Rock' in Britain," 172.

68. Bill Schwarz, *Memories of Empire*, vol. I: *The White Man's World* (Oxford: Oxford University Press, 2011), introduction.

69. Countries in the Commonwealth possessed most powers of self-determination, but participated in global trade and defense arrangements with Great Britain. The Nationality Act of 1948 made Commonwealth citizens de facto citizens of the UK. On the other hand, countries in the empire experienced more direct control from London. White settler colonies were admitted to the Commonwealth earlier and at a higher rate than nonwhite lands.

70. On how the "Rivers of Blood" speech came in a deeper context, see Peter Brooke, "India, Post-imperialism and the Origins of Enoch Powell's 'Rivers of Blood' Speech," *The Historical Journal* 50, no. 3 (2007): 669–687, esp. footnote 8.

71. It's quite possible that the "fearful pensioner" was an invention, as many journalists rushed to find her in the aftermath of the speech and failed. Listen to a BBC story on the possible invention here: www.bbc.co.uk/sounds/play/b007737v.

72. For the full text of the "Rivers of Blood" speech, see www.telegraph.co.uk/comment/3643823/Enoch-Powells-Rivers-of-Blood-speech.html.

73. Clive Webb, "Enoch Powell's America/America's Enoch Powell," in Daniel Geary, Camilla Schofield, and Jennifer Sutton, eds., *Global*

White Nationalism: From Apartheid to Trump (Manchester: Manchester University Press, 2020), 105–130, 110–111.

74. Camilla Schofield, *Enoch Powell and the Making of Postcolonial Britain* (Cambridge: Cambridge University Press, 2013), 237; Shirin Hirsch, "Reverberations from 'Rivers of Blood,'" in *In the Shadow of Enoch Powell: Race, Locality and Resistance* (Manchester: Manchester University Press, 2018), 49–71, 49.

75. See American Historical Association director Dr. Jim Grossman, quoted in Miles Parks, "Confederate Statues Were Built to Further a 'White Supremacist Future,'" National Public Radio News, August 20, 2017, www.npr.org/2017/08/20/544266880/confederate-statues-were-built-to-further-a-white-supremacist-future.

76. Seth Forman, "The Unbearable Whiteness of Being Jewish: Desegregation in the South and the Crisis of Jewish Liberalism," *American Jewish History* 85, no. 2 (1997): 121–142, 125–126 and elsewhere; Clive Webb, "Closing Ranks: Montgomery Jews and Civil Rights, 1954–1960," *Journal of American Studies* 32, no. 3 (1998): 463–481, 471; Melissa Fay Greene, "From *The Temple Bombing*," *The Georgia Review* 66, no. 3 (2012): 667–671.

77. Interview of unnamed white Little Rock high school student shown in the documentary *Eyes on the Prize: America's Civil Rights Years*, episode 2, "Fighting Back (1957–1962)" at 22:00.

78. National Museum of Australia, "Defining Moments: Aboriginal Land Rights Act," www.nma.gov.au/defining-moments/resources/aboriginal-land-rights-act.

79. Scott Rutherford, *Canada's Other Red Scare: Indigenous Protest and Colonial Encounters during the Global Sixties* (Montreal: McGill-Queen's University Press, 2020).

80. Troy R. Johnson, *The Occupation of Alcatraz Island: Indian Self-Determination and the Rise of Indian Activism* (Urbana-Champaign, IL: University of Illinois Press, 1996).

81. King's article "My Pilgrimage to Nonviolence" relates how he was inspired by Gandhi's writings and pored over them. See Martin Luther King, Jr., "My Pilgrimage to Nonviolence," *Fellowship* 24, no. 17 (September 1958): 4–8.

82. Mohandas Gandhi, "Our Shortcomings," in *Young India, 1919–1922* (New York: Huebsch, 1923), 623–629, 629.

83. Richard Toye, *Churchill's Empire: The World That Made Him and the World He Made* (New York: Macmillan, 2010), 176.

84. As a young lawyer in South Africa, Gandhi initially expressed a belief in Aryan supremacy – Indians supposedly being descended from Aryans along with whites. Later, he repented of such views and

recognized the common cause of Black Africans and Indians. See Chima Jacob Korieh, *Minorities and the State in Africa* (Amherst, NY: Cambria Press, 2010), 74–75 and elsewhere. For Mandela's recognition of Gandhi, see Elleke Boehmer, *Nelson Mandela: A Very Short Introduction*, 2nd ed. (Oxford: Oxford University Press, 2023), 16, 19, and elsewhere. Later, ANC posters appealed to India-descended South Africans by asking, "who would Gandhi have voted for?" See J. Piombo and L. Nijzink, *Electoral Politics in South Africa: Assessing the First Democratic Decade* (New York: Springer, 2005), 122.

85. Jake Hodder, "The Elusive History of the Pan-African Congress, 1919–27," *History Workshop Journal* 91, no. 1 (April 2021): 113–131, 117.

86. Tiffany Angel Player, "The Anti-lynching Crusaders: A Study of Black Women's Activism" (MA Thesis, University of Georgia, 2008); Angelina Weld Grimké, *Press, Platform, Pulpit: Black Feminist Publics in the Era of Reform* (Knoxville, TN: University of Tennessee Press, 2011), 161–164 and elsewhere; Thomas L. Bynum, *NAACP Youth and the Fight for Black Freedom, 1936–1965* (Knoxville, TN: University of Tennessee Press, 2013).

87. Samuel Roberts, *Infectious Fear: Politics, Disease, and the Health Effects of Segregation* (Chapel Hill, NC: University of North Carolina Press, 2009), 5 and elsewhere.

88. Anton Weiss-Wendt, *Racial Science in Hitler's New Europe, 1938–1945* (Lincoln, NE: University of Nebraska Press, 2013), 354.

89. James Samuel Stemons, *As Victim to Victims; an American Negro Laments with Jews* (New York: Fortuny's, 1941). Published in 1941, it's a safe guess that Stemons wrote this 280-page book in 1940.

90. Stephen Menendian, Samir Gambhir, and Chih-Wei Hsu, "Roots of Structural Racism: The 2020 Census Update" (Berkeley, CA: University of California Othering and Belonging Institute, 2021), https://belonging.berkeley.edu/roots-structural-racism-2020.

91. NBC News and BridgeDetroit, "Built to Keep Black from White: Eighty Years after a Segregation Wall Rose in Detroit, America Remains Divided. That's Not an Accident," July 19, 2021, www.nbcnews.com/specials/detroit-segregation-wall.

92. Francis Markham and Nicholas Biddle, "Indigenous Residential Segregation in Towns and Cities, 1976–2016," June 9, 2018, 1, https://caepr.cass.anu.edu.au/sites/default/files/docs/2024/11/CAEPR_Census_Paper_4_2018_0.pdf.

93. Joe T. Darden, "Homeownership among Immigrants in Canada and the United States: Similarities and Differences," in Carlos Teixeira and Wei Li, eds., *The Housing and Economic Experiences of Immigrants*

in U.S. and Canadian Cities (Toronto: University of Toronto Press, 2015), 43–68

94. Abhay Aneja and Guo Xu, "The Costs of Employment Segregation: Evidence from the Federal Government under Woodrow Wilson," Working Paper (Cambridge, MA: National Bureau of Economic Research, 2021), www.nber.org/system/files/working_papers/w27798/w27798.pdf.

95. Dalton Conley, *Being Black, Living in the Red: Race, Wealth, and Social Policy in America*, 10th anniversary ed., with a new afterword (Berkeley, CA: University of California Press, 2010), 25.

96. Donn Feir, Elijah Moreno, and Lakota Vogel, "Data from a Native CDFI Yield New Insights on Wealth Gap in Indian Country" (Federal Reserve Bank of Minneapolis, August 2022), www.minneapolisfed .org/article/2022/data-from-a-native-cdfi-yield-new-insights-on-wealth-gap-in-indian-country.

97. Elizabeth P. Weissert, "Get Out of Jail Free? Preventing Employment Discrimination against People with Criminal Records Using Ban the Box Laws," *University of Pennsylvania Law Review* 164, no. 6 (2016): 1529–1555, 1533–1536.

98. Marianne Bertrand and Sendhil Mullainathan, "Are Emily and Greg More Employable Than Lakisha and Jamal? A Field Experiment on Labor Market Discrimination," *American Economic Review* 94, no. 4 (2004): 991–1013.

99. Wouter Zwysen, Valentina Di Stasio, and Anthony Heath, "Ethnic Penalties and Hiring Discrimination: Comparing Results from Observational Studies with Field Experiments in the UK," *Sociology* 55, no. 2 (April 2021): 263–282.

100. Mehrsa Baradaran, *The Color of Money: Black Banks and the Racial Wealth Gap* (Cambridge, MA: Harvard University Press, 2017), 110.

101. These "cultural" arguments were made by Lawrence M. Mead, in an article retracted by its journal after an uproar: Lawrence M. Mead, "Poverty and Culture," *Society*, July 21, 2020.

102. Paul Djupe, "'Anglo-Saxon' Hits the Campaign Trail," *PRRI*, July 26, 2012, www.prri.org/spotlight/anglo-saxon-hits-the-campaign-trail; Christopher Bratt, "Is It Racism? The Belief in Cultural Superiority across Europe," *European Societies* 24, no. 2 (March 2022): 207–228.

103. Views of the violent nonwhite immigrant persist despite immigrants being charged with fewer violent crimes even though they're disproportionately policed. See Frank R. Baumgartner, Derek A. Epp, and Kelsey Shoub, *Suspect Citizens: What 20 Million Traffic Stops Tell Us about Policing and Race* (Cambridge: Cambridge University Press, 2018), 149.

104. Michelle Alexander, *The New Jim Crow: Mass Incarceration in the Age of Colorblindness*, revised ed. (New York: New Press, 2012), 51–60.

105. Ibid., 71–72, 133. For Clinton, see Richard C. Fording and Sanford F. Schram, *Hard White: The Mainstreaming of Racism in American Politics* (Oxford: Oxford University Press, 2020), 3. For Reagan, see Elizabeth Hinton , *From the War on Poverty to the War on Crime: The Making of Mass Incarceration in America* (Cambridge, MA: Harvard University Press, 2016), 307–309 and elsewhere.

106. Pew Foundation, "Racial Disparities Persist in Many U.S. Jails," *Pew Issue Brief*, May 2023, www.pewtrusts.org/-/media/assets/2023/05/racial_disparities_persist_in_many_us_jails_brief_digital.pdf.

107. Michael Shiner, Zoe Carre, Rebekah Delsol, and Niamh Eastwood, "The Colour of Injustice: 'Race,' Drugs and Law Enforcement in England and Wales" (London School of Economics, Release, and Stopwatch, 2018), 13, www.lse.ac.uk/united-states/Assets/Documents/The-Colour-of-Injustice.pdf; Lara Vomfell and Neil Stewart, "Officer Bias, Over-patrolling and Ethnic Disparities in Stop and Search," *Nature Human Behaviour* 5, no. 5 (May 2021): 566–575.

108. Joel H. Suss and Thiago R. Oliveira, "Economic Inequality and the Spatial Distribution of Stop and Search: Evidence from London," *The British Journal of Criminology* 63, no. 4 (July 1, 2023): 828–847.

109. Amy M. Alberton, Kevin M. Gorey, and Naomi G. Williams, "Individual and Community Predictors of Arrests in Canada: Evidence of Over-policing of Indigenous Peoples and Communities," *Journal of Ethnic & Cultural Diversity in Social Work* 34, no. 1 (May 2023): 5–17, 6.

110. Emma Pierson, Camelia Simoiu, Jan Overgoor et al., "A Large-Scale Analysis of Racial Disparities in Police Stops across the United States," *Nature Human Behaviour* 4, no. 7 (July 2020): 736–745.

111. Laura Santhanam, "A Majority of Americans Say Policing Should Be Reformed. But Most White People Still Don't Think Police Treat Black People Differently," *PBS News*, May 17, 2021, www.pbs.org/newshour/nation/a-majority-of-americans-say-policing-should-be-reformed-but-most-white-people-still-dont-think-police-treat-black-people-differently.

112. US Government Accountability Office, "K-12 Education: Discipline Disparities for Black Students, Boys, and Students with Disabilities" (March 2018), www.gao.gov/assets/gao-18-258.pdf; Alison Cooke, Amy Halberstadt, and Pamela Watkins Garner, "New Teachers Mistakenly Assume Black Students Are Angry," *The Conversation*, July 2020, https://theconversation.com/new-teachers-mistakenly-assume-black-students-are-angry-142237.

113. Ronet Bachman, Heather Zaykowski, Rachel Kallmyer, Margarita Poteyeva, and Christina Lanier, "Violence against

American Indian and Alaska Native Women and the Criminal Justice Response: What Is Known" (National Institute of Justice, Office of Justice Programs, and US Department of Justice, August 2008), 5 and elsewhere, www.ojp.gov/pdffiles1/nij/grants/223691.pdf; Tina Hotton Mahony, Joanna Jacob, and Heather Hobson, "Women and the Criminal Justice System" (Canadian Ministry of Industry, Statistics Canada, June 2017), 12 and elsewhere, https://www150 .statcan.gc.ca/n1/en/pub/89-503-x/2015001/article/14785-eng.pdf? st=YDiJppWY; Chay Brown, Connie Shaw, Kayla Glynn-Braun, and Shirleen Campbell, "The Report on Murdered and Missing Indigenous Women and Children Fails to Hold Anyone to Account. It's Not Enough," *The Conversation*, August 16, 2024, https://the conversation.com/the-report-on-murdered-and-missing-indigenous-women-and-children-fails-to-hold-anyone-to-account-its-not-enough-236941.

114. Brian Cathcart, *The Case of Stephen Lawrence* (London: Penguin, 2000).

115. Frank Edwards, Hedwig Lee, and Michael Esposito, "Risk of Being Killed by Police Use of Force in the United States by Age, Race–Ethnicity, and Sex," *Proceedings of the National Academy of Sciences* 116, no. 34 (August 20, 2019): 16793–16798.

116. Carlton W. Reeves, "Demographic Differences in Federal Sentencing" (United States Sentencing Commission, November 2023), 29, www .ussc.gov/sites/default/files/pdf/research-and-publications/research-publications/2023/20231114_Demographic-Differences.pdf.

117. Terrance MacMullan, *Habits of Whiteness: A Pragmatist Reconstruction*, 2nd ed. (Bloomington, IN: Indiana University Press, 2022), 194; Eric L. Goldstein, *The Price of Whiteness: Jews, Race, and American Identity* (Princeton, NJ: Princeton University Press, 2019), 139.

118. Anita Harris, "Making Whiteness and the Racialisation of Australian Youth Citizenship," *Journal of Intercultural Studies* 45, no. 4 (July 3, 2024): 589–606; Jennifer Martin, Dharma Arunachalam, and Helen Forbes-Mewett, *Identity and Belonging among Chinese Australians: Phenotype, Ethnic Language and Cultural Values*, vol. 7: *Migration, Minorities and Modernity* (Cham: Springer Nature Switzerland, 2023), 29–30.

119. For an overview of these developments, see Ian Haney-López, *Dog Whistle Politics: How Coded Racial Appeals Have Reinvented Racism and Wrecked the Middle Class* (Oxford: Oxford University Press, 2014).

120. Rick Perlstein, "Exclusive: Lee Atwater's Infamous 1981 Interview on the Southern Strategy," *The Nation*, November 13, 2012, www.the

nation.com/article/archive/exclusive-lee-atwaters-infamous-1981-interview-southern-strategy.

121. Janell Ross, "Joe Biden Didn't Just Compromise with Segregationists. He Fought for Their Cause in Schools, Experts Say," *NBC News*, June 26, 2019, www.nbcnews.com/news/nbcblk/joe-biden-didn-t-just-compromise-segregationists-he-fought-their-n1021626; Jill Barshay, "The Children of Children Who Went to Desegregated Schools Reap Benefits, Too, Study Finds," *The Hechinger Report*, May 23, 2016, https://hechingerreport.org/two-generations-desegregation; Rucker C. Johnson and Alexander Nazaryan, *Children of the Dream: Why School Integration Works*, 1st ed. (New York: Basic Books, 2019).

122. For an overview of these developments, see Haney-López, *Dog Whistle Politics*.

123. Tim Soutphommasane, *Reclaiming Patriotism: Nation-Building for Australian Progressives* (Melbourne: Cambridge University Press, 2009), 17, 23, and elsewhere.

124. Carol Johnson, "John Howard's 'Values' and Australian Identity," *Australian Journal of Political Science* 42 (June 2007): 195–209.

125. Lalaie Ameeriar, *Downwardly Global: Women, Work, and Citizenship in the Pakistani Diaspora* (Durham, NC: Duke University Press, 2017), 78.

126. Christopher Kyriakides, Satnam Virdee, and Tariq Modood, "Racism, Muslims and the National Imagination," *Journal of Ethnic and Migration Studies* 35, no. 2 (February 1, 2009): 289–308.

127. Kiran S. K. Arora, "Reflections on the Experiences of Turbaned Sikh Men in the Aftermath of 9/11," *Journal for Social Action in Counseling & Psychology* 5 (April 2013): 116–121; Victoria Mason, "Strangers Within in the 'Lucky Country': Arab-Australians after September 11," *Comparative Studies of South Asia, Africa and the Middle East* 24 (2004): 233–243.

128. Maria Golovnina, "Britain's Sikhs Reeling from Wisconsin Attack," *Reuters*, August 6, 2012, www.reuters.com/article/world/britains-sikhs-reeling-from-wisconsin-attack-idUSBRE87516X.

129. Aurelien Mondon and Aaron Winter, "Articulations of Islamophobia: From the Extreme to the Mainstream?" *Ethnic & Racial Studies* 40, no. 13 (October 2017): 2151–2179, 2151. "Muslim rage" got dusted off quite a few times. To name only two, see Bernard Lewis, "The Roots of Muslim Rage; Why Many Followers of Islam Resent the West and Why Their Bitterness Will Not Easily Be Mollified," *Daily News of Los Angeles (CA)*, December 9, 1990; Bernard Lewis, "The Roots of Muslim Rage," *Atlantic Monthly* 266, no. 3 (September 1990): 47–60.

130. John M. Hobson, "The Clash of Civilizations 2.0: Race and Eurocentrism, Imperialism and Anti-imperialism," in Mahmoud Eid and Karim H. Karim, eds., *Re-imagining the Other: Culture, Media, and Western–Muslim Intersections*, 1st ed. (New York: Palgrave Macmillan, 2014), chapter 5.

131. Christopher Caldwell, *Reflections on the Revolution in Europe: Immigration, Islam, and the West* (New York: Doubleday, 2009), 120.

132. Nadeem Badshah, "Tory MP Paul Scully Claims There Are 'No-Go' Areas in Birmingham and London," *The Guardian*, February 26, 2024, www.theguardian.com/news/2024/feb/26/tory-mp-paul-scully-claims-there-are-no-go-areas-in-birmingham-and-london; Tara Suter, "Chip Roy: 'Sharia Law' Will Soon Be 'Forced upon the American People,'" *The Hill*, May 8, 2024, https://thehill.com/homenews/house/4651114-chip-roy-sharia-law-will-soon-be-forced-upon-the-american-people.

133. Lothrop Stoddard, *The New World of Islam* (London: Chapman and Hall, 1922), 175–299.

134. Webb, "Enoch Powell's America," 107.

135. "We have been made to believe that differences of race and region . . . have separated us into warring factions . . . It is a vision of America that's been exploited and encouraged by pundits and politicians who need this division to score points and win elections. But it is a vision of America that I am running for President to fundamentally reject – not because of a blind optimism I hold, but because of a story I've lived. . . . Our family's story is one that spans miles and generations; races and realities. . . . It's a varied and unlikely journey, but one that's held together by the same simple dream. And that is why it's American. That's why I can stand here and talk about how this country is more than a collection of Red States and Blue States – because my story could only happen in the United States. That's why I believe that we are not as divided as our politics suggests; that the dream we share is more powerful than the differences we have – because I am living proof of that ideal." Barack Obama speech in El Dorado, Kansas, January 29, 2008, UC Santa Barbara American Presidency Project, www.presidency.ucsb.edu/documents/remarks-el-dorado-kansas-reclaiming-the-american-dream.

136. Gary Gerstle, "Civic Ideals, Race, and Nation in the Age of Obama," in Julian E. Zelizer, ed., *The Presidency of Barack Obama: A First Historical Assessment* (Princeton, NJ: Princeton University Press, 2018), 261–280.

137. Myra Mendible, "The Politics of Race and Class in the Age of Obama," *Revue de Recherche en Civilisation Américaine*, no. 3 (January 30, 2012): 1–12, 8 footnote 25; Ben Carrington, "Fear of a Black President," *Soundings* 43, no. 43 (December 1, 2009): 114–124.

138. Marc Ambinder, "'Pals Around with Terrorists': Palin Wasn't That Rogue, After All," *The Atlantic* (blog), July 10, 2009, www.theatlan tic.com/politics/archive/2009/07/-pals-around-with-terrorists-palin-wasnt-that-rogue-after-all/21044.

139. Andy Barr, "The GOP's No-Compromise Pledge," *Politico*, October 28, 2010, https://www.politico.com/story/2010/10/the-gops-no-compromise-pledge-044311. Republican House representative Tom Tancredo argued that Obama voters were illegitimate, as well. "People who could not even spell the word 'vote' or say it in English put a committed socialist in the White House." Tancredo quoted in E. J. Dionne Jr., "Does Race Drive Tea Partiers?" *The New Republic*, February 12, 2010; Robb Willer, Matthew Feinberg, and Rachel Wetts, "Threats to Racial Status Promote Tea Party Support among White Americans," SSRN Scholarly Paper (Rochester, NY, May 4, 2016), https://pacscenter.stanford.edu/publication/threats-to-racial-status-promote-tea-party-support-among-white-americans.

140. Alan Abramowitz, *The Great Alignment: Race, Party Transformation, and the Rise of Donald Trump* (New Haven, CT: Yale University Press, 2018), 123; Paul Banahene Adjei, "Race to the Bottom: Obama's Presidency, Trump's Election Victory, and the Perceived Insidious Greed of Whiteness," *Race, Gender & Class* 25, no. 3/4 (2018): 43–67.

141. Daniel Tope, Justin T. Pickett, Ryon J. Cobb, and Jonathan Dirlam, "Othering Obama: Racial Attitudes and Dubious Beliefs about the Nation's First Black President," *Sociological Perspectives* 57, no. 4 (2014): 450–469, 452.

142. Mahmoud Haddad, "Fudging the Boundaries between Concept(s) of Race, Class, and Religion: The Two Cases of Donald Trump and Lothrop Stoddard," *Contemporary Arab Affairs* 12, no. 4 (2019): 121–140, 122.

143. Fording and Schram, *Hard White*, 40.

144. Adam Serwer, "Trump Tells America What Kind of Nationalist He Is," *The Atlantic*, July 15, 2019, www.theatlantic.com/ideas/archive/2019/07/trumps-white-nationalist-attack-four-congresswomen/594019.

145. January 6 Select Committee, *The January 6th Report: Findings from the Select Committee to Investigate the January 6th Attack on the United States Capitol* (New York: Random House Publishing Group, 2023), 38, 429, 529, 563.

146. William D. Hicks, Seth C. McKee, and Daniel A. Smith, "The Determinants of State Legislator Support for Restrictive Voter ID Laws," *State Politics & Policy Quarterly* 16, no. 4 (2016): 411–431; Lorraine C. Minnite, *The Myth of Voter Fraud* (Ithaca, NY: Cornell University Press, 2011).

147. Carol Anderson, *One Person, No Vote: How Voter Suppression Is Destroying Our Democracy* (New York: Bloomsbury USA, 2018); Stephen Fowler, "Why Do Nonwhite Georgia Voters Have to Wait in Line for Hours? Too Few Polling Places," *NPR and ProPublica*, October 17, 2020, www.npr.org/2020/10/17/924527679/why-do-non white-georgia-voters-have-to-wait-in-line-for-hours-too-few-polling-pl.

148. Steven V. Miller and Nicholas T. Davis, "The Effect of White Social Prejudice on Support for American Democracy," *Journal of Race, Ethnicity, and Politics* 6, no. 2 (July 2021): 334–351.

149. James Oliphant, "Trump Likely to Challenge Any Election Loss. His Options Have Narrowed." *Reuters*, October 17, 2024, www.reuters .com/world/us/what-could-happen-if-trump-rejects-us-election-results-2024-10-16.

150. Diversity, equity, and inclusion. The phrase is often used for programs or offices in agencies, corporations, or schools. These programs often promote awareness of difference or encourage opportunities for historically disadvantaged groups. Upon being elected a second time, the Trump administration demanded federal agencies remove any reference to diversity and inclusion from their publications and websites.

151. Amanda Terkel, "'Dumb' and a 'DEI' Candidate: Trump and Allies Attack Kamala Harris Based on Race, Gender." *NBC News*, July 24, 2024, www.nbcnews.com/politics/2024-election/republican-attacks-kamala-harris-center-race-gender-dumb-dei-candidate-rcna162570.

152. Nik Popli and Eric Coretellessa. "Exclusive: Trump Says 'Anti-White Feeling' Is a Problem in the U.S.," *Time*, April 30, 2024, https://time .com/6972270/donald-trump-anti-white-bias-exclusive.

153. Merlyn Thomas and Mike Wendling. "Donald Trump Repeats Baseless Claim about Haitian Immigrants Eating Cats and Dogs in Springfield, Ohio," September 15, 2024, https://www.bbc.co.uk/news/articles/c77l28myezko.

154. Michelle L. Price, "Trump Says Migrants Who Have Committed Murder Have Introduced 'a Lot of Bad Genes in Our Country,'" *AP News*, October 7, 2024, https://apnews.com/article/donald-trump-immigration-2024-election-2157777f240142e5aed38be192a52b25.

155. Kathryn Bromwich, "Boris Johnson and Nigel Farage: Their Wit and Wisdom," *The Observer*, August 30, 2014, www.theguardian.com/politics/2014/aug/31/boris-johnson-nigel-farage-in-quotes; Rowena Mason and political correspondent, "Nigel Farage Asked Former Conservative MP Enoch Powell to Back Ukip," *The Guardian*, December 13, 2014, www.theguardian.com/politics/2014/dec/13/nigel-farage-enoch-powell-endorsement-russell-brand.

156. Leo McKinstry, "Opening National Borders Has Been an Abject Failure," *Daily Express*, September 3, 2015, www.express.co.uk/

comment/columnists/leo-mckinstry/602556/Leo-McKinstry-national-borders-failure. The September 3, 2015 edition was emblazoned with "EU BLAMED FOR MIGRANT CHAOS."

157. Chris Lawton and Robert Ackrill, "Hard Evidence: How Areas with Low Immigration Voted Mainly for Brexit," *The Conversation*, July 8, 2016, https://theconversation.com/hard-evidence-how-areas-with-low-immigration-voted-mainly-for-brexit-62138.

158. Paul B. Hutchings and Katie E. Sullivan, "Prejudice and the Brexit Vote: A Tangled Web," *Palgrave Communications* 5, no. 1 (January 15, 2019): 1–5; Tina G. Patel and Laura Connelly, "'Post-Race' Racisms in the Narratives of 'Brexit' Voters," *Sociological Review* 67, no. 5 (September 2019): 968–984.

159. Jon Burnett, *Racial Violence and the Brexit State* (London: Institute of Race Relations, 2018).

160. Jennifer Hassan, "After Far-Right Riots, Brits of Color Contemplate Their Safety," *Washington Post*, August 12, 2024, www.washingtonpost.com/world/2024/08/12/uk-riots-racism-muslims; Matt Dathan, "Nigel Farage Calls for Ukip Unity as He Declares: 'We Want Our Country Back,'" *The Independent*, September 25, 2015, www.independent.co.uk/news/uk/politics/nigel-farage-we-want-our-country-back-10516726.html.

161. Arsalan Iftikhar, "Christchurch Anniversary: The Islamophobic 'Great Replacement' Theory," Georgetown University, Bridge Initiative, March 14, 2020, https://bridge.georgetown.edu/research/christchurch-anniversary-the-islamophobic-great-replacement-theory; Les Perreaux, "Quebec Mosque Shooter Told Police He Was Motivated by Canada's Immigration Policies," *The Globe and Mail*, April 13, 2018, www.theglobeandmail.com/canada/article-mosque-shooter-told-police-he-was-motivated-by-canadas-immigration.

162. Ten days after the murderous Charlottesville march, President Trump said, in a speech in Phoenix, that the news media was part of a conspiracy "trying to take away our history and our heritage." See Jacqueline Thomsen, "Trump: Media Is Trying 'to Take Away Our History and Our Heritage,'" *The Hill*, August 22, 2017, https://thehill.com/homenews/administration/347587-trump-media-is-trying-to-take-away-our-history-and-our-heritage. For the terrorist's praise of Trump as a white leader, and also the New Zealand and Canadian media's reluctance to call a white terrorist a terrorist – and comfort with calling a Muslim or nonwhite terrorist a terrorist, see Houssem Ben Lazreg, "The Hypocritical Media Coverage of the New Zealand Terror Attacks," *The Conversation*, March 25, 2019, https://theconversation.com/the-hypocritical-media-coverage-of-the-new-zealand-terror-attacks-113713.

163. Kurt Sengul, "Pauline Hanson Built a Political Career on White Victimhood and Brought Far-Right Rhetoric to the Mainstream," *The Conversation*, June 22, 2020, https://theconversation.com/pauline-hanson-built-a-political-career-on-white-victimhood-and-brought-far-right-rhetoric-to-the-mainstream-134661.

164. Lynne Olson, *Those Angry Days: Roosevelt, Lindbergh, and America's Fight over World War II, 1939–1941* (New York: Random House, 2013), 383.

165. James Baldwin, *Notes of a Native Son* (Boston, MA: Little, Brown, 1955), 175. I'm grateful for Dr. Jane Dailey turning me to this quote.

166. Andrew Carter and Paul Swinney, "Brexit and the Future of the UK's Unbalanced Economic Geography," *The Political Quarterly* 90 (2019): 72–83, María C. Latorre, Zoryana Olekseyuk, Hidemichi Yonezawa, and Sherman Robinson, "Brexit: Everyone Loses, but Britain Loses the Most," Peterson Institute for International Economics (March 2019), www.piie.com/sites/default/files/documents/wp19-5.pdf. In spring 2024, the Tory government's Office for Budget Responsibility reported that "exports and imports will be around 15 per cent lower in the long run than if the UK had remained in the EU." See "Brexit Analysis," UK Office for Budget Responsibility (March 2024), https://obr.uk/forecasts-in-depth/the-economy-forecast/brexit-analysis/#assumptions.

167. Anna Maria Mayda and Giovanni Peri, "The Economic Impact of US Immigration Policies in the Age of Trump," in Chad Bown, ed., *Economics and Policy in the Age of Trump* (London: CEPR Press, 2017), 69–78.

168. Pankaj Mishra, *Bland Fanatics: Liberals, Race, and Empire* (New York: Farrar, Straus and Giroux, 2020), 59.

Final Reflections and Prospects for the Future

1. Ursula K. Le Guin, "Speech in Acceptance of the National Book Foundation Medal for Distinguished Contribution to American Letters," November 19, 2014, www.ursulakleguin.com/nbf-medal.

2. Coates interview with Chris Hayes, "All in with Chris Hayes," MSNBC, February 3, 2023.

3. Billy Perrigo, "Crowds Protest in New Zealand against George Floyd's Death," *Time*, June 1, 2020.

4. Angela Skujins, "'You're Going to Hear Us – Really Hear Us,'" *CityMag*, June 9, 2020, https://citymag.indaily.com.au/culture/youre-going-to-hear-us-really-hear-us.

SUGGESTIONS FOR FURTHER READING

Sticking only to books, I offer this brief list that should start the reader down the main paths of my chapters. This list is far from exhaustive and favors books that I hope the reader can actually acquire at a library near them.

Introduction

Coates, Ta-Nehisi. *Between the World and Me*. New York: One World, 2015.

DiAngelo, Robin. *Nice Racism: How Progressive White People Perpetuate Racial Harm*. Boston, MA: Beacon Press, 2021.

Eddo-Lodge, Reni. *Why I'm No Longer Talking to White People about Race*. London: Bloomsbury Circus, 2017.

Fredrickson, George. *Racism: A Short History*. Princeton, NJ: Princeton University Press, 2002.

Kendi, Ibram X. *Stamped from the Beginning: The Definitive History of Racist Ideas in America*. New York: Bold Type Books, 2017.

Chapter 1

Adi, Hakim, ed. *Black British History: New Perspectives*. London: Zed, 2019.

Dabydeen, David, John Gilmore, and Cecily Jones. *Oxford Companion to Black British History*. Oxford: Oxford University Press, 2008.

Fields, Karen E. and Barbara J. Fields. *Racecraft: The Soul of Inequality in American Life*, reprint ed. London: Verso, 2014.

Jackson, Jr., John P. and Nadine M. Weidman. *Race, Racism, and Science*. New Brunswick, NJ: Rutgers University Press, 2004.

Kaufmann, Miranda, ed. *Black Tudors: The Untold Story*. London: Oneworld Publications, 2017.

Morris-Reich, Amos and Dirk Rupnow. *Ideas of "Race" in the History of the Humanities*. Cham: Palgrave Macmillan, 2017.

Olusoga, David. *Black and British: A Forgotten History*, revised and updated. New York: Picador, 2021.

Rio, Alice. *Slavery after Rome, 500–1100*. Oxford: Oxford University Press, 2017.

Schwartz, Stuart B., ed. *Tropical Babylons: Sugar and the Making of the Atlantic World, 1450–1680*. Chapel Hill, NC: University of North Carolina Press, 2004.

Vlassopoulos, Kostas. *Historicising Ancient Slavery*. Edinburgh: Edinburgh University Press, 2021.

Chapter 2

Belew, Kathleen and Ramón A. Gutiérrez, eds. *A Field Guide to White Supremacy*. Berkeley, CA: University of California Press, 2021.

Berlin, Ira. *Many Thousands Gone: The First Two Centuries of Slavery in North America*. Cambridge, MA: Belknap Press of Harvard University Press, 1998.

Blackburn, Robin. *The Making of New World Slavery: From the Baroque to the Modern, 1492–1800*. London: Verso, 1997.

Canizares-Esguerra, Jorge. *Entangled Empires: The Anglo-Iberian Atlantic, 1500–1830*. Philadelphia, PA: University of Pennsylvania Press, 2018.

Evans, William McKee. *Open Wound: The Long View of Race in America*. Urbana, IL: University of Illinois Press, 2009.

Gallay, Alan. *Indian Slave Trade: The Rise of the English Empire in the American South, 1670–1717*. New Haven, CT: Yale University Press, 2002.

Morgan, Edmund S. *American Slavery, American Freedom*, reissue ed. New York: W. W. Norton & Company, 2003.

Morgan, Jennifer L. *Reckoning with Slavery: Gender, Kinship, and Capitalism in the Early Black Atlantic*. Durham, NC: Duke University Press, 2021.

Newell, Margaret Ellen. *Brethren by Nature: New England Indians, Colonists, and the Origins of American Slavery*. Ithaca, NY: Cornell University Press, 2016.

Chapter 3

Craciun, Adriana and Mary Terrall. *Curious Encounters: Voyaging, Collecting, and Making Knowledge in the Long Eighteenth Century*. Toronto: University of Toronto Press, 2019.

Guasco, Michael. *Slaves and Englishmen: Human Bondage in the Early Modern Atlantic World*. Philadelphia, PA: University of Pennsylvania Press, 2017.

Hannaford, Ivan. *Race: The History of an Idea in the West*. Baltimore, MD: Johns Hopkins University Press, 1996.

Malcolmson, Cristina. *Studies of Skin Color in the Early Royal Society: Boyle, Cavendish, Swift*. Oxford: Routledge, 2016.

McCarthy, Thomas. *Race, Empire, and the Idea of Human Development*. Cambridge: Cambridge University Press, 2009.

Stovall, Tyler. *White Freedom: The Racial History of an Idea*. Princeton, NJ: Princeton University Press, 2021.

Vartija, Devin J. *The Color of Equality: Race and Common Humanity in Enlightenment Thought*. Philadelphia, PA: University of Pennsylvania Press, 2021.

Chapter 4

Baum, Bruce. *The Rise and Fall of the Caucasian Race: A Political History of Racial Identity*. New York: New York University Press, 2006.

Brown, Christopher Leslie. *Moral Capital: Foundations of British Abolitionism*. Chapel Hill, NC: University of North Carolina Press, 2006.

Hall, Catherine. *Civilising Subjects: Metropole and Colony in the English Imagination 1830–1867*. Chicago, IL: University of Chicago Press, 2002.

Hall, Catherine, Nicholas Draper, Keith McClelland, Katie Donington, and Rachel Lang. *Legacies of British Slave-Ownership: Colonial Slavery and the Formation of Victorian Britain*, illustrated ed. Cambridge: Cambridge University Press, 2014.

Harris, Ron. *Going the Distance: Eurasian Trade and the Rise of the Business Corporation, 1400–1700*. Princeton, NJ: Princeton University Press, 2020.

Morgan, Cecilia. *Building Better Britains?: Settler Societies in the British World, 1783–1920*. Toronto: University of Toronto Press, 2016.

Sinha, Manisha. *The Slave's Cause: A History of Abolition*. New Haven, CT: Yale University Press, 2016.

Wilson, Kathleen. *The Island Race: Englishness, Empire and Gender in the Eighteenth Century*. London: Routledge, 2003.

Zoellner, Tom. *Island on Fire: The Revolt That Ended Slavery in the British Empire*. Cambridge, MA: Harvard University Press, 2020.

Chapter 5

Adams, Francis D. and Barry Sanders. *Alienable Rights: The Exclusion of African Americans in a White Man's Land, 1619–2000*. New York: HarperCollins, 2003.

Brantlinger, Patrick. *Dark Vanishings: Discourse on the Extinction of Primitive Races, 1800–1930*. Ithaca, NY: Cornell University Press, 2014.

Curthoys, Ann and Jessie Mitchell. *Taking Liberty: Indigenous Rights and Settler Self-Government in Colonial Australia, 1830–1890*. Cambridge: Cambridge University Press, 2018.

Dain, Bruce. *A Hideous Monster of the Mind: American Race Theory in the Early Republic*. Cambridge, MA: Harvard University Press, 2002.

Dunbar, Erica Armstrong. *Never Caught: Ona Judge, the Washingtons, and the Relentless Pursuit of Their Runaway Slave*. New York: Simon & Schuster, 2017.

Guyatt, Nicholas. *Bind Us Apart: How Enlightened Americans Invented Racial Segregation*. New York: Basic Books, 2016.

Madley, Benjamin. *An American Genocide: The United States and the California Indian Catastrophe, 1846–1873*, illustrated ed. New Haven, CT: Yale University Press, 2016.

O'Brien, Jean M. *Firsting and Lasting: Writing Indians Out of Existence in New England*. Minneapolis, MN: University of Minnesota Press, 2010.

Ostler, Jeffrey. *Surviving Genocide: Native Nations and the United States from the American Revolution to Bleeding Kansas*. New Haven, CT: Yale University Press, 2019.

Chapter 6

Bell, Duncan. *The Idea of Greater Britain: Empire and the Future of World Order, 1860–1900*. Princeton, NJ: Princeton University Press, 2011.

Bowler, Peter J. *Evolution: The History of an Idea*, 25th anniversary ed. Berkeley, CA: University of California Press, 2009.

Braun, Lundy. *Breathing Race into the Machine: The Surprising Career of the Spirometer from Plantation to Genetics*. Minneapolis, MN: University of Minnesota Press, 2014.

Evans, Julie, Patricia Grimshaw, David Philips, and Shurlee Swain. *Equal Subjects, Unequal Rights: Indigenous People in British Settler Colonies, 1830–1910*. Manchester: Manchester University Press, 2003.

Hawkins, Mike. *Social Darwinism in European and American Thought, 1860–1945: Nature as Model and Nature as Threat*. Cambridge: Cambridge University Press, 1997.

Keevak, Michael. *Becoming Yellow: A Short History of Racial Thinking*. Princeton, NJ: Princeton University Press, 2001.

Nightingale, Carl Husemoller. *Segregation: A Global History of Divided Cities*. Chicago, IL: University of Chicago Press, 2012.

Paul, Diane B., John Stenhouse, and Hamish G. Spencer, eds. *Eugenics at the Edges of Empire: New Zealand, Australia, Canada and South Africa*. Cham: Palgrave Macmillan, 2018.

Stote, Karen. *An Act of Genocide: Colonialism and the Sterilization of Aboriginal Women*. New York: Columbia University Press, 2015.

Willoughby, Christopher D. E. *Masters of Health: Racial Science and Slavery in U.S. Medical Schools*. Chapel Hill, NC: University of North Carolina Press, 2022.

Chapter 7

Alexander, Michelle. *The New Jim Crow: Mass Incarceration in the Age of Colorblindness*, revised ed. New York: New Press, 2012.

Cecelski, David S. and Timothy B. Tyson. *Democracy Betrayed: The Wilmington Race Riot of 1898 and Its Legacy*. Chapel Hill, NC: University of North Carolina Press, 2000.

Haney-López, Ian. *Dog Whistle Politics: How Coded Racial Appeals Have Reinvented Racism and Wrecked the Middle Class*. Oxford: Oxford University Press, 2014.

Mishra, Pankaj. *Bland Fanatics: Liberals, Race, and Empire*. New York: Farrar, Straus and Giroux, 2020.

Roberts, Samuel. *Infectious Fear: Politics, Disease, and the Health Effects of Segregation*. Chapel Hill, NC: University of North Carolina Press, 2009.

Rothstein, Richard. *The Color of Law: A Forgotten History of How Our Government Segregated America*, reprint ed. New York: Liveright, 2018.

Schofield, Camilla. *Enoch Powell and the Making of Postcolonial Britain*. Cambridge: Cambridge University Press, 2013.

Whitman, James Q. *Hitler's American Model: The United States and the Making of Nazi Race Law*. Princeton, NJ: Princeton University Press, 2018.

INDEX

Printed in the United Kingdom by TJ Clays Ltd.